Smell and History

Smell

AND HISTORY
A READER

Edited by
MARK M. SMITH

West Virginia University Press
Morgantown 2019

Copyright © 2019 by West Virginia University Press
All rights reserved
First edition published 2019 by West Virginia University Press
Printed in the United States of America

ISBN:
Cloth 978-1-946684-67-7
Paper 978-1-946684-68-4
Ebook 978-1-946684-69-1

Library of Congress Cataloging-in-Publication Data is available from the
    Library of Congress

Book and cover design by Than Saffel / WVU Press

For my Rose; naturally.

Contents

Editor's Introduction

Smelling the Past

Mark M. Smith

The historical study of sight, sound, smell, taste, and touch—commonly known as sensory history—is burgeoning. Almost two decades ago, Douglas Kahn argued in the *Australian Review of Books* that the historical study of sound was booming; today, an equally reliable claim might be made about the historical study of the senses generally and about the sense of smell specifically.[1] The rapid emergence of sensory history, an increasing scholarly attention to the history of smell, and the aim of introducing the topic to a new generation of undergraduate and graduate students has inspired this collection of essays. This reader aims to introduce the history of smell and smelling to a variety of students, not simply those studying history but also those who hold cognate interests in, say, environmental studies, public health, anthropology, media and communications studies, science and technology, and even the natural sciences. It is my hope that students whose work attends to human perception and the context of that perception will find much of interest here.

Sensory history—understood as a habit of historical inquiry that takes smells, sounds, tastes, and touches as seriously as sights—has never been more popular or more widely practiced than it is today. From its origins in the writings of the early Annales school, sensory history—as both methodological habit and as distinct field of inquiry—has emerged as an important way of thinking about and writing history in many historical subfields. Because sensory history is not limited to time or place, historians of every period, antiquity to the present, and of a variety of locations are increasingly practicing sensory history. So too with historians of all interests and persuasions. Diplomatic historians and historians of science and technology, for example, have recently joined cultural and social historians, historians of the environment, and historians of medicine in framing their work sensorially. What is increasingly clear from this work is not only how attention to the senses helps texture and deepen our understanding of, say, environmental history but also how it holds the potential to expand our very interpretations of what constitutes the environment. As environmental historians have shown, studies of pollution that are not attentive to sound, noise, and smell—how noises and odors constituted recognized public nuisances and even dangers—not only limit our definition of the environment but tacitly limit what is and is not pollution. Indeed, the study of history generally can benefit enormously from attention to the nonvisual senses not simply in an expansive, empirical sense but also in a methodological one. Sensory history, after all, demands that historians read conventional sources with, ironically, an eye to nonvisual evidence.[2]

The increasing popularity of sensory history is reflected in the existence of several important essays on the topic as well as in the number of book series dedicated to sensory studies generally. Prominent journals have devoted precious space to the topic, including the *Journal of American History*, the *American Historical Review*, the *Hispanic American Historical Review*, and the *American Quarterly*, as have more specialized journals, such as the *Journal of Sport History* and the *Public Historian*. There is also a relatively new journal, *The Senses and Society*, focused on the interdisciplinary exploration of the senses. Most recently we have an impressive multivolume treatment of the senses from antiquity to the modern period, edited by Constance Classen and covering a very wide array of subjects.[3] The subject also pops up in mainstream culture with pieces in major newspapers reporting what histories of the senses have long known—that sensory perception, smell included, is as much about culture as about biology.[4] The senses have been popularized in literature, most notably in Patrick Süskind's 1985 bestselling work, *Perfume: The Story of a Murderer* (subsequently made into a film in 2006). The sensory is here to stay.

The history of smell and olfaction has been central to this sensory turn. Historians of olfaction have in many ways written some of the most wide-ranging yet most theoretically sophisticated work on any of the senses, and this reader presents some of it. As is sensory history generally, the history of smell and smelling is best understood in plural form, reflecting not only the fact that the past was populated by myriad smells but that the way contemporaries understood those smells varied a great deal depending on time, place, and whose nose was doing the smelling. That much said, the history of smell and olfaction is a lot deeper than is historians' writing on the topic. Certainly, historians have peppered their historical writings with references to whiffs and stenches for years, but self-conscious writing on the subject is relatively much newer.[5] Some of this early work was important for establishing what we might think of the modern foundation of the history of smell and olfaction, one we can reliably trace to the French historian of the senses, Alain Corbin. Corbin's seminal work on olfaction, *Le miasme et la jonquille: L'odorat et l'imaginaire social, XVIIIe–XIXe siècles*, first published in 1983 and made available in English in 1986 as *The Foul and the Fragrant: Odor and the French Social Imagination*, offers an important interpretive foundation for work on the history of smell. Corbin's introduction to this critical work is included in this reader. Beyond the French influence, the work of several historians and sensory anthropologists during the 1990s was central for shaping the emergence of the field. Constance Classen, David Howes, and Anthony Synnott gave us in 1994 the sweeping *Aroma: The Cultural History of Smell. Aroma*, still a widely referenced book, did as much to introduce English-language readers to the broad temporal and spatial history of smell and, while well over twenty years old, remains an important work in the history of olfaction.[6]

From these early interventions, writing on the history of smell has grown in recent years; it has burgeoned and is probably second only to the history of sound and hearing in popularity among historians of the senses (with the exception of the history of vision). This reader collects ten of the most recent and important articles and essays detailing the history of smell and smelling from antiquity through the twentieth century. Naturally, it is not catholic, and many excellent treatments are necessarily not found in this collection. The section on further reading directs interested readers to many of these additional sources. But this collection does offer an up-to-date selection of articles that examine the history of olfaction throughout history, primarily in the West. With the exception of the piece by Corbin, all of the essays were published between 2003 and 2016. And with the exception of David Howes's extremely thoughtful epilogue, there is little material on the history of smell outside Western culture included in this reader. This is simply a reflection of the state of the field. While sociologists and anthropologists (including Howes) have begun to explore the role of olfaction in non-Western cultures, historians have yet to pay sustained attention to the topic.[7]

The collection opens with an extract from Corbin's influential *The Foul and the Fragrant*. Unlike every other essay offered in this collection, Corbin's contribution is older. It is included here because, as is made clear by the following chapters, his work is foundational, offering an interpretive framework for many other historians working on the subject. As Corbin outlines, his interest in the history of smell was inspired by his reading on the history of public health and hygiene. That work tethered smells to disease and highlighted efforts in eighteenth- and nineteenth-century France to measure and map urban stench. Corbin detected an emerging collective hypersensitivity to odors, good and bad, which allowed him to ask the essential question: what was behind this increasing attentiveness to smells, and why did the French in this period seemingly want to deodorize their world? His book is dedicated to answering these basic questions. For Corbin, olfaction—the way people choose to smell and what they deem offensive or fragrant—is central to and constitutive of social power and reflected in the social order. He suggests that historians, at least when he first wrote on the topic, often unwittingly inherited assumptions associating smell with mere animalism and sensualism as opposed to the supposedly more intellectual and rational (and hence more happily embraced by historians) senses of sight and, to some extent, hearing. Corbin reminds us that if we ignore the nonvisual senses generally, and smell in particular, then we are in danger of reinscribing past conceits and prejudices against smell that are quite unfounded. Corbin suggests that smell and habits of smelling matter and shows how the nose was central to the creation of the nineteenth-century French social order and iterations of power.[8]

Logically, we begin the collection proper with antiquity. Chapter 1 reprints part of Susan Ashbrook Harvey's highly influential 2006 book, *Scenting Salvation: Ancient Christianity and the Olfactory Imagination*. As Harvey explains, olfaction conferred important meaning in the ancient world and was inextricable to the foundation of Christian identity. As she details various scents, she places special emphasis on how scent informed the Christian association with sacrifice. Incense, because it was ephemeral, was a humble but meaningful form of sacrifice, and burning incense was transformative, changing ordinary matter into fragrance, traveling upward, and inspiring piety in those whom it penetrated. Harvey claims that alone among the ancient Mediterranean religions, early Christianity thought of incense as a spiritual fragrance, a symbol of prayer, divorced from its earthly source. Odor developed a revelatory quality because it could confer knowledge of God even if one

could not see him. Smell, then, was as powerful as vision and functioned as a unifier of God and people.

In his recent essay "Urban Smells and Roman Noses," the second
chapter of this reader, historian Neville Morley offers us both a
detailed description of the urban smells of Rome and sober remind-
ers about the difficulties and dangers of "doing" olfactory history.
In addition to narrating the common urban Roman smellscape,
explaining how Romans used smells to navigate their worlds physically and socially, he also helpfully explains that we need to be very
precise in our use of evidence. Contextualization is critical, suggests
Morley, and we must be careful not to cast the Roman past as either
intolerably smelly—as is often the case with historical treatments
concerning smell—or as unduly fragrant. Smells, their meanings,
and their interpretations, he shows, were highly contingent on who,
when, and where, and it is only this attention to context that allows
us to move beyond our idealizing and often binary views of the past
generally and of antiquity in particular. Here, olfactory scholarship
departs from some popular treatments of olfaction that sometimes
treat smell as transcendent, roving over the centuries with little
change in meaning, when in reality the meaning of smells, as all of
the essays collected here show, is highly contingent on time, place,
and constituency.[9]

Indeed, as historians of antiquity have argued, precisely by
paying attention to the broadest possible swath of time, we can
profitably rethink the connection, established by Corbin, between
the rise of a modern sensibility and the idea of deodorization. As
Morley argues, there is a tendency to associate the modern period
with attempts to control smells, thanks in part to Corbin's pioneering work; the default position, at least until sustained work on the
history of smell for antiquity, medieval, and early modern periods
appeared, was that the further we venture back into the past, the
smellier it becomes. This point has been made by several historians,
most notably by Mark S. R. Jenner, whose work has done a great

deal to complicate the modern-deodorized/premodern-odorized binary, especially for early modern England.[10]

Less interpretive but still insightful is chapter 3, C. M. Woolgar's exceptionally detailed narration of smells in the medieval world. In addition to chronicling a very wide range of smells, Woolgar asks us a deceptively simple question: why did things smell? In the context of medieval Europe, he shows, the answer was complicated. Central to this question was a sensitivity to whose nose was doing the smelling. Social standing mattered, but so did the humoral makeup of the individual: melancholic men, for example, says Woolgar, avoided good smells and frequented places that were rank. Smells were also, as in ancient Christianity, tightly indexed to sanctity and grace in the medieval world; evil too had its own fragrance. And as in Rome, smell was associated with disease, a relationship that proved tenacious and meaningful even in the modern era. Woolgar details the emerging role of perfume and an increasing tendency for individuals to scent their bodies beginning in the late fourteenth century. As in urban Rome, what seems to matter in the medieval world was context in determining how smells were evaluated and attributed meaning.

In chapter 4, thanks to the pioneering work of Holly Dugan, we encounter a sense of how people experienced olfaction in the New World, beginning in the sixteenth and seventeenth centuries. A great deal has been written on the sensory worlds of the early modern period, but relatively little attention has been paid to smell in the New World.[11] Dugan shows how early explorers to North America experienced the environment in terms of sensory zones, ranging from Newfoundland to Virginia. In many ways, these encounters were multisensory, and travel accounts of the sounds, tastes, and smells of these regions served to create sensory images in the minds of those in Europe reading these accounts. Given the commercial imperatives animating European exploration of the New World, at first glance it might seem surprising that smell had much at all to do with these ventures. Dugan suggests otherwise. She focuses on the way the English in particular tried to capitalize on their "discovery" by exploiting the olfactory success of the highly fragrant and aromatic sassafras tree. Although today most commonly associated with a taste, sassafras in the early modern period was very much a smell, associated with perfume and scent, that had several applications itself. As Dugan shows, sassafras became popular in Europe for its putative medicinal qualities and as an ingredient in perfume. But Dugan also examines just how sassafras became the smell most commonly associated with the New World, at once a scent associated with English failures and difficulties and a ubiquitous scent lending the place an Edenic quality in the noses and minds of explorers. Smell as much as sight, argues Dugan, bestowed meaning on European adventures into the New World and impinging on contemporary ideas about national identity, science, and encounters with Native Americans.

A welcome attention to gender informs chapter 5, Jennifer Evans's piece on "Gender, Medicine, and Smell in Seventeenth-Century England." Evans is concerned with the way smell was used to obviate the limits of touch and sight when it came to "treating" the "problem" of female barrenness in seventeenth-century England. Attentive to a multisensory analysis, Evans is nevertheless intrigued by the way aromatic treatments for infertility allowed male physicians—as well as women themselves—to access women's bodies. At base Evans's article shows with powerful clarity how men could circumvent dictates counseling against direct touch of women's bodies by using olfaction—a powerfully transgressive sense that allowed men to invade infertile women's bodies and sexually stimulate them with the use of particular scents. Her article speaks directly to the gendered nature of sensory protocols in the seventeenth century and reveals how somatic histories of the gendered body are inextricably tied to histories of the senses.[12]

As I have argued elsewhere, one of the most refreshing qualities about writing on the history of smell is the emerging tension
within the field. Historians of olfaction, unlike historians of some
of the other senses, seem willing to engage in interpretive debate in
an effort to further develop the subject. Despite its deeper geneal-
ogy, historical acoustemology, for example, is quite a long way from
this sort of critical examination. Historians of olfaction also tend to
engage more critically with methodological questions. Scholars of
olfaction tend to embrace the idea that smells and their meanings is
a product of their historical context, understandable in reference to
the values prevailing in that context and not in any real way reproducible in or exportable to the present. By contrast, some historians
of acoustemology have tended to write as though the sounds of the
past can be recreated in the present with some fidelity. Why this
is the case is not altogether clear, but it might well have something
to do with the simple fact that technologies of odor reproduction
are in their infancy, certainly when compared to those of sound.
Technologies of recording can have the seductive effect of lulling us
into thinking that a recorded sound retains the same meaning upon
being replayed as it held when it was originally recorded.[13] Plainly,
though, careful thinking on the matter suggests otherwise: not only
have most sounds of the past not been subject to electromagnetic
recording, but even those that have cannot be heard with the same
or even similar meaning by modern ears. Contexts change; technologies alter perceptions. This is why a tornado, for example, can
only sound like a freight train once trains have been invented and
populated the soundscape. Despite efforts by some museums and
historic homes, smell has been much more difficult to reproduce,
and this may explain in part why historians of olfaction have been
less inclined to claim that scents are transcendent.[14]

Healthy debate, then, characterizes the state of historical writing on smell. As Jonathan Reinarz shows in chapter 6, "Smell and
Victorian England," not only do historians of smell argue about

the legitimacy of, for example, Alain Corbin's claims about the connection between modernity and deodorization, but they are increasingly concerned with disrupting established and unhelpful interpretive binaries (foul versus fragrant, for example) by reconceptualizing smell as far more varied, subtle, and even intersensorial. As chapter 6 shows, many smells did not fall into either the fetid or fragrant category, but they remain as worthy of study as the more extreme iterations of smell. Reinarz is also concerned with the act of smelling—not simply with the sources of smells—and is especially interested in how the nose was used for productive purposes in an age of manufacturing.[15]

In his wide-ranging chapter on smells in the modern era—principally the twentieth century—historian Robert Jütte, in chapter 7, charts a number of significant olfactory developments, from the legal challenges to and politicization of smell and air pollution, to the way Adolf Hitler used olfactory stereotypes to demonize Jews. Jütte also examines national preoccupations with smell. Whereas Corbin focused on the French in the nineteenth century, Jütte considers the German and Western fascination with bad breath, perfume, and aromatherapy and from there makes an intriguing claim that the process of nineteenth-century deodorization in France saw a German twentieth century fascinated with reodorization. Jütte, in effect, reminds us that the history of olfaction is not beholden to a teleology in which the distant stinking past served as mere prelude to a more fragrant and deodorized era. Rather, the particular technologies and cultural, political, and social imperatives of a given time and place help define the scentscape and its multiple meanings.[16]

In chapter 8, I attempt to show through comparative analysis how olfactory stereotypes of European Jews and African Americans, while sharing many similarities, were very much products of particular cultural and political values born of specific times and places. In both instances, modernity—in particular the more extreme instances of the modern era's preoccupation with categorization and demarcation—relied as much if not more on putative smells as it did on sight. In fact, in this chapter I contend that modern iterations of racism depended heavily on olfactory stereotypes and were used to shore up a growing instability in vision.[17]

The reader concludes with an epilogue by David Howes, the esteemed anthropologist of the senses, from whom historians can and have learned a great deal. Howes's piece considers what we might think of as profitable areas of future inquiry for scholars of scent, historians in particular. Howes encourages us to think about smell as an aesthetic, which in turn opens up ways for historians to think of how olfaction informs art, how modes of past thinking have served to exclude smells from aesthetics, and how thinking outside of Western culture—notably in India, China, and Japan—can introduce us to different religious, temporal, and spatial understandings of olfaction. He reminds us that smell, like vision and hearing, does have an intellectual history, that it can engage the mind, and that to treat olfaction as a non-aesthetic sense serves only to reinscribe Kantian conceits and stereotypes and denies us access to the ways that smell is a robustly intellectual sense.[18]

Inevitably, as with any collection of essays, there are gaps. The sheer volume of work published on the history of smell in the past twenty years means that the reader lacks utter comprehensiveness. Some important work not published here—such as articles by Jenner and the book *Aroma* by Classen, Howes, and Synnott—is discussed in several chapters, giving readers a good sense of the main arguments offered in those texts.

Similarly, no reader can publish work yet to emerge. But this is not to say that we cannot speculate on the likely topics that historians of smell and smelling will work on in the near future. It seems likely, for example, that preliminary work on the smell of war—how war stretches the sense of smell, testing its very limits, sometimes inducing a feeling of sensory throwback—will continue.

We already have books and essays on the smells of the US Civil War and World Wars I and II, and it seems likely and desirable that other wars will be investigated not only for their smellscapes but for the technologies underwriting how they smelled (and to whom) and for examples of the tactical and strategic uses of scent. Work on the olfactory aspects of modern wars especially reminds us poignantly of the basic fact that olfaction is transgressive: to live is to breathe, and to breathe is to smell. There are no nose-lids. Except in cases of anosmia and the loss of the sense of smell, the world must be smelled. The stench of death generally, especially in war time, punches its way into nostrils, which cannot deny the scent and fetor; in warfare where gas is deployed, to smell—to inhale—is to court death.[19]

It also seems both probable and, again, desirable for much more work to be done not only on the history of smell and smelling outside of Europe and the United States but also on how migrations of goods and people, especially in the post–World War II era, rearranged habits of smelling. Here, historians of tariffs and business might well consider investigating how economic policy shaped the trade in perfume—which scents populated which places. Historians of demography could also shed light on how modern migration patterns reworked smells associated with nation-states. Food studies have an obvious role to play here but could profitably think about the smell of food, not just its taste. Cultural and social historians have done much of the work underwriting sensory history, but this is not to say that historians of business and economics should not have a role to play in the shaping of sensory history. Indeed, their interventions would be most welcome.

Finally, as with the history of the senses generally, historians of olfaction might consider how sensory history intersects with disability studies in an effort to further understand specificities of smell. We know something about how deaf studies intersects with sound studies, but what would a history of anosmia—the inability to smell—look like? Is there such a thing as social or cultural anosmia, whereby smells become so familiar that they are no longer smelled or retain the same meaning? Clearly, there is such a thing, and this in turn will help historians of smell think carefully about their sources. We know that travel accounts, while immensely useful, tend to profile the exceptional and rarely speak to the normative when it comes to the senses. After all, travelers comment on the sounds, sights, smells, tastes, and touches they found new and intriguing when visiting a place for the first time. Historians of sound have been especially attentive to this methodological issue, and historians of olfaction can use their work to think carefully about how smells become habituated, normalized, and slip in and out of the written historical record.[20]

There are, of course, literally hundreds of topics left to explore through the nose. The above list is certainly not exhaustive. Whatever the future of the field of olfactory history, it is my hope that the essays in this reader might, in some small way, help future scholars think about the challenges of writing history per the nose but also recognize the immense dividends of the approach.

NOTES

1. Douglas Kahn, "Sound Awake," *Australian Review of Books* (July 2000), 21–22. For an overview, see my "Making Sense of U.S. History," *American Historian* 7 (February 2016): 18–23.

2. On the origins and evolution of sensory history, see my *Sensing the Past: Seeing, Hearing, Smelling, Tasting, and Touching in History* (Berkeley: University of California Press, 2007). On environmental historians and the senses, see, for example, the pioneering work of Raymond Smilor, "Cacophony at 34th and 6th: The Noise Problem in America, 1900–1930," *American Studies* 18 (Spring 1977): 23–38; and, more recently, Peter Coates, "The Strange Stillness of the Past: Toward an Environmental History of Sound and Noise," *Environmental History* 10 (October 2005): 636–65.

3. An especially astute essay is Peter Denney, "Looking Back, Groping Forward: Rethinking Sensory History," *Rethinking History* 15 (November 2011): 601–16. See too my "Producing Sense, Consuming Sense, Making

Sense: Perils and Prospects for Sensory History," *Journal of Social History* 40 (Summer 2007): 841–58; "Making Sense of Social History," *Journal of Social History* 37 (September 2003), 165–86. For the various round-table discussions, see *Journal of American History* 95 (September 2008); *American Historical Review* (April 2011); *Hispanic American Historical Review* 96 (2016); *American Quarterly* 63 (September 2011); *Journal of Sport History* 40 (Spring 2013); *Public Historian* (November 2015). On the book series, see my own Interdisciplinary Studies in Sensory History published by Penn State University Press; the Sensory Studies Series, edited by David Howes; and the Senses in Antiquity Series, published by Routledge and edited by Mark Bradley and Shane Butler. Constance Classen, ed., *A Cultural History of the Senses*, 6 vols. (New York: Bloomsbury, 2014).

4.   T. M. Luhrmann, "Can't Place That Smell?: You Must Be Americans," *New York Times*, September 7, 2014, 6.

5.   Jim Drobnick is certainly right, however, to point to the relatively uneven evolution of writing on olfaction generally prior to the 1980s. See his "Introduction: Olfactocentrism," in *The Smell Culture Reader*, ed. Jim Drobnick (Oxford: Berg, 2006): 3–4. On historians deploying sensory language for literary effect, see my *The Smell of Battle, The Taste of Siege: A Sensory History of the American Civil War* (New York: Oxford University Press, 2014), 4–5.

6.   Constance Classen, David Howes, and Anthony Synnott, *Aroma: The Cultural History of Smell* (New York: Routledge, 1994). See also David Howes, ed., *Varieties of Sensory Experience: A Sourcebook in the Anthropology of the Senses* (Toronto: University of Toronto Press, 1991); Constance Classen, *Worlds of Sense: Exploring the Senses in History and Culture* (New York: Routledge, 1993).

7.   See especially Kelvin Low, *Scents and Scent-sibilities: Smell and Everyday Life Experiences* (Newcastle-upon-Tyne: Cambridge Scholars Publishing, 2009). There is some excellent anthropological and sociological work on smell in India (most notably, James McHugh's important study *Sandalwood and Carrion: Smell in Indian Religion and Culture* [Oxford: Oxford University Press, 2012]). On Japan, see Brian Morean, *Making Scents of Smell: Manufacturing Incense in Japan*, June 2007, Copenhagen Business School, Creative Encounters Working Paper no. 1.

8.   Corbin's work still informs us. Take, for example, very recent work on the olfactory history of nineteenth-century urban America, which takes seriously many of Corbin's ideas and applies them to the history of (mainly) Chicago and New York in an effort to show how smell influenced urban policy and sanitation. See Melanie Kiechle, *Smell Detectives: An Olfactory History of Nineteenth-Century Urban America* (Seattle and London: University of Washington Press, 2017). Note also, Rodolphe El-Khoury, "Polish and Deodorise: Paving the City in Late Eighteenth-Century France," in *Smell Culture Reader*, 18–28.

9. Randy Kennedy, "What's That Smell?: Rare Books and Artifacts from a 1906 Library," *New York Times*, March 3, 2017; Carmen Drahl, "Smelling the Moon," *Chemical and Engineering News*, December 14, 2011. Even some of the science of olfaction points to the nose of the beholder, though less to the historical context in which the particular nose does the smelling. See Sophie L. Rovner, "The Smell of Sweaty Guys," *Chemical and Engineering News*, September 19, 2007.

10. On this topic see too the earlier and important work of D. S. Potter, "Odor and Power in the Roman Empire," in J. I. Porter, ed., *Constructions of the Classical Body* (Ann Arbor: University of Michigan Press, 1999), 169–89; and, generally, the excellent collection of essays on the topic in Mark Bradley, ed., *Smell and the Ancient Senses*, from which Morley's essay is drawn. Mark S. R. Jenner, "Civilization and Deodorization?: Smell in Early Modern English Culture," in *Civil Histories: Essays Presented to Sir Keith Thomas*, ed. Burke, B. Harrison, and Slack (Oxford: Oxford University Press, 2000), 127–44; Mark S. R. Jenner, "Follow Your Nose?: Smell, Smelling, and Their Histories," *American Historical Review* (April 2011): 335–51.

11. See, for example, Hermann Roodenburg, ed., *A Cultural History of the Senses in the Renaissance* (New York: Bloomsbury, 2017); Bruce R. Smith, *The Acoustic World of Early Modern England: Attending to the O-Factor* (Chicago: University of Chicago Press, 1999); Matthew Milner, *The Senses and the English Reformation* (Burlington, VT: Ashgate, 2011); Jeffrey Chipps-Smith, *Sensuous Worship: Jesuits and the Art of the Early Catholic Reformation in Germany* (Princeton, NJ: Princeton University Press, 2002). Note as well Hristomir A. Stanev, "The City out of Breath: Jacobean City Comedy and the Odors of Restraint," *Postmedieval* 3 (Winter 2012): 423–35.

12. Note too Clare Brandt, "Fume and Perfume: Some Eighteenth-Century Uses of Smell," *Journal of British Studies*, 43, no. 4 (2004): 444–63; Emily Cockayne, *Hubbub: Filth, Noise, and Stench in Early Modern England, 1600–1700* (New Haven: Yale University Press, 2007).

13. On this, see my critique in "Producing Sense and Consuming Sense."

14. Mark Jenner believes that the historical study of smell coincided with an increasing tendency to use smell and scent to evoke the past at various historic sites, see Jenner, "Civilization and Deodorization," 128.

15. See my "In Praise of Discord: Injecting Noise into Sound History," Vanderbilt History Seminar, Nashville, Tennessee, April 10, 2017; "A Sensory History Manifesto," Centre for Interdisciplinary Studies in Society and Culture, Concordia University, Montreal, Canada, October 6, 2017; and the indispensable book by Jonathan Reinarz, *Past Scents: Historical Perspectives on Smell* (Urbana: University of Illinois Press, 2014). Note too Adam Mack, *Sensing Chicago: Noisemakers, Strikebreakers, and Muckrakers* (Urbana: University of Illinois Press, 2015).

16. For an intriguing related treatment on the invention of scent, see Andrew Kettler, "Making the Synthetic Epic: Septimus Piesse, the Manufacturing of Mercutio Frangipani, and Olfactory Renaissance in Victorian England," *Senses and Society*, 10 no. 1 (March 2015). Note too the important work on the modern period by Joy Parr, *Sensing Changes: Technologies, Environments, and the Everyday, 1953–2003* (Burnaby: University of British Columbia Press, 2010).

17. See also my *How Race Is Made: Slavery, Segregation, and the Senses* (Chapel Hill: University of North Carolina Press, 2008); William Tullett, "Grease and Sweat: Race and Smell in Eighteenth-Century English Culture," *Cultural and Social History* (2016). We are now in possession of a masterful treatment of race and olfaction in the Atlantic world. See Andrew Kettler, "Odor and Power in the Americas: Olfactory Consciousness from Columbus to Emancipation," (PhD dissertation, University of South Carolina, 2017).

18. On this topic, see too Jim Drobnick, "Towards an Olfactory Art History: The Mingled, Fatal, and Rejuvenating Perfumes of Paul Gaugin," *Senses and Society* 7 (2012): 196–208.

19. Smith, *Smell of Battle*, 66–83; Franco Nicolis, "The Scent of Snow at Punta Linke: First World War Sites as Sense-scapes, Trentino, Italy," and Susannah Callow, "Odour and Ethnicity: Americans and Japanese in the Second World War," in *Modern Conflict and the Senses*, ed. Nicholas J. Saunders and Paul Cornish, (New York: Routledge 2017), 61–75, 157–70. Other areas of inquiry attesting to how the senses are stretched and pummeled include the sensory history of natural disasters. See my *Camille, 1969: Histories of a Hurricane* (Athens: University of Georgia Press, 2011), ch. 1; "'The Sensorium on a Constant Strain': A Sensory History of Natural Disasters in the Danish West Indies in 1867," Danish National Archives, Copenhagen, Denmark, June 10, 2017.

20. On deafness and sound, see Mara Mills, *On the Phone: Deafness and Communication Engineering* (Durham: Duke University Press, 2017). The travel account bias is discussed in Bruce R. Smith, *The Acoustic World of Early Modern England*; some of the methodological issues are explored in my exchange with Professor Smith in "Echoes in Print: Method and Causation in Aural History," *Journal of The Historical Society* 2 (Summer/Fall, 2002): 317–36. A good example of the issue can be found in Richard Mullen and James Munson, *"The Smell of the Continent": The British Discover Europe* (London: Macmillan, 2009).

Why Smell the Past?

Alain Corbin

The idea of writing a book about the perception of odors came to me as I was reading the memoirs of Jean-Noël Hallé, a member of the Société Royale de Médecine under the ancien régime and the first incumbent of the chair of public hygiene established in Paris in 1794.

Let us follow him through three episodes of his tireless struggle, beginning with February 14, 1790. More than six months have passed since the storming of the Bastille. The situation has calmed down. Mild temperatures announce the end of winter. On this day the thermometer rises to four degrees Réaumur; there is a south-easterly breeze; near the Pont de la Tournelle the Seine reaches a level of five feet. Accompanied by his friend Boncerf, Jean-Noël Hallé has gone out early in the morning to explore the odors on the riverbanks, or rather, to sniff them out. Both scientists have been entrusted with this task by the Société Royale de Médecine. Starting at the Pont Neuf, they stride along the right bank up to La Rapée. They cross the river almost opposite the sewer of the Salpêtrière in order to return on the left bank to their departure point. The meticulous record of their walk of more than ten kilometers provides an accurate picture of the variety of odors. There is no reference anywhere in the text to anything visual.

Hallé's report makes rather unsatisfactory reading for amateurs of the picturesque; similarly, there is no mention of the chatter of washerwomen or of the noisy bustle of dockers on either side of the Seine. Nothing but odors—the discontinuous mapping of a walk that favors rubbish and ignores those parts of the river where the quays or houses are built directly into the water and where no stench can be perceived.

This olfactory survey is not without danger. One incident shows how necessary it is to guard against excessive boldness. At the mouth of the dreadful Gobelin tributary Hallé's companion, *facing the breeze,* walks along the edge of the water and wades through the black mud: "Monsieur Boncerf, who at this point had turned more directly into the southeasterly breeze and had descended to the riverbank, was overcome by a biting, alkaline, stinging, and stinking odor. It affected his respiratory system so badly that his throat began to hurt within half an hour and his tongue became noticeably swollen. Affected by these poisonous vapors, he warned me to return to the road straightaway; because I had remained at the easternmost point of the bank that had been infested by these sediments, and hence with my back to the wind, I myself did not experience anything unpleasant."[1]

But this was no more than a minor skirmish. The long battle with stench provided incomparably more dramatic episodes. Consider another incident eight years earlier. On March 23, 1782, the most famous experts in hygiene and chemistry gather in front of the Hotel de la Grenade in the rue de la Parcheminerie. The cesspool of the building is to be cleaned out. The fatal character of its effluvia is well known. Moreover, the landlady is certain that the medical students have buried beneath the feces arms, legs, and other parts of the human body by the bucketful. The extent of the danger is without precedent. The Académie Royale des Sciences has dispatched the academicians Lavoisier, Le Roy, and Fougeroux to make an on-the-spot inspection. The chemists Macquer and Fourcroy and the duc de La Rochefoucauld, the abbé Tessier, and Jean-Noël Hallé have come by order of the Société Royale de Médecine. They all are supposed to test the effectiveness of a new antimephitic substance; its inventor, Sieur Janin, has daringly asserted that it will destroy foul smells and quell miasmas.

It is a cold day, a mere two degrees Réaumur around noon. The wind is blowing from the north. There has been a heavy snowfall during the morning. In short, meteorological conditions appear favorable. While Janin sprinkles his substance, Jean-Noël Hallé and abbé Tessier climb up and down ladders in order to measure the varying intensity of the stench. For hours the experiment, which began between eight and nine in the morning, proceeds without incident. Then, around three in the afternoon, comes a dramatic turn of events: one of the cesspool cleaners suffers a fit of asphyxiation and slips off the ladder into the cesspool. He is pulled out with extreme difficulty.

The onlookers lean over the mortally ill cleaner. A young man tries in vain to save him by administering artificial respiration. At this point Monsieur Verville, an expert, intervenes. He is an inspector for a company that makes the ventilators which have been used for some years during the cleaning of cesspools. Hallé graphically describes the fate of the hapless Verville.

> He had scarcely inhaled the air that was coming from the mouth of the mortally ill man when he shouted "I am a dead man!" and fell down unconscious. . . . I saw that he was making an extreme effort to regain his breath; he was held by the arms, as he reared up with a loud groan; his chest and his stomach moved up and down alternately in violent convulsive movements. He had lost consciousness; his limbs were cold; his pulse became weaker and weaker. . . . Occasionally his mouth even filled with foam, his limbs became stiff, and the sick man appeared to be having a genuine epileptic fit.[2]

Fortunately Monsieur Verville regains consciousness. He has done no more than inhale the breath of a mortally ill person, and he is soon able to go home. But for a long time he suffers from after-effects. As he explains, "cesspool gases that have been transmitted" are even more terrifying than those that threaten to suffocate the cleaner at the bottom of the cesspool.

Stay with Jean-Noël Hallé a moment longer, this time to accompany him on his general medical practice. The following report is highly detailed, but not a single word should be omitted; it describes the various pathogenic odors that develop in that olfactory inferno, the hospital.

There is a stench that is similar to the one exuded by clothes, and there is a moldy smell that is less noticeable but nevertheless more unpleasant because of the general revulsion it arouses. A third, which might be called the odor of decomposition, may be described as a mixture of the acidic, the sickly, and the fetid; it provokes nausea rather than offending the nose. This mixture accompanies decomposition and is the most repellent among all the odors to be encountered in a hospital. Another odor, which makes the nose and eyes burn, results from uncleanliness. It gives the impression that the air contains something like powder, and, if one looks for the source, one is certain to find damp moldy laundry, a pile of rubbish or clothes and bedclothes infested by fermenting miasmas. Each infectious material has its distinctive exhalation. Doctors know the special smell of a septic wound, of a cancerous agent, and the pestilential odor that is spread by caries. But what physicians have learned of this subject from experience can be tested by anyone who compares the various odors in the wards. In the pediatric ward the smell is sour and stinking; in the women's wards it is sweet and putrid; the men's wards, on the other hand, exude a strong odor that merely stinks and hence is not so repulsive. Although there is now a greater emphasis on cleanliness than in earlier times, in the wards occupied by the good poor of Bicêtre there prevails a flat odor that produces an effect of nausea in delicate constitutions.[3]

Hallé's statements and behavior are by no means unusual. A careful reading of contemporary texts reveals a collective hypersensitivity to odors of all sorts. Pleasure at the sight of the landscape of an English garden or the blueprint of an ideal city is paralleled by horror of the city air, which is infested by miasmas.[4] But we moderns risk an anachronistic perspective. From the anguished quest of Jean-Noël Hallé onward, something changes in the way smells are perceived and analyzed.

What is the meaning of this more refined alertness to smell? What produced the mysterious and alarming strategy of deodorization that causes us to be intolerant of everything that offends our muted olfactory environment? By what stages has this far-reaching, anthropological transformation taken place? What are the social stakes? What kinds of interests are behind this change in our evaluative schemas and symbolic systems concerning the sense of smell?

Lucien Febvre was among the first to recognize the problem; the history of olfactory perception is one of the many avenues of investigation that he has opened up.[5] Since then historians have turned their attention to the senses of sight and smell; in the case of sight, a project stimulated by the discovery of the great panoptic dream (its claim to attention further strengthened by developments in aesthetic theory); in the case of taste, a project sheltered behind the desire to analyze the rituals and forms of sociability of everyday life. In this sphere as well, the sense of smell has suffered from an unremitting process of discrediting since the time when a new offensive against the olfactory intensities of public space was being sketched out.[6]

The time has come to trace the conflict-laden history of the perception of smells and to study the logic of the systems of images from which that history has been generated. But it is also necessary to relate divergent modes of perception to social structures. It would be futile to analyze social tensions and conflicts without account-ing for the different kinds of sensibilities that decisively influence them. Abhorrence of smells produces its own form of social power. Foul-smelling rubbish appears to threaten the social order, whereas the reassuring victory of the hygienic and the fragrant promises to buttress its stability.

Initially there seems to be considerable accord between Hallé's behavior and the philosophical positions of his time. The subtle sen-sitivity with which he approaches the phenomena of sensory per-ception reflects the influence of sensualism upon scientific method. Sensualist theory, which was based on the thought of Locke, had been developed in basic outline by Maubec as early as 1709.[7] A gen-eration later it had been given greater precision by David Hartley, whose writings were translated into French in 1755. The theory had been transformed into a logical system by the time Condillac published his two main works, *Essai sur l'origine des connaissances humaines* (1746) and *Traité des sensations* (1754). For Locke, under-standing was an "autonomous principle endowed with activity of its own"; for Condillac, in contrast, it was no more than "the sum total of a combination of psychic activities."[8] Judgment, desire, lust, and craving are nothing but modified expressions of sensation. And everyone remembers Condillac's proof of this: the fictitious statue that, in coming alive, confuses the sense of its own existence with the fragrance of a rose it first smells.

Thenceforth all scientists, all philosophers have found them-selves obliged to engage with sensualism. However great their resistance, they have been unable to escape its influence.[9] These, however, are mere episodes in the history of philosophy during the Enlightenment. The important point here concerns the devel-oping alertness to the sensory environment. The senses "increas-ingly [became] analytical tools, sensitive gauges for the degree of pleasantness or unpleasantness of the physical environment."[10] While Hallé with his sensitive nose pursued the menace of germs, an optimist like Abbé Pluche invited his readers to enjoy the spectacle of nature.[11]

The philosophers, however, paid little attention to the sense of smell. This neglect reinforces Lucien Febvre's argument that the sense of smell has declined in importance since the beginning of the modern period.[12] Moreover, scientific discourse has been reluctant to address this issue, given the extent to which it is riddled with contradictions; science has oscillated between appreciating and depreciating olfactory phenomena. The baffling poverty of the language,[13] lack of understanding of the nature of odors, and the refusal of some scientists to abandon the *spiritus rector* ("guiding spirit") theory all help to explain the abundance of muddled thinking and tortuous writing on the subject.[14] A few fairly simple stereotypes demonstrate the paradoxical nature of the sense of smell. Olfaction as the sense of lust, desire, and impulsiveness is associated with sensuality. Smelling and sniffing are associated with animal behavior.[15] If olfaction were his most important sense, man's linguistic incapacity to describe olfactory sensations would turn him into a creature tied to his environment.[16] Because they are ephemeral, olfactory sensations can never provide a persistent stimulus of thought. Thus the development of the sense of smell seems to be inversely related to the development of intelligence.

Unlike the senses of hearing and sight, valued on the basis of a perpetually repeated Platonic prejudice, olfaction is also relatively useless in civilized society. According to Count Albrecht von Haller, "The sense of smell was less important to [man], for he was destined to walk upright; he was to discover from a distance what might be his food; social life and language were designed to enlighten him about the properties of the things that appeared to him to be edible."[17] The best proof of this claim is that the sense of smell is more highly developed among savages than among civilized men; Père du Tertre, Père Lafitau, Humboldt,[18] Cook, and the early anthropologists[19] were agreed on this point. Even if some anecdotes on this subject seem exaggerated, observations of adolescent savages have confirmed that people who have been raised outside civilized society have a superior sense of smell.[20]

All these scientific convictions produced a whole array of taboos on the use of the sense of smell. Sniffing and smelling, a predilection for powerful animal odors, the erotic effect of sexual odors—all become objects of suspicion. Such interests, thought to be essentially savage, attest to a proximity to animals, a lack of refinement, and ignorance of good manners. In short, they reveal a basic failure at the level of social education. The sense of smell is at the bottom of the hierarchy of senses, along with the sense of touch. Furthermore, Kant disqualified it aesthetically.

Jean-Noël Hallé's behavior contradicts all these assertions and demonstrates the first paradox: the sense of smell is an animal sense—and at the same time, and precisely because of this, the sense of self-preservation. The nose, as the vanguard of the sense of taste, warns us against poisonous substances.[21] Even more important, the sense of smell locates hidden dangers in the atmosphere. Its capacity to test the properties of air is unmatched. The increased importance attributed to the phenomenon of air by chemistry and medical theories of infection put a brake on the declining attention to the sense of smell. The nose anticipates dangers; it recognizes from a distance both harmful mold and the presence of miasmas. It is repelled by what is in a state of decomposition. Increased recognition of the importance of the air led to increased acknowledgment of the importance of the sense of smell as an instrument of vigilance. That vigilance produced the guidelines for the reordering of space when the rise of modern chemistry made that reordering unavoidable.

A second paradox is that olfactory sensations are ephemeral, and thus defy comparisons through memory; any attempt to train the sense of smell always results in disappointment. This is why olfaction would not be taken into account in designing the

English garden as the privileged place of sensory education and fulfillment.

On the other hand, doctors since ancient times have untiringly stressed the importance of the nose as the sensory organ closest to the brain, the "origin of sensation."[22] Moreover, "all the fine threads of the olfactory nerves and plates are extremely loose and full of life. Those that are more removed from this source are firmer and less penetrable, in line with the general laws on nerves."[23] Thus, in contrast to the claims made in association with the first paradox, the extraordinary subtlety of the sense of smell appears to *grow* with the development of intelligence. The culminating aesthetic proof is that the exquisite fragrance of flowers "appears to be made for man alone."[24]

As the sense of affective behavior and its secrets (in Rousseau's frame of reference, the sense of imagination and of desire),[25] the sense of smell was viewed as capable of shaking man's inner life more profoundly than were the senses of hearing or of sight. It seemed to reach to the roots of life.[26] In the nineteenth century it was elevated to being the privileged instrument of recollection, that which reveals the coexistence of the self and the universe, and, finally, the precondition of intimacy. Furthermore, the rise of narcissism was also to favor this hitherto discredited form of sensory life, in the same way that the obsessive fear of polluted air and the battle against infectious disease emphasized its importance.[27]

Clearly, the theoretical discourse devoted to olfaction reflects a maze of fascinating taboos and mysterious attractions. The required vigilance toward the threat of putrid miasmas, the exquisite enjoyment of fragrant flowers and the perfume of narcissus counterbalance the proscription of sensuous animal instinct. It would be therefore an overhasty move to exclude the sense of smell from the history of sensory perceptions simply because of the infatuation with the prestige of sight and hearing.

NOTES

1. J.-N. Hallé, "Procès-verbal de la visite faite le long des deux rives de la rivière Seine, depuis le pont-Neuf jusqu'à la Rappée et la Garre, le 14 février 1790," *Histoire et mémoires de la Société Royale de Médecine* 10 (1789), lxxxvi.

2. J.-N. Hallé, *Recherches sur la nature et les effets du méphitisme des fosses d'aisances* (1785), 57–58.

3. J.-N. Hallé, "Air des hôpitaux de terre et de mer," in *Encyclopédic méthodique: Médecine* (1787), 571.

4. On the pleasures of sight in the eighteenth century, see Mona Ozouf, "L'Image de la ville chez Claude-Nicolas Ledoux," *Annales: Economies, Sociétés, Civilisations* 21 (November–December 1966), 1276.

5. Lucien Febvre, *Le problème de l'incroyance au XVI⁰ siècle* (Paris, 1942).

6. In his *Introduction à la France moderne: Essai de psychologie historique, 1500–1640* (Paris, 1961), Robert Mandrou, influenced by Lucien Febvre, devotes a long chapter to the history of perception at the dawn of modern times; as far as I know this is the only attempt at a synthesis of the subject.

   Since the publication of Pierre Francastel's work, the historical analysis of sight has inspired numerous books, most recently those by Michael Baxandall. Number 40 of *Actes de la recherche en sciences sociales* (1981) is devoted entirely to this aspect of the sociology of perception. In *La fantasmagorie* (Paris, 1982), a masterly work devoted to the study of the mirror image and the transfiguration of the perceptive universe in the literature of fantasy, Max Milner analyzes the bonds that, according to Kant, link sensory history and the inquiry into identity.

   As early as 1967, Jean-Paul Aron's *Essai sur la sensibilité alimentaire à Paris au XIXe siècle* (Paris) inaugurated a long series of works devoted to the history of taste. The Institut Français du Goût periodically endeavors to bring together at Tours all researchers into the human sciences concerned with psychosociology and the history of eating behavior. However, very few of these studies concern the gustative sensation, the poverty of which is well known: it is in fact the sense of smell that contributes the refinement of flavors.

   Mention must also be made of the interesting book by Ruth Winter, a journalist for the *Los Angeles Times: Scent Talk among Animals* (New York, 1977). It contains a copious bibliography of recent works in physiology and experimental psychology and, notably, references to books by J. Le Magnen and by A. Holley, French experts in these aspects of osmology. The aesthetics of the sense of smell is the subject of Edmond Roudnitska's remarkable *L'Esthéique en question* (Paris, 1977), which includes an interesting study of Kant's rejection of the sense of smell.

   Finally, mention should be made of the whole body of work by Peter

Reinhart Gleichmann. For some years he has been extending the research of Norbert Elias and studying the interrelationships between the change in emotions, the transformation of the images of the body, and the techniques of social control that the construction of cleansing systems reveals. Especially relevant to our purposes are his articles on the integration of the physiological functions in the domestic sphere and the extent of the chain reactions engendered by this domestication; see, for example, "Des villes propres et sans odeur," *Urbi*, April 1982. However, his primary focus is central Europe between 1866 and 1930; he says nothing about the pre-Pasteurian mythologies and minimizes the importance of the period studied here. In the same field see also Dominique Laporte, *Histoire de la merde* (Paris, 1979).

7. See Jean Ehrard, *L'Idée de nature en France dans la première moitié du XVIIIe siècle* (Paris, 1963), 676.

8. Ibid., 685.

9. A survey of these episodes in Enlightenment philosophy is beyond the scope of this book. Claire Salomon-Bayet, *L'Institution de la science et l'expérience du vivant* (Paris, 1978), 204 ff., has successfully analyzed how scholars use the observations of the *homo ferus*, the philosophical fiction (Condillac's statue), the experimental fictions (the healed blind man of Maupertuis), or unforeseen accidents (Rousseau's fall during his second promenade) to try to solve the problems posed by empirical knowledge.

10. Jacques Guillerme, "Le malsain et l'économie de la nature," *XVIIIe Siècle* 9 (1977), 61.

11. "All the diversities of flavors, odors, sounds, colors, in a word, all our sensations are only the action of God upon us, diversified according to our needs"; Pluche, *Spectacle de la nature,* vol. 4 (1739), 162.

12. Febvre, *Le problème de l'incroyance,* 461–72.

13. Emphasized by Locke, *An Essay Concerning Human Understanding* (London, 1947), 36 (1st ed., 1755).

14. Robert Boyle, *The General History of the Air* (London, 1692) had noted that musk, despite the strong odors it emitted, lost nothing, or almost nothing, of its substance. Albrecht von Haller, *Elementa physiologiae corporis humani*, vol. 5 (Lausanne, 1763), 157, kept papers perfumed by a single grain of ambergris for more than forty years with no diminution in their odor. Herman Boerhaave propounded as many observations confirming the *spiritus rector* theory. In his view, far from being the emanation of corpuscles separated from the smelling body, odor was a subtle fluid, "a volatile being, very fleeting, very expansible, weightless, completely invisible, inaccessible to the senses were it not for the olfactory membrane"; quoted in Hippolyte Cloquet, *Osphrésiologie ou traité des odeurs,* 2nd ed. (1821), 39–40. For the majority of scholars, that guiding spirit, called *aroma* at the end of

the eighteenth century, was oily in nature. It seemed obvious, however, that it did not assume the same form everywhere, and Pierre Joseph Maquer, one of the most eminent chemists of the day, strove to catalog its various manifestations.

It was precisely this variety that eventually discredited Boerhaave's theory. Since aroma perpetually proved different from itself, its existence as a principle could no longer be sustained. This at least is what Nicolas Le Cat (*Traité des sensations et des passions en général et des sens en particulier*, vol. 2 [1767], 234) and the chevalier Louis de Jaucourt ("Odorat," in the 1765 Encyclopédie) already thought. Although the corpuscular theory, already formulated by Theophrastus and approved by the Cartesians, remained hypothetical until Fourcroy and Berthollet proved it well founded, a number of Hallé's contemporaries thought that bodies emitted several particles of smell that formed part of their substance.

15. Especially for Buffon.

16. See Condillac's view of the role of language; Ehrard, *L'Idée de nature*, 686.

17. Haller, quoted in "Odorat," *Encyclopédie*, supplement (1777).

18. Père du Tertre, *Histoire naturelle et morale des îles Antilles . . .* (1658); Père Joseph François Lafitau, *Moeurs des sauvages américains . . .* (1724); Alexander von Humboldt, *Essai politique sur le royaume de la Nouvelle-Espagne* (1811).

19. Notably Samuel Thomas von Soemmerring and Johann Friedrich Blumenbach.

20. "There have been observations," wrote Haller again in 1777, "of a child raised in a wilderness sniffing the grass as a sheep would, and choosing by the odor the piece he would like to eat. Having been returned to society and become accustomed to different foods, he lost this trait"; quoted in "Odorat."

21. See Le Cat, *Traité de sensations*, 230.

22. An opinion also found in Haller, *Eléments de physiologie*, 2 vols. (1769), 2:33.

23. Jaucourt, quoted in "Odorat."

24. Haller, quoted in "Odorat."

25. Rousseau, *Emile* (Paris, 1966), 200–201; odors "exert an influence not so much by what they give forth as by what they hold in abeyance."

26. Jaucourt, quoted in "Odorat": "There is a mysterious rapport between the vital principle and fragrant bodies."

27. "I began to see calmly and to hear effortlessly when a light, fresh breeze brought me scents that caused me to blossom inwardly and gave me a feeling of love for myself," declares the first man in Buffon's account; *De l'homme* (Paris, 1971), 215.

CHAPTER 1

Scent and Sacrifice in the Early Christian World

Susan Ashbrook Harvey

Religious symbols . . . reek of meaning.

—Clifford Geertz

Around the year 15 CE, the elderly bishop Polycarp was martyred in the city of Smyrna on charges of refusal to sacrifice to the Roman gods. Christian witnesses to Polycarp's execution wrote a letter reporting the event to their neighboring church in the city of Philomelium in Phrygia. But they addressed their letter further to "the holy Church in every place"; it quickly circulated throughout the Christian communities of the Roman Empire and beyond. By their epistle the Christians of Smyrna intended to render account of the hardships they had suffered in persecution, culminating in the death of their renowned and beloved leader. They also needed to make sense of his death, for themselves and for Christians everywhere.

Accordingly, the letter abounds with allusions to the rich literary traditions surrounding the classical concept of the "noble death,"[1] amply demonstrated with descriptions of Polycarp's serenity, steadfastness under torture, and calm acceptance of execution. More importantly, the writers declared that Polycarp had chosen his death on behalf of all believers and not simply for his own salvation.

Overt parallels were drawn between Polycarp's final days and the passion narratives of Jesus of Nazareth. Such presentation depicts Polycarp's death in unequivocal terms as a true martyrdom honorable to divine as well as human eyes.

A further interpretive strategy of the letter was the Smyrnaeans' use of familiar sensory impressions to articulate what had taken place. The witnesses told of Polycarp's arrest, his brief trial, and his execution in the public stadium of the city in the presence of the gathered populace. Then they described their own experience of Polycarp's martyrdom:

> The men in charge of the fire started to light it. A great flame
> blazed up and those of us to whom it was given to see beheld
> a miracle. And we have been preserved to recount the story
> to others. For the flames, bellying out like a ship's sail in the
> wind, formed into the shape of a vault and thus surrounded
> the martyr's body as with a wall. And he was within it not
> as burning flesh but rather as bread being baked, or like gold
> and silver being purified in a smelting furnace. And from it
> we perceived such a delightful fragrance as though it were
> smoking incense or some other costly perfume.
>
> At last when these vicious men realized that his body
> could not be consumed by the fire they ordered a *confector*
> to go up and plunge a dagger into the body. When he did this
> there came out such a quantity of blood that the flames were
> extinguished.[2]

The experience these Christian witnesses claimed was one in which their senses redefined the event. The fire they saw enshrined rather than destroyed their bishop. The air they breathed billowed with the aroma of baking bread—the comforting promise of daily sustenance, and for Christians the center of (sacrificial) fellowship in the name of Christ. Moreover, the fire seemed not to destroy Polycarp's body, but rather to purify it as in a crucible, until the air no longer carried the stench of burning flesh, but instead a fragrance as sweet as frankincense, the precious savor of sacrifice pleasing to God. The dove recalled the presence of the Holy Spirit at Christ's baptism (Mk 1:10; Mt 3:16; Lk 3:22), and blood pouring from the martyr's side recalled Christ's own crucifixion (Jn 19:34). Visuality framed this scene, starting with fire and ending with blood. But olfactory experience marked its meaning, as the smells of bread and frankincense signaled the supreme moment of Christian offering ("This is my body . . . broken for you"). With a few, deft, sensory images—a glimpse, a fragrance, a texture—Polycarp's followers rendered a deeply traumatic event into a theological teaching that would become foundational for the emerging Christian identity. Their bishop's death was neither meaningless nor a defeat. Rather, it had been a pure and holy sacrifice acceptable to God. Like the death of Jesus Christ to which it conformed in style and manner, it heralded the promise of salvation, eternal life, for all believers.

Of all the imagery that laced the Smyrnaeans' letter, that of frankincense carried particular poignancy because of its universal association with sacrificial offering.[3] In the religious systems of the ancient Mediterranean world, sacrifice was the central component of community order and identity. In its most basic sense, sacrifice was a relational activity. The ritual processes of sacrifice established and maintained the relationships that bound the human order to the divine one. Moreover, through ritual roles, functions, and sequenced actions, sacrifice articulated the ties that constituted the human social order. It demarcated distinctions and connections within the local community, and of the local community in relation to larger political and ethnic structures. Sacrifice maintained an ordered cosmos, inclusive of human and divine domains.[4]

From the simple to the complex, Mediterranean sacrificial practices could be—and in ancient texts almost always were—characterized by the smells they generated. Incense was burned along the route the ritual procession would follow, and at the location where the rite was held. Flowers, wreaths, and perfumes adorned altars, cult statues, sacrificial victims, ritual leaders, ritual garments, and participants. Libations added the scent of (perfumed) wine. On the occasions of animal sacrifice, the smell of blood and roasting or boiling meat deepened the multiple aromas.[5] Because fire was a frequent component, these smells were associated further with their accompanying smoke. In the smoke, the combined smells of the ritual process could be seen to pass, literally, from earth to heaven. Lucian described animal sacrifice in just such terms, as olfactorily visual: "A godly steam, and fit for godly nostrils, rises heavenwards, and drifts to each quarter of the sky."[6]

The "scent" of sacrifice was thus diverse, comprised of the offering and all that attended and adorned the sequence of ritual actions. It might be as simple as frankincense alone; it might carry the grand fragrances of extravagant ceremony.[7] But to the ancients— whether Greek, Roman, Egyptian, Syrian, Jew—the savor of sacrifice required "beauty" if it was to be worthy, or even appropriate, for the deity to whom it was offered. Fragrance was itself an attribute of divinity, and of everything characterizing the divine. Gods and goddesses could be recognized by the perfumed scent they wafted; their divine abodes were redolent with sweet scents.[8] Rich flora and fauna adorned the places dear to them in the natural world,[9] and the marvelous utopias of legend where the inhabitants dwelled always in the gods' favor.[10] Those humans whose lives demonstrated exceptional blessing themselves exhaled a wondrous scent, near to the divine as they were.[11] Altars, devotees, and sacrificers bedecked with flowers were known to be especially cherished by the gods.[12] The stench of wounds or illness—marks of human mortality—could invalidate religious activities: in Greek myth, Philoctetes had been exiled on the island of Lemnos when Odysseus and his men feared the stink from his wound would pollute their sacrifices.[13]

Incense was not necessarily the only offering, nor the most important or powerful one, but it was a general accompaniment to sacrificial rituals of all kinds. Its scent was a marker of the occasion, and in any context "incense" could be a term equivalent to "sacrifice." Unlike animal sacrifice, which provided meat for the priests and community to eat, incense offerings left no usable product. Hence incense was the quintessential example of the whole burnt offering, the holocaust—a cheaper, simpler alternative to animal holocaust, and one that effectively represented the sacrificial process in larger terms. In Roman times especially, it gained exalted status for just this reason. Eunapius described the "poor and humble" house of the philosopher Julian of Cappadocia as so fragrant with incense that it resembled "a holy temple."[14] Apollonius of Tyana offered only frankincense, but could tell from the path of the smoke and the qualities of the fire as it burned that his prayer was accepted.[15] Plutarch spoke with admiration of the Egyptian practice of offering incense three times daily to the sun: resin in the morning, myrrh at noon, and a compound of sixteen spices at evening. The last, he noted, was "not put together haphazardly, but whenever the unguent-makers are mixing these ingredients, sacred writings are read out to them."[16]

The burning of incense was understood to be transformative rather than destructive. It changed the ordinary matter of resin or gum into exquisite fragrance, a substance intangible yet perceptible both by scent and by sight of the fragrant smoke. Altered or "purified" by burning, incense traveled heavenward: a physical image of ascent that mirrored both polytheistic and Jewish cosmologies. The image of prayer rising up like incense to the deity was common across religious traditions. Christians themselves cited Psalm 141:2 on innumerable occasions: "Let my prayer be counted as incense before thee, / and the lifting up of my hands as an evening sacrifice!" At the same time, sacrificial incense was not only itself a transformed substance. It had the capacity to transform the human worshiper who offered it, or even encountered it, into a state of exceptional piety. Its lingering scents attuned the mind to devotion and adoration both before and long after the act of sacrifice had taken place. Thus the extraordinary beauty of the temple to the Syrian goddess in Phoenician Hierapolis was measured by its fragrance, a fragrance that marked the faithful indelibly thereafter: "An ambrosial fragrance comes [from that temple], such as they say comes from the land of Arabia. And as you approach even from a distance it sends forth a scent that is very pleasant. And as you depart, it does not leave you. Your clothes retain the scent for a long time, and you remember it forever."[17]

Incense carried similar significations in the various religions of the ancient Mediterranean.[18] Christians, however, took scripture as their conceptual guide. They drew their imagery from the elaborate traditions of ancient Judaism where the smells of burnt sacrifice were remembered as part of their earliest cultic activities and textually represented in such terms.[19] Cain and Abel had made the first burnt offerings, Abel's acceptable to God and Cain's not (Gen 4:3–5). When Noah offered sacrifice "of every clean animal and every clean bird" after the flood subsided, "the Lord smelled the pleasing odor" and granted divine blessing in return (Gen 8:20–9:1). Incense offerings were prominent in the cultic system institutionalized in the First Temple.[20] In the Second Temple period, the prescriptions of Exodus 30 and Leviticus 2 and 16 were taken as programmatic and upheld as the ideal in any depiction of proper Jewish worship thereafter.[21] Jews used these passages as their guides, whether opposing the Jerusalem Temple cult, as did the Qumran communities on the grounds that the priestly line was corrupt, or, after the destruction of the temple in 70 CE, when envisioning its reestablishment at some future time.[22] These same passages would also prove foundational for Christian incense imagery and, later, for Christian incense practices.

In their representations of the ideal temple and its ideal use, the biblical texts set incense among a complex of fragrances that served to demarcate sacred space, sacred action, and sacred identity.

Exodus 30 gave instructions for building the incense altar, which was to be made of the odoriferous acacia wood. Set in place before the veil of the ark of the covenant, the altar was to be used for incense offerings only; other burnt offerings or cereal offerings or libations were to be performed elsewhere. Incense was to be burned by the priest twice daily, at morning and evening, as "a perpetual incense before the Lord throughout your generations" (Ex 30:8). Instructions follow for making the holy oil with which to anoint the tabernacle, the ark of the covenant, the ritual furniture and implements, and the incense altar, as well as the priests. It should be composed of liquid myrrh, cinnamon, aromatic cane, cassia, and olive oil, "blended as by the perfumer" (Ex 30:25). In turn, the holy incense was to be composed of sweet spices in equal parts: stacte, onycha, galbanum, frankincense, and salt. Both the holy oil and the holy incense were to be utterly exclusive in their usage: God commands, "This shall be my holy anointing oil. . . . It shall not be poured upon the bodies of ordinary men, and you shall make no other like it in composition. . . . [This incense] you shall not make for yourselves; it shall be for you holy to the Lord. Whoever makes any like it to use as perfume shall be cut off from his people."[23] It was this holy incense of which the high priest was to take two handfuls, "beaten small," to offer once a year at the mercy seat on the Day of Atonement, that its clouds might protect him in the presence of God.[24]

In whatever forms these prescriptions were enacted, holy oil and holy incense gave unique fragrance to the temple and its rituals. Other fragrances heightened the sensory quality of cultic activity. Cereal and bread offerings were spiced with frankincense.[25] Lamps scented the air with their oil; the cleansing rituals mandated for the temple area, the priests, and their garments would also have contributed distinctive smells. While animal slaughter and cooking meat are often thought to be the primary odors of sacrifice, Jewish tradition—like that of their Greek and Roman neighbors—set its sacrifices in the midst of air already dense with complex and pungent ritual aromas.

Although we may rightly expect that there was diversity in practice, the ideal paradigm formulated during the Second Temple period restricted burnt sacrifices, including incense, to the Jerusalem temple. The role of sacred smells in Jewish ritual practices performed in other locations is not entirely clear. Spices were set out for the Sabbath observance, but there is no evidence that they were burned as an incense offering.[26] Archaeological evidence from synagogues of the Roman period may indicate incense use despite the temple restriction. Whether or not certain implements found in excavations were incense shovels or burners and whether or not they were employed as such as part of sacred rituals remain contested questions.[27] Since, as we will see, the burning of incense was also a standard means of cleaning buildings, the presence of implements for that purpose need not indicate more than hygienic usage— which, in a special building, could well have been conducted with special utensils even when not part of sacred ritual. Nonetheless, the centralization of the priestly cultic system during the Second Temple period meant that the destruction of the Jerusalem temple in 70 CE forced dramatic changes in Jewish ritual practices. While certain rituals were eventually relocated to the synagogues, the sacrificial system as a cultic one was not reconstituted in another form. Other activities emerged in Jewish practice as sacrificial in nature. But Jews did not cease to understand themselves as belonging to a religion that practiced temple sacrifice involving burnt offerings. Instead, burnt sacrifice was understood to be suspended until such time as the temple would again be built and consecrated. In the meantime, holy tradition upheld the memory of the richly scented temple: "from Jericho they could smell the smell at the compounding of the incense. R. Eleazar b. Diglai said: My father's house kept goats in the mountain of Machwar, and they used to sneeze from the smell of the compounding of the incense."[28]

Within the ideal put forward in Exodus 30 and Leviticus 16, incense as a component of Jewish sacrificial ritual is shown to have had certain characteristics. Most often (but not always), it was an accompaniment to the sacrificial system and not a central focus. Varieties of offerings were mandated in the Torah: incense, libations, grains, birds, animals. Varieties of functions were identified for those sacrifices: they expiated sins, propitiated blessings, offered thanks, offered praise, marked covenants, defined identity and location. Overall, however, animal sacrifice held a certain primacy. Blood—its shedding, collection, sprinkling, and pouring—was a major concern.[29] Animal sacrifice allowed for offerings shared between God and God's people, when certain portions were burned and others cooked for consumption by the priests or the community.[30] For ancient Israel, its most potent form was the holocaust, or whole burnt offering: that offering wholly destroyed and thereby wholly given to God. In biblical texts, incense offerings were often contributions to sacrifice rather than its constituent element.

Even so, incense appears to have been uniquely significant in function. Biblical texts apart from those related to the temple cult refer to incense as a sweet savor pleasing to God. Within the cultic system proper, the Jerusalem temple itself could not operate as required without incense. Incense offerings demarcated temple space as sacred, yielding fragrance unique to the God whose temple it was; incense offerings shielded and protected its priests at its most sacred ritual, the annual Day of Atonement. The mere scent of incense could image the cultic tradition as a whole.

Alone of the ancient Mediterranean religions, early Christianity followed the customs neither of animal sacrifice nor of incense offerings. These omissions of practice are striking because both were integral to Jewish temple cult as well as to the many pagan cults of the Mediterranean world out of which Christianity emerged. Yet Christians assumed themselves to be, and presented themselves as, a sacrificing people. Biblical literature provided them a ready means to do so. Clement of Alexandria could give a "spiritual" reading of a biblical text, interpreting it in ethical rather than literal terms, and his reading assumes an audience already familiar with such modes of interpretation: "If anyone object that the great High Priest, the Lord, offers up to God incense of sweet odor, let this not be understood as the sacrifice and good odor of incense, but as the acceptable gift of love, a spiritual fragrance on the altar, that the Lord offers up."[31] Again, Origen could offer a "symbolic" reading, likening the composition of holy incense in Leviticus 24:7 to the diverse virtues that, when compounded together, constitute pure prayer. The relationship was typological. Certainly, he admonished, God had not commanded such elaborate instructions simply to encourage the international spice trade: "The type of incense symbolizes prayer. . . . For do not think that the omnipotent God commanded this and consecrated this in the Law that incense be brought from Arabia. But this is the incense that God seeks to be offered by human beings to him, from which he receives a 'pleasing odor,' prayers from a pure heart and good conscience in which God truly receives a pleasing warmth."[32]

Yet Christians had no reason to think of themselves as other than a sacrificing people. Jesus and his followers had been active participants in the Jerusalem temple cult. Jewish biblical traditions provided ample means for interpreting the death of Jesus in sacrificial terms, and allusions to the Psalms or the prophets that carried such sense were sprinkled through gospel accounts, particularly in the passion narratives.[33] Epistolary admonitions drew on the same motifs, as in Ephesians 5:2: "And walk in love, as Christ loved us and gave himself up for us, a fragrant offering and sacrifice to God." The letter to the Hebrews directly negotiated the sacrificial heritage of Judaism when it relocated temple cult into the person and action of Jesus Christ, sacrifice and sacrificer.[34] Revelation 5:8 and 8:3–5 presented incense offerings as continual in the heavenly sanctuary.

The apostle Paul filled his letters with allusions to the temple practices that he himself observed along with others of the apostolic community, prior to the temple's destruction in 70 CE.[35] Thus he described the gifts the Philippians sent to him as "a fragrant offering, a sacrifice acceptable and pleasing to God."[36] So, too, did he describe the consequences of his work: "Even if I am to be poured as a libation upon the sacrificial offering of your faith, I am glad and rejoice with you all."[37] In one particularly trenchant passage, Paul used the olfactory dimensions of sacrifice to indicate the critical epistemological qualities carried by the experience of smell. In 2 Corinthians 2:14–16 he wrote: "But thanks be to God, who in Christ always leads us in triumph, and through us spreads the fragrance (*osmen*) of the knowledge of him everywhere. For we are the aroma (*euodia*) of Christ to God among those who are being saved and among those who are perishing, to one a fragrance (*osme*) from death to death, to the other a fragrance (*osme*) from life to life."

Scholars have long debated Paul's use of imagery in this passage, and the degree to which its sacrificial language drew more strongly from Jewish or pagan practices.[38] Some have wished to see it as evidence for distinctive ritual anointings in the earliest Christian communities, although there is little evidence to support such a view.[39] Rather, in literary terms, Paul engages a number of *topoi* familiar from both biblical and philosophical traditions: the notion that divine wisdom gives forth a fragrance or that virtue itself yields fragrance;[40] that divine knowledge yields moral transformation in the one who receives it and so too that the wise person's speech or character has a transformative impact on his or her followers; the belief that inhaling the breath of a divinity, or of a wise person, can instill wisdom or virtue.[41] These were the same *topoi* to be used, for example, when Ignatius of Antioch instructed the Ephesians, "For this reason did the Lord receive ointment on his head (Mt 26:6–7) that he might breathe immortality on the Church. Be not anointed with the evil odor of the doctrine of the prince of this world."[42]

At this point, however, it is worth noting how Paul's imagery in 2 Corinthians 2:14–16 engaged the simple processes of olfactory encounter to represent the progression of divine revelation in human history.[43] Here Paul takes the essential action of sacrifice, the forging of relationship through an offering; that action he characterizes by its resulting smell. The smell is a "good odor" (*euodia*) because it is yielded by the action that binds Christ to God. By this "good odor" alone, one can recognize God—have "knowledge of him"—even in the absence of any visible or explicit presence. Further, as with any smell, this "good odor" travels afar ("everywhere"), spreading its signification ("knowledge of him") as it goes. The apostles are the bodied enactment of this olfactory process, for they travel abroad spreading the gospel of Christ's sacrifice in exactly the same way that the aroma of a sacrifice wafts far beyond altar or temple precinct, invisibly yet tangibly encountered. But Paul does more with these images, using a further, crucial aspect of olfactory experience to express the difficulties of the apostolic effort: smells are ambiguous in their effects. Perception of a smell, reception of its qualities, will not be uniformly experienced. A sweet odor to one person will be malodorous to another. To some people, then, the "aroma of Christ" will seem foul, a perception that proves the falsity of their understanding and will lead therefore "from death to death." To others, this aroma will be experienced as truly "good": already open to God's initiative, these people will be led "from life to life." Paul's statement here identifies the importance of Christ's relationship to God, the revelatory quality of that relationship, and the nature of apostolic activity all by invoking fundamental aspects of ancient olfactory experience—its indication of relationship (sacrifice), its capacity to convey knowledge, and its ambiguous effect upon those receiving it. As we will see, this text more than any other scriptural passage provided the ancient Christian paradigms for considering the experience of smell.

The New Testament rhetoric of sacrifice was formulated in a context actively engaged in Jewish sacrificial traditions. When the temple was destroyed, there was no immediate conviction of change to the nature of the Jewish ritual activities but rather the suspension of cultic practices until the temple would be reconstituted. As Christians and Jews clarified and hardened their separate religious identities, Christians already had a biblical inheritance in which the sacrificial language and imagery of the Hebrew Bible were recast for their use through the writings of the earliest Christian communities. As in the letter to the Hebrews, Christians could—and did— see traditional sacrificial practices, whether Jewish or pagan, to be superseded by the actions of Christ. Paul's letters gave Christians models for seeing their biblical inheritance embodied in their own activities on behalf of the gospel message. Sacrifice was one theme used to characterize the communion ritual of bread and wine that Christians celebrated and by the third century had become its dominant motif. The flexibility and variety of sacrificial imagery available to early Christian writers is as evident as it is pervasive in the extant texts, demonstrating that sacrificial motifs could allow for wide variations in application. Christians understood themselves to belong to a religion in which sacrifice was a central activity.

Most poignantly, sacrifice was the obvious language by which to eulogize those Christians who died in persecution, as in the case of Polycarp. Paul had used it for himself; so too did Ignatius of Antioch employ its imagery for his own pending death in the letters he wrote en route to his trial and death in Rome.[44] Provoked by capricious circumstance and at the whim of local governor or imperial decree, persecution was a sporadic but always terrifying threat for Christian communities of the Roman Empire prior to their legalization in 312–313 by the emperor Constantine.[45] Outbreaks brought the arrest and torture of Christians and sometimes their execution. The order to participate in sacrificial rites was the usual test to which accused Christians were put. As early as Pliny's limited execution of Christians in Bithynia around the year 112, the refusal to offer incense to the Roman gods was a criterion for condemnation.[46] Apostates who succumbed to threats or torture became known as "incense-burners" (*turificati*).[47]

The death of Jesus at the hands of Roman officials and the martyrdoms of Christians that followed were events that lent dramatic force to the rhetoric of sacrifice that Christians employed as the religion began to form its own distinctive identity and practices. Such rhetoric was concise in expression and effective in its significance: Polycarp was one of many whose deaths were said to have scented the air with a "sweet savor pleasing to God." To represent the martyr as the incense offering was not only to appropriate an ancient religious practice but further to make the symbolic reading a starkly physical one.

While there was neither occasion nor means by which early Christians could have arrived at consensus on the issue, abstinence from incense offerings in their own rituals seems to have marked the first three centuries of Christian worship. Not until long after their legalization in the fourth century did Christians begin to burn incense in their liturgical gatherings and private devotional practices. The abstention is notable not only for its singularity in Mediterranean religious practice but further in light of the lavish incense piety that late antique Christianity would subsequently develop. Yet from the view of discourse, at least, there was no discontinuity in Christian rituals whether incense was used or not. The language by which Christians characterized themselves and their religious practices across these first centuries was consistently one that used the rhetoric of sacrifice—and often the imagery of incense—to express identity and meaning.[48] Commenting on Malachi 1:11, "for from the rising of the sun to its setting my name is great among the nations, and in every place incense is offered to my name, and a pure offering," Irenaeus wrote: "The oblation of the church, therefore, which the Lord commanded to be offered throughout the world, has been accounted by God a pure sacrifice and is acceptable to Him. . . . And the class of oblations in general has not been done away with, for there were oblations then, and there are oblations now; there were sacrifices among the People, there are sacrifices in the church. Rather, the kind alone has been changed."[49]

Christians were indeed a sacrificing people. The aroma of bread adorned their altars; the odor of burning flesh accompanied their martyrs. Christians used these smells to explain their actions and interpret the events they experienced; they articulated them specifically as the smells of sacrifice.

NOTES

Epigraph. Clifford Geertz, *Negara: The Theatre State in Nineteenth Century Bali* (Princeton: Princeton University Press, 1980), 105; cited in Catherine Bell, *Ritual Theory, Ritual Practice* (New York: Oxford University Press, 1992), 44.

1. Exemplified for Christians in texts such as 4 Maccabees with its strongly Stoic character; e.g., Stanley K. Stowers, "4 Maccabees," *Harpers Bible Commentary*, ed. James L. Mays (San Francisco: Harper and Row, 1988), 922–34.

2. *Martyrdom of Polycarp* 15.I–16.I; trans. Musurillo, *Acts of the Christian Martyrs*, 2–21, at 14–15.

3. For an important discussion of Christian martyrdom as a sacrificial system competing with and opposed to that of the pagan Roman Empire, see Robin Darling Young, *In Procession Before the World: Martyrdom as Public Liturgy in Early Christianity* (Milwaukee: Marquette University Press, 2001). On the vast geographical spread of the ancient frankincense trade, see Gus W. Van Beek, "Frankincense and Myrrh," *Biblical Archaeologist* 23 (1960): 70–95.

4. I have been helped most by Marcel Detienne and Jean-Pierre Vernant, *The Cuisine of Sacrifice among the Greeks*, trans. Paula Wissing (Chicago: University of Chicago Press, 1989); Nancy Jay, *Throughout Your Generations Forever: Sacrifice, Religion and Paternity* (Chicago: University of Chicago Press, 1992); Stanley K. Stowers, "Greeks Who Sacrifice and Those Who Do Not: Towards an Anthropology of Greek Religion," in *The Social World of the First Christians: Essays in Honor of Wayne A. Meeks*, ed. L. Michael White and Larry A. Yarbrough (Minneapolis: Fortress Press, 1995). 293–33.

5. See esp. Mary Beard, John North, and Simon Price, eds., *Religions of Rome*, vol. 2, A *Sourcebook* (Cambridge: Cambridge University Press, 1998), 78–115, 148–65; Simon Price, *Religions of the Ancient Greeks* (Cambridge: Cambridge University Press, 1999), 25–46, 97, 177–78; Louise Bruit Zaidman and Pauline Schmitt Pantel, eds., *Religion in the Ancient Greek City*, trans. Paul Cartledge (Cambridge: Cambridge University Press, 1992), 27–45. For a summary listing of the ritual components of Greek sacrifice, see Walter Burkert, *Greek Religion*, trans. John Raffan (Cambridge, MA: Harvard University Press, 1985), 55–118. For some Hellenistic and Roman examples, see, e.g., Ovid, *Fasti* 4.247–348, and Livy, *Annals of Rome* 29.14, both on the origins of the cult of the Great Mother in Rome; Pausanias, *Description of Greece*, Elis, 1.20.2–3 on worshiping Eileithyia and Sosipolis; Ovid, *Fasti* 4.133–62, on washing the statue of Venus; Theocritus, *Idyll* 15 on the Festival of Adonis; Athenaeus, *Deipnosophists* 11.462 on sacrifice made at sea, 15.674 on wreaths worn to honor specific deities, 15.678b on the bones of the heroine Europa carried in wreaths; Philostratus, *Life of Apollonius* 1.10–11, 31–32 on excessive and moderate sacrifices; Eusebius, *Preparation of the Gospel* 4.9.1–2 on proper animals, birds, grains, and incense for sacrifice (oracle of Apollo), 5.11.1–12.2 on herbs, spices, and resin to mix for purifying statues of Hecate.

6. Lucian, *Of Sacrifice* 13; trans. Harmon, 1:189. See Saara Lilja, *The Treatment of Odours in the Poetry of Antiquity* (Helsinki: Societas Scientiarum Fennica, 1972), 31–47, for numerous citations.

7. Although blood sacrifice was not always required, other basic elements such as incense, lamps, and hymns were deemed essential for daily rites in the late antique period. The use of incense appears to have increased during the Hellenistic and Roman periods due to changes in trade. See Martin Nilsson, "Pagan Divine Service in Late Antiquity," *HTR* 38 (1945): 63–69.

8. Examples are legion, but see, e.g., the *Homeric Hymn to Demeter*, passim; Plutarch, *On Isis and Osiris*, ch. 15; Apuleius, *Metamorphoses* 11; Louis V. Zabkar, *Hymns to Isis in Her Temple at Philae* (Hanover, NH: Brandeis University Press, 1988); Erik Hornung, *Conceptions of God in Ancient Egypt: The One and the Many*, trans. John Baines (Ithaca, NY: Cornell University Press, 1982), 133–34; Cynthia W Shelmerdine, "Shining and Fragrant Cloth in Homeric Epic," in *The Ages of Homer: A Tribute to Emily Townsend Vermeule*, ed. Jane B. Carter and Sarah Morris (Austin: University of Texas Press, 1995), 99–107; Lilja, *Treatment of Odours*, 19–30; Marcel Detienne, *The Gardens of Adonis: Spices in Greek Mythology*, trans. Janet Lloyd (Princeton: Princeton University Press, 1994). Saul Levin, "The Etymology of *Nectar* and Exotic Scents in Early Greece," *Studi Micenei ed Egeo-anatolici* 13 (1971): 31–50 has an interesting discussion of

etymology, the foods and drinks of the gods as opposed to humans, and the ancient spice trade.

9. As Libanius extolled in his praise for the region of Daphne on the outskirts of Antioch, in his *Oration* 11: *The Antiochikos*, sec. 235–36: "Of Daphne, there has never yet been a fitting description, nor will there ever be . . . with shady paths, harmonious bird songs, a gentle breeze, and odours sweeter than incense." Trans. Norman, 55.

10. E.g., A. Lallemand, "Le parfum comme signe fabuleux dans les pays mythiques," in *Peuples et pays mythique: Actes du Ve Colloque du Centre Recherches Mythologiques de l'Université de Paris X*, ed. François Jouan and Bernard Deforge (Paris: Les Belles Lettres, 1988), 73–90; Joël Thomas, "La nourriture d'immortalité en Grèce et à Rome," and Alain Moreau, "Le fabuleux, le divin, le parfum: Aphrodite maîtresse des odeurs," both in *Saveurs, Senteurs: Le Goût de la Méditerranée*, ed. Paul Carmignani, Jean-Yves Laurichesse, and Joël Thomas, Actes du Colloque Université de Perpignan Novembre 1997 (Perpignan: Presses Universitaires, 1998), 13–22 and 41–58, respectively.

11. Plutarch, *Lives*, "Alexander" 4.2–6; Philostratus, *Life of Apollonius* 1.5.

12. Athenaeus, *Deipnosophists* 15.674e, 675f–76a.

13. The theme is prominent in Sophocles's *Philoctetes*. See also Detienne, *Gardens of Adonis*, 10–11, 24–25, 90–91, 92–98.

14. Eunapius, *Lives of the Sophists* 483; trans. Wright, 467.

15. Philostratus, *Life of Apollonius* 1.31.

16. Plutarch, *On Isis and Osiris* 79–80; trans. Gwyn Griffiths, 244–46.

17. Lucian (?), *On the Syrian Goddess* 30; trans. Attridge and Oden, 43. The authorship for this text remains contested, but the dating (second century CE) seems solid.

18. To reduce the function of sacrificial incense to the masking of the odor of animal slaughter, as has sometimes been done by scholars, is to miss entirely the complex of aesthetic and ritual issues for which incense was the prime signifier. Yet such a view has been commonplace in scholarly literature.

19. An especially helpful guide may be found in Jacob Milgrom, Leviticus 1–16, Anchor Bible (New York: Doubleday, 1991), 54, 236–38, 597, 628–32, 1014–15, 1024–31. For the broader context of ancient near eastern sacrificial practices, see, e.g., J. Quaegebeur, ed., *Ritual and Sacrifice in the Ancient Near East*, OLA 55 (Leuven: Peeters and Departement Oriëntalistiek, 1993).

20. The difficulty of dating the biblical texts and especially of ascertaining the impact of later redactors on earlier sources makes the evidence for the First Temple sacrificial system extremely tenuous. In addition to Milgrom, *Leviticus* 1–16, a helpful study utilizing archaeological evidence is Victor Avigdor Hurowitz, "Solomon's Golden Vessels (1 Kings 7:48–50) and the Cult of the First Temple," in *Pomegranates and*

Golden Bells: Studies in Biblical, Jewish, and Near Eastern Ritual, Law, and Literature in Honor of Jacob Milgrom, ed. David Wright, David Noel Freedman, and Avi Hurvitz (Winona Lake, IN: Eisenbrauns, 1995), 151–64. Various implements in this study indicate the use of incense (incense shovels, burners, or firepans, altars) and point to other odors that may have marked sacred ritual (floral motifs decorating the menorah, tongs that appear to have been used either with the incense altar or to trim or remove lampwicks—lamp oil made a pungent odor, whether scented or simple—and libation cups).

21. Kjeld Nielsen, *Incense in Ancient Israel*, SVT 38 (Leiden: E. J. Brill, 1986); Paul Heger, *The Development of Incense Cult in Israel* (New York: Walter de Gruyter, 1997). Heger curiously restricts himself to the biblical texts, with no use of archaeological evidence. See also, e.g., Menahem Haran, *Temples and Temple Service in Ancient Israel: An Inquiry into Biblical Cult Phenomena and the Historical Setting of the Priestly School*, 2nd ed. (Winona Lake, IN: Eisenbrauns, 1985); E. Sanders, *Judaism, Practice and Belief, 63 B.C.E.–60 C.E.* (London: SCM Press, 1992), 77–102, esp. 83, for the casting of lots among the priests to see who would offer incense. Although dated in some respects, the classic study for the development of Christian practice and doctrine remains Robert Daly, *Christian Sacrifice: The Judeo-Christian Background before Origen* (Washington, DC: Catholic University of America Press, 1978).

22. Lawrence H. Schiffman, "Communal Meals at Qumran," *RQ* 10 (1979): 45–56.

23. Ex 30:31–38.

24. Lev 16:1–14. See C. Houtman, "On the Function of the Holy Incense (Exodus XXX 34–8) and the Sacred Anointing Oil (Exodus XXX 22–33)," *VT* 42 (1992): 458–65.

25. Lev 2:1–2, 2:15–16, 24:7.

26. Gregory Dix, *The Shape of the Liturgy*, 2nd ed. (1945; repr. London: A. and C. Black, 1993), 425–26.

27. Béatrice Caseau, "*Euodia*: The Use and Meaning of Fragrances in the Ancient World and Their Christianization (100–900 A.D.)" (PhD diss., Princeton University, 1994), 82–90.

28. Tamid 2:8; trans. Herbert Danby, *The Mishnah* (Oxford: Clarendon Press, 1933). 585.

29. See William K. Gilders, *Blood Ritual in the Hebrew Bible: Meaning and Power* (Baltimore: Johns Hopkins University Press, 2004).

30. In addition to Gilders, *Blood Ritual in the Hebrew Bible*, see the important discussion comparing Israelite and Greek cultic uses of blood in Stanley K. Stowers, "On the Comparison of Blood in Greek and Israelite Ritual," in *Hesed Ve-Emet: Studies in Honor of Ernest S. Frerichs*, ed. Jodi Magness and Seymour Gitin, (Atlanta: Scholars Press, 1998), 179–94.

31. Clement, *Christ the Educator* 2.8.67; trans. Wood, at 151.

32. Origen, *Homilies on Leviticus* 13.5.2; trans. Barkley, at 242.

33. Notably Psalm 22.

34. Two recent studies addressing this issue are Marie E. Isaacs, *Sacred Space: An Approach to the Theology of the Epistle to the Hebrews* (Sheffield: JSOT Press, 1992); and John Dunnill, *Covenant and Sacrifice in the Letter to the Hebrews* (Cambridge: Cambridge University Press, 1992).

35. Also mentioned in Acts 2:46, 3:1.

36. Phil 4:18.

37. Phil 2:17. Cf. 2 Tim 4:6: "For I am already on the point of being sacrificed; the time of my departure has come."

38. Above all, see the masterful study by Harold W Attridge, "Making Scents of Paul: The Background and Sense of 2 Cor. 2:14–7," in *Early Christianity and Classical Culture*, ed. John T. Fitzgerald, Thomas H. Olbricht, and L. Michael White (Leiden: E. J. Brill, 2003), 71–88. Attridge gives both a thorough review of the scholarship and a strong argument for a coherently interwoven joining of traditions in Paul's choice of terminology.

39. Against such a mechanical reading see Jeffrey John, "Anointing in the New Testament," in *The Oil of Gladness: Anointing in the Christian Tradition*, ed. Martin Dudley and Geoffrey Rowell (London: SPCK, 1993), 69–70.

40. E.g., Sirach 24:1–21, 39:12–16.

41. E.g., Plutarch, *Lives*, "Alexander" 4.2–6; Philo, *de Som.* 1.49–51. For a late antique example, Paulinus of Nola, *Poem* 27.148–68, 235–45.

42. Ignatius, *To the Ephesians* 17.1; trans. Lake, *Apostolic Fathers* 1:191.

43. Mark Johnson, *The Body in the Mind: The Bodily Basis of Meaning, Imagination, and Reason* (Chicago: University of Chicago Press, 1987), argues that scholars have often ignored the degree to which bodily experience underlies basic metaphorical language.

44. See esp. Ignatius, *To the Ephesians* 8.1, 11.2, 21.1; *To the Romans* 2.2, 3.2, 4.1–3, 5.1–6.3; *To Polycarp* 6.1. On the role of letters in directing Christian perceptions of martyrdom, see Young, *In Procession before the World*.

45. As Caroline Bynum has commented, the fact that recent scholarship has shown the actual numbers of martyrs to be fewer than previously thought (or claimed) does not diminish the degree to which the threat of persecution or martyrdom exercised profound fear among early Christian communities. Caroline Walker Bynum, *The Resurrection of the Body in Western Christianity, 200–1336* (New York: Columbia University Press, 1995), 21–58.

46. Pliny, *Letters* 10.96.

47. Caseau, "*Euodia*," 92–98. Consider Cyprian, *On the Lapsed* 8: "Was not that altar, where [the apostate] was going to his death, in fact his funeral pyre? When he saw that altar of the devil, smoking and reeking with its

foul stench, should he not have fled in terror, as from the place where his soul must burn?" (trans. Bévenot, 19). Compare Eusebius, *HE* 4.41.9.

48. So too Young, *In Procession before the World*; and Philip A. Harland, "Christ-Bearers and Fellow-Initiates: Local Cultural Life and Christian Identity in Ignatius' Letters," *JECS* 11 (2003): 481–99.

49. Irenaeus, *Against Heresies* 4.18.1–2; trans. Sheerin, *The Eucharist*, 246–47.

CHAPTER 2

Urban Smells and Roman Noses

Neville Morley

At the time of which we speak, the cities were dominated by a stench that we moderns can scarcely imagine. The streets stank of dung, the back yards stank of urine, the stairwells stank of rotten wood and rat droppings, the kitchens of rotten cabbage and mutton fat; the unventilated rooms stank of must and dust, the bedrooms of greasy sheets, damp feather beds and the penetrating sweet smell of chamberpots. From the chimneys came the stench of sulphur, from the tanneries the stench of pungent liquids, from the slaughterhouses the stench of spilt blood. The people stank of sweat and unwashed clothes; from their mouths came the stench of rotten teeth, from their stomachs the stench of onion juice, and from their bodies, if they were no longer young, the stench of old cheese and sour milk and tumours. The rivers stank, the squares stank, the churches stank; it stank under the bridges and in the palaces. The farmer and the priest stank, the journeyman and the master's wife; the whole nobility stank, even the king stank, he stank like a predator, and the queen like an old goat, summer and winter. For in the eighteenth century there was no control on the way that bacteria caused everything to decompose, and so there was no human activity, neither creative nor destructive, no expression of growing or decaying life, that would not have been accompanied by stench.

—Patrick Süskind, *Das Parfum*

It is conventional to begin any discussion of smell in history with a lament about the neglect of this theme in modern scholarship. "Today's history comes deodorized," Roy Porter argued in his foreword to the English translation of Alain Corbin's *Le miasme et la jonquille*, because researchers were repelled by their own (modern, and hence overdeveloped) hygienic sensibilities even from contemplating past stenches.[1] Others have blamed a modern tendency, even among scientists, to devalue smell compared with sight and hearing, whether because it is harder to study (not least because it has proved difficult to establish an objective measure of the intensity of an aroma but also because responses to smell are clearly in part cultural and psychological rather than solely physiological) or because of a widespread perception that it *is* less important and has been since early humans switched to bipedalism, or because of an association of smell (and smells) with the primitive and childish.[2] In the case of classical antiquity, we might also note the well-established tradition of conceiving of the Greco–Roman world in terms of light, space, cleanliness and flowing water; ancient, especially Roman, cities are celebrated as model urban environments organized on rational lines and provided with exemplary public facilities.[3] This antiquity, constructed by historians on the basis of the literary writings, architectural remains, and art works of the wealthy elite, was indeed largely odorless; if the scenes depicted by the likes of Laurence Alma-Tadema smelled of anything, it was fresh air, well-laundered clothes, the scent of flowers, and perhaps a touch of incense.

In recent decades, as the heirs of the *Annales* school and their interest in social, economic and mental structures have combined with the New Historicists and their wish to reconstruct and represent past experience, there has been a small but perceptible increase in scholarly attention to the history of smell, especially bad smells with their connection to health and ideas of pollution, and especially bad smells in the premodern city.[4] There is a new sense that the past *must* have been smellier than the world with which we are familiar. This implies that we cannot hope to appreciate the nature of past experience if we concentrate only on the visual and literary or if we consider only the refined and hygienic aspects of past societies—the concern that an interest in such vulgar things may itself carry a certain whiff of vulgarity is firmly rejected. This trend can be seen in ancient history as well, not only in the limited number of studies specifically on this topic, but in the attention paid to the histories of the body and of health, both topics with olfactory overtones, and more general and popular attempts at bringing the past to life.[5] Thus Keith Hopkins, in *A World Full of Gods*, ensures that the imaginary time travelers he has sent back to Pompeii are regularly assailed with strong and disconcerting smells like rotting fish and especially urine and imagine to themselves what other unfamiliar aspects of the ancient world might smell like (for example, the cremation of a corpse in the open air is imagined to smell like roast pork).[6] One might argue that a modern visitor to Pompeii or Rome would surely have been wholly overwhelmed by the sensory (and especially olfactory) experience rather than occasionally inconvenienced or disturbed, but that would hardly serve the historian's purpose. What is significant for this discussion is that smell is very definitely part of the past that the historian seeks to bring to life—and, conversely, an emphasis on strange smells and the implicit contrast with modern hygiene is one of the tools at the historian's disposal for presenting the past as different and distant from the present.

This does create the risk that the resulting picture of the past ends up just as distorted as the sanitized version, characterized by an excess of odor and ordure rather than by their absence. Jenner's account of the limitations of the contemporary historiography of smell, which is still largely confined to popularizing presentations and museum reconstructions like the Jorvik center and its scratch 'n' sniff cards, should be a warning to ancient historians working in

this area.[7] The conviction that the modern West has been deodorized (an idea that appears to be largely mythical) leads to the conviction that a smelly past must be an authentic one and vice versa.
Replacing one set of clichés that present the past as familiar and
sympathetic with another set that present it as alien and alienat-
ing represents at best only a marginal development in historical
understanding.

After all, it is not the case that until recent decades portrayals
of the Roman city have only ever been scrubbed and deodorized;
there is an equally strong tradition of portraying all cities, especially
Rome, in terms of the worst excesses of modern urbanism: pollution, poverty, squalor, filth, and stench.[8] The techniques of such
accounts are familiar. A different selection of the limited literary
and archaeological evidence is employed—the satires of Juvenal
and Horace rather than the works of Vitruvius or Frontinus, the
architecture of everyday life rather than the temples and palaces—to
convey to the reader a world that is remarkably close to Süskind's
fictional account of eighteenth-century Paris.[9] Rodolfo Lanciani's
anecdote about the stench released when his excavators uncovered
a mass grave on the Esquiline, so that they had to be given time
to recover, is repeated time and again, with the implicit or explicit
conclusion that the smell must have been far worse two thousand
years earlier.[10] Jérome Carcopino offers an extensive impressionistic
account of the different sources of smells in the city, from fullers and
tanners to slaughterhouses and graveyards—which is virtually the
sole source for the reconstruction offered by Classen, Howes, and
Synnott of the olfactory world of ancient Rome. As Ray Laurence
has noted, such accounts are wholly descriptive rather than analytical, and largely fictional, interpreting the limited amount of evidence (itself largely fictional, or at least poetic) in terms of a template
derived directly from nineteenth-century conceptions of the urban
slum. There is a clear tendency to emphasize those elements that
precisely contrast with the idealizing view of antiquity—the grime

to set against the gleaming marble, the vulgar hubbub and racket of the street scene against the calm of the aristocratic interior, and the smells of cooking, rubbish, and decomposing corpses against the scent of rose petals.

For polemical purposes, especially in asserting the importance of the history of the masses rather than just that of the elite, such accounts have their uses, but they do also limit our understanding. What we really need is an olfactory history of the Roman city that is comparable to the sophisticated studies of Roman visual culture that have appeared in recent years—not just the power of images and buildings produced for deliberate effect but the overall visual experience of urban inhabitants and visitors.[11] This must be part of a wider study of how Romans received and interpreted sensory information and made use of it in navigating their immediate environment, identifying threats and opportunities, locating themselves within different orders of space and society: in brief, understanding how the sense of smell worked in different ways as a more or less essential part of everyday human life rather than treating it just as a marker of difference or familiarity.

Smells in the Roman Urban Environment

One basic issue for such a study is that, like the other senses, smell always works through a combination of the physiological and the psychological or cultural: on the one hand, what molecules are present in the atmosphere at a given location and how far an individual can detect them, and on the other, how a particular odor or combination of odors is interpreted, consciously or unconsciously, and what reaction it produces. Different traditions of smell studies have tended, inevitably, to favor either materialist or culturalist approaches, each one locating the nature/culture divide differently; in general, the physical and physiological are treated as more or less ahistorical and timeless, the cultural and psychological as context dependent.[12] In simplistic terms, we should be able to identify the likely source of smells with relative ease, as they will produce odors in any circumstances (especially in centuries before the development of masking agents and deodorants); how those smells will be understood and evaluated, however, varies from culture to culture.[13]

The study of the visual aspects of the Roman sensorium is relatively well advanced, not only because there is a much longer tradition of taking the visual seriously as the subject of historical research, but also because we have a reasonably substantial corpus of evidence for both parts of the subject: not only the archaeological remains of buildings, enabling the reconstruction of the topography and appearance of different cities, but also the accounts (inevitably mainly from the literate elite) of how different individuals viewed buildings and cityscapes and representations of those buildings and cities in other media. Apart from a few exceptional cases like Lanciani's burial pits or rancid olive oil on Monte Testaccio, smells do not themselves survive the passage of millennia well; the reconstruction of the physical sources of smells is therefore a matter of extrapolation, based on modern knowledge of odor-producing substances, from the physical remains of certain kinds of buildings and the traces of the activities that took place within them, and from literary descriptions of cities, their buildings, and their different districts.[14] Further, ancient literary sources have relatively little to say about smells compared with their treatment of visual images (which may itself be significant but clearly represents a problem for this kind of study), and there are no surviving representations of smells in other media. Certainly we do not have the rich source-material used by Corbin and other historians of the early modern and modern periods, the diaries, letters, and pamphlets written by people for whom the smell of the city was clearly a theme of great significance.

The typical Roman city incorporated a number of activities and businesses that could be extremely odorous: laundries that used

urine to clean and bleach clothes (perhaps not detectable from any
great distance, but the smell of the pots of stale urine, and still more
the stench if one broke, is taken by Martial as one of the archetypal
bad smells in 6.93); tanneries that used equally noxious liquids to
remove the flesh and hairs from the animal skins; and slaughterhouses and the meat and fish markets.[15] There is some evidence, at
least in the case of Rome, for a limited amount of zoning, so that
the more antisocial industries (the main exception were the food
markets) were pushed toward the margins of the city; likewise, the
dead were cremated and buried outside the city, whereas the smell
from cemeteries was one of the most notorious sources of nausea
in eighteenth- and nineteenth-century Paris (of course, the Roman
custom of cremating their dead rather than burying them would
also have reduced the persistence of odor).[16] This certainly creates
the impression that some areas would have been more odorous than
others and that one might indeed to some extent be able to navigate
through the city according to different smells, following the scent of
incense and sacrificial meats to the monumental center rather than
the stench of industrial chemicals to the outskirts.

It is also possible that different classes of residential district
were olfactorily marked.[17] Certainly it was the perception of at
least one elite writer, Martial, that poor households smelled much
worse than rich households: in 12.32 he lists the various smells to
be encountered in the former, from the cracked chamber pot to
the jar of stinking fish, the whole ensemble smelling worse than
a marine pond (an interesting choice of comparator). The wealthy
could afford to mask their bodily odors with various perfumes, they
avoided soiling their clothes, and they attended the baths regularly,
whereas the poor were either excluded from the latter altogether
or at any rate were limited to the less salubrious public bathhouses
and were a fortiori less likely to change their clothes or use perfume.[18] However, it is next to impossible to disentangle the genuine
evidence from the class prejudice in such accounts, and certainly

impossible to determine whether such differences led to genuine
and perceptible differences between districts—not least because
the majority of residential *insulae* in Roman cities were inhabited
by a mix of social classes, from the large apartments at the bottom
to the garrets at the top.[19] Further, there was at least one powerful odor that was produced by all classes of dwelling and that in
any case would have been diffused throughout the city, potentially
masking lesser smells: wood smoke, from the primary source of
heating and cooking fuel.

Discussion of smells in the city, whether ancient or early modern,
almost invariably focus on a different sort of pollution: human
waste, the archetypal source of filth.[20] All inhabitants of Roman
cities produced substantial quantities of feces and urine, day in
and day out, as well as other rubbish (above all, food waste). This
is recognized as one of the most significant problems for the management of any modern urban center; discussions of sanitation in
premodern cities, as in modern Third World cities, make it clear
that failure to deal with this problem adequately has serious implications for the health and well-being of the urban population—and,
given the universal response of disgust to the smell of privies and
human excrement, at least in the modern West, implications for the
olfactory environment as well.[21] When it comes to the sanitation
systems of Roman cities, once again we find two clear traditions of
interpretation, echoing Hermansen's characterization of different
approaches to urban housing: "von Gerkan sees Rome as a serene
group of upper-middle-class residences, very remote from medieval
conditions, while Calza and Lugli believe in a slummy metropolis."[22] The first tradition emphasizes the extensive infrastructure
constructed by the Romans in every city, not just in the capital,
for the purposes of sanitation, and above all the vast quantities of
water brought in by aqueducts to flow through the fountains, along
the sides of the streets and down into the drains. In Frontinus's
account of the water system, pride of place is given to the aqueducts

that improve the *salubritas* and *securitas* of the city and remove the causes of *gravius caelum*, foul air, far more impressive monuments than the pyramids or the temples of the Greeks (*De aquis* preface 1, 88). In other accounts, it is the famous Cloaca Maxima, the great sewer that ran from the forum to the Tiber, constructed in monumental stone and large enough for sightseers to travel along it in boats.[23] Other cities had less spectacular infrastructure than the capital but still displayed Roman expertise in channeling water into and out of the center and Roman willingness to expend substantial resources on this. Certainly these systems were extremely impressive compared with the typical medieval or early modern city, where the "sanitation system" normally consisted of no more than the expectation that liquids would drain or leach away, while refuse collectors would collect the solid waste and carry it out into the countryside to be spread on the fields as fertilizer; these methods were certainly known in classical antiquity—human waste was indeed a well-regarded source of nutrients for the land—but they were only one part of the typical Roman system, rather than the sole means for dealing with human waste and its accompanying smell.

In this tradition, emphasis on the relative sophistication of Roman urban sanitation tends to bring with it an assumption about its efficacy; waste was flushed away, so the city must have been more healthy and also much less smelly. On the other hand, there is the alternative historical tradition that largely owes its existence to Alex Scobie's classic article on "Slums, Sanitation, and Mortality in the Roman World," which emphasizes the limitations of the Roman sanitary infrastructure compared with modern expectations. First, Roman sewers were designed primarily for drainage, to remove water from low-lying areas like the forum, in an environment that was prone to cloudbursts and serious flooding in autumn and winter.[24] Certainly the constant flow of water from the fountains into the gutters would have helped wash away liquid waste and small pieces of rubbish into the drains, but it is as yet unproven whether the flow was powerful enough to remove substantial quantities of human feces effectively, let alone things like the bodies of dead animals. It is instructive to compare the situation in Paris, where the sewers were similarly intended primarily for drainage. Even after extensive sanitation reforms in the later nineteenth century, local ordinances insisted that the sewers should be used for the removal of liquids only, for fear that they would clog up; the city's inhabitants continued to rely on cesspits and chamber pots, which were emptied by the same dung collectors as before.[25] It is clear from the archaeological evidence from the Roman period that scarcely any residence was connected directly to the sewers, whether because of the cost, or the fear that the system would back up if the Tiber flooded, or perhaps because of a similar belief that the sewers were for drainage rather than waste disposal.[26] The inhabitants of Roman cities relied on cesspits—often situated next to the kitchen, for ease of rubbish disposal—and chamber pots; some of their waste presumably found its way into the sewer system (one of the hazards of Roman urban life recounted in Juvenal's third satire is being hit by the contents of a chamber pot, emptied from an upper-story window: 3.268ff) but the basic principle of the cesspit is that its contents accumulated over a period of time and were carted off at intervals by professional dung collectors, rather than being constantly flushed away by the sewage system before they could emit too many odors.

The net result was that human waste remained within or close to human habitations for much longer periods, often adjacent to the living quarters; this significantly increased the likelihood of infections from various pathogens, contributing to the well-established phenomenon of the city having a higher death rate than the countryside, and must also have produced unpleasant smells from the slow decomposition of urine and excrement.[27] The reliance on cesspits rather than some kind of flushing system was common to all classes of dwelling; it was not that the poorer quarters were significantly smellier—indeed, the likelihood that the diet of the poor was predominantly based on cereals and vegetables rather than meat implies that their excrement may have been significantly less smelly—but rather the whole city would have been pervaded with the smell of human waste.[28] Poor sanitation increased the incidence of gastric infections and diarrhea, which then both increased the likelihood of further contamination and added to the mess and the smell. The unhealthiness of the city could not always be detected by the nose, contrary to ancient beliefs in foul air as the direct causes of sickness—most illnesses produce only the most subtle changes in the smell of the person's breath or skin, and even ketoacidosis (e.g., from diabetes mellitus) or rotting teeth are detectable only at close quarters—but the inadequacies of the sanitation system in disposing of noxious, polluting substances was certainly detectable, forming a constant background to the other smells of everyday life.

The Roman Olfactory Experience

Considering the physical evidence for the various sources of unpleasant, polluting smells in the city, there seems little reason to disagree with David Potter's forthright declaration: "There can be no question but that the urban air of the Roman empire stank."[29] The strange thing is that the Romans themselves apparently failed to notice this, or at any rate to comment on it. Individual sources of bad smells in the city were certainly identified as such, such as the *fullonica*, while Roman legal writings on the importance of keeping the public drains clear of rubbish note the threat of a pestilential atmosphere if they become clogged with filth (*Digest* 43.23.1.2). However, there is nothing to compare with the numerous eighteenth- and nineteenth-century examples, documented by Corbin and others, of complaints about the stench of the city as a whole. It does not even feature explicitly as a theme in the most obvious place for such a diatribe, Juvenal's third satire. In the whole of Umbricius's scatter-gun condemnation of every unpleasant and dangerous aspect of urban life, smell is hardly ever explicit; it is arguably implied by his condemnation of those who take on contracts for public toilets (37–38) and by the chamber pot incident referred to above, but compared with modern examples of the genre Juvenal's satire entirely passes up the chance to characterize the city in terms of its stench, real and/or metaphorical—the closest we get is the use of smell of indicate the foreignness of some of Rome's *nouveaux riches* in another poem. Umbricius moves to Campania on the grounds that it is less dangerous and more hospitable to good old Roman values, not that it smells less bad.

Despite the widespread ancient belief in the dangers of foul smells as the source of disease, the city is not identified in these terms. On the contrary, it appears as somewhere that may be threatened by such odors drifting in from elsewhere, if it is situated in the wrong place, as in Vitruvius's account—"For when the morning breezes blow toward the town at sunrise, if they bring with them mist from marshes and, mingled with the mist, the poisonous breath of creatures of the marshes to be wafted into the bodies of the inhabitants, they will make the site unhealthy" (1.4.1). The idea of the city as itself the source of dangerous vapors, threatening not only its own inhabitants but those in its vicinity—a theme in modern accounts of urban pollution—does not feature. Indeed, far from the Romans identifying the city as a place of stench and pollution, as would appear natural to us, the opposite appears to have been the case: it is country folk rather than city dwellers who are identified in several sources as being smelly (above all, they smell of goats and garlic), and one of the best-known examples of a member of the elite using a nosegay to ward off unpleasant smells occurs when he is traveling through the countryside between cities, not living in one.[30]

Given the physical evidence for inadequate sanitation discussed above, how is this apparent blindness to the appalling stench of the city, even among the wealthy elite who regularly sought refuge in the *suburbium* or down in the Bay of Naples, to be explained?[31] One possibility is that we should make a qualified return to the more positive interpretation of Roman urbanism, in which the constant flow of fresh water through the streets (perhaps combined with the virtues of a predominantly vegetarian diet) kept the smell of human waste to a minimum. The alternative is to focus on the psychological and cultural aspects of the sense of smell and to emphasize that both "filth consciousness" and sensitivity to particular odors vary over time rather than being universal responses to biological processes. In other words, given the physical conditions to be found in Rome and other Roman cities, if we were able to experience them directly we would be overwhelmed by the stench, but the Romans did not experience this in the same way.

There are two different ways of interpreting such a—to us—lack of sensitivity to external stimuli. The first is implied by Süskind's fictional account of Paris, echoing the assumptions of historians like Corbin: the inhabitants have had their sense of smell destroyed, or at any rate impaired, by living for so long in the midst of such appalling stench. This is known technically as adaptation and is a well-known physiological phenomenon in which the perceived intensity of a smell reduces over time even if the measured intensity remains the same (this is not the same as the permanent loss of smell experienced by workers operating with certain especially noxious substances such as cadmium).[32] In other words, a writer like Juvenal has simply lived in Rome too long to be able to distinguish anything but the most powerful of smells (a fullery, for example) in his immediate vicinity; he does not detect smells that would be obvious to a visitor from the countryside (or from the deodorized future). If this was the case, we might then speculate on the implications for the Roman sense of taste, something that is closely linked to the sense of smell. Is an impaired olfactory sensitivity the reason why Roman recipes to modern taste buds often seem so sweet and over-spiced, and the explanation for the Roman taste for the salty and pungent garum?

However, this would not explain the apparent sensitivity of upper-class Roman noses to the smells of the countryside—which to the modern nose would also have been smelly, given the use of human excrement as fertilizer, but substantially less so.[33] It seems better to interpret Roman indifference to urban stench not as adaptation but as habituation, analogous to the way that someone can become oblivious to the loud ticking of a clock or the noise of traffic outside their house without having suffered any deterioration in their hearing.[34] It is not that the olfactory organs do not register the odor but rather that they do not register it as any sort of threat. "Odour preferences are acquired by learning to adapt to the environment"; small children, as is well established, do not instinctively find the smell of excrement disgusting but rather learn or are taught to do so.[35] Corbin notes the indifference of the Parisian masses to the issue of smell that so preoccupied the educated classes in the eighteenth century, and their resistance to many of the measures introduced to improve sanitation; as Jenner argues, it was not that they were less sensitive than their social superiors (though that was the dominant opinion of the latter) but that they had not been taught to perceive the characteristic smell of the city as a threat to their health and well-being and hence did not react to it in the same way.[36]

In other words, the characteristic smell of a Roman city—a mixture of urine, shit, decay, smoke, incense, cooked meat, and boiled cabbage, among other things, in unknown proportions—would be a stench to us, because that is our characteristic response to most of those odors. For the regular inhabitants of ancient cities, it was the smell of home—and perhaps even of civilization, as opposed to the more backward countryside where those smells were less intense and barbaric regions where many of them might be absent altogether. Within that complex of odors one might well favor some over others, tolerating the smells of the industrial areas or the fish market while gravitating toward the smell of sacrifice. But even the smell of the sewers was not perceived as intrinsically unpleasant, let alone threatening, and so not interpreted as such. Did this unsanitary Rome and her unsanitary daughters across the empire stink, as Potter argues? Not, perhaps, to the majority of their inhabitants.

NOTES

Epigraph. Patrick Süskind, *Das Parfum* (Zurich: Diogenes, 1984), 5–6 (author's own translation).

1. A. Corbin, *The Foul and the Fragrant: Odor and the French Social Imagination*, trans. M. Kochan (New York: Berg, 1986), v.

2. As argued by, for example, C. Classen, D. Howes, and A. Synnott, *Aroma: The Cultural History of Smell* (London: Routledge, 1994), 1–11; generally, see T. Engen, *The Perception of Odors* (New York: Academic Press, 1982); T. Engen, *Odor, Sensation and Memory* (New York: Praeger, 1991); and M. Jenner, "Follow Your Nose?: Smell, Smelling, and Their Histories," *American Historical Review* 116, no. 2 (2011), 335–51.

3. N. Morley, "The Salubriousness of the Roman City," *Health in Antiquity*, ed. H. King (London and New York: Routledge), 192–204.

4. See works mentioned in notes 2 and 3 above. Also see W. A. Cohen and S. Johnson, eds., *Filth: Dirt, Disgust, and Modern Life* (Minneapolis and London: University of Minnesota Press, 2005); E. Cockayne, *Hubbub: Filth, Noise, and Stench in England, 1600–1770* (New Haven: Yale University Press, 2007); A. Cowan and J. Steward, eds., *The City and the Senses: Urban Culture since 1500* (Aldershot: Ashgate, 2007).

5. Work on smells and smell-related topics include R. Parker, *Miasma: Pollution and Purification in Early Greek Religion* (Oxford: Clarendon Press, 1983); A. Scobie, "Slums, Sanitation and Mortality in the Roman World," *Klio* 68 (1986), 399–433; J. I. Porter, ed., *Constructions of the Classical Body* (Ann Arbor: University of Michigan Press, 1999); V. M. Hope and E. Marshall, eds., *Death and Disease in the Ancient City* (London and: Routledge, 2000); H. King, ed., *Health in Antiquity* (London: Routledge, 2005); M. Bradley, ed., *Rome, Pollution, and Propriety: Dirt, Disease, and Hygiene in the Eternal City from Antiquity to Modernity* (Cambridge: Cambridge University Press, 2012).

6. K. Hopkins, *A World Full of Gods: Pagans, Jews and Christians in the Roman Empire* (London: Weidenfeld and Nicolson, 1999), 10, 11, 13, 19.

7. Jenner, "Follow Your Nose," 335–37.

8. See Bradley, *Rome, Pollution, and Propriety*, part 2: "Modernity."

9. R. Laurence, "Writing the Roman Metropolis," in *Roman Urbanism: Beyond the Consumer City*, ed. Helen Perkins (London: Routledge, 1997), 1–20.

10. R. Lanciani, *Ancient Rome in the Light of Recent Discoveries* (London: Macmillan, 1888).

11. See, for example, Zanker, *Der Kaiser baut fürs Volk* (Leipzig: Fock, 1901); M. Beard, "The Triumph of the Absurd: Roman Street Theatre," in *Rome the Cosmopolis*, ed. C. Edwards and G. Woolf (Cambridge: Cambridge University Press, 2003), 21–42; D. Favro, "The IconiCITY of Ancient Rome," *Urban History* 331 (2006), 20–38.

12. Jenner, "Follow Your Nose," 342–43, 348.

13. A. O. Koloski-Ostrow, "Roman Urban Smells: The Archaelogical Evidence," in *Smell and the Ancient Senses*, ed. M. Bradley (London: Routledge, 2015), 90–109.

14. L. Bartosiewicz, "'There's Something Rotten in the State . . .': Bad Smells in Antiquity," *European Journal of Archaeology* 6 (2003), 175–95.

15. Generally, see Bartosiewicz, "'There's Something Rotten in the State,'" and J. E. Davies, "Pollution, Propriety and Urbanism in Republican Rome," in *Rome, Pollution, and Propriety: Dirt, Disease, and Hygiene in the Eternal City from Antiquity to Modernity*, ed. M. Bradley, (Cambridge: Cambridge University Press, 2012), 667–80.

16. J. R. Patterson, "On the Margins of the City of Rome," in *Death and Disease in the Ancient City*, ed. V. M. Hope and E. Marshall (London: Routledge, 2000), 85–103; H. Lindsay, "Eating with the Dead," in *Meals in a Social Context*, ed. I. Nielsen and H. S. Nielsen (Aarhus: Aarhus Studies in Mediterranean Antiquity 1, 1998), 67–80; J. Bodel, "'Dealing with the Dead': Undertakers, Executioners and Potter's Fields in Ancient Rome," in *Death and Disease in the Ancient City*, 128–51.

17. Suggested, for example, by D. S. Potter, "Odor and Power in the Roman Empire," in *Constructions of the Classical Body*, ed. J. Porter (Ann Arbor: University of Michigan Press, 1999), 169–89.

18. On the poor in Rome and their relative exclusion, see Morley, "The Poor in the City of Rome," in *Poverty in the Roman World*, ed. R. Osborne and M. Atkins (Cambridge: Cambridge University Press, 2006), 21–39.

19. J. E. Packer, *The Insulae of Imperial Ostia* (Rome: American Academy at Rome, 1971).

20. Generally, see Cohen and Johnson, eds., *Filth: Dirt, Disgust, and Modern Life*; and G. Jansen, A. O. Koloski-Ostrow, and E. Moormann, *Roman Toilets: Their Archaeology and Cultural History* (Leuven: BABESCH, 2011).

21. On the universal Western dislike of privy smells, see Engen, *Perception of Odors*, 135–36.

22. G. Hermansen, "The Population of Imperial Rome: The Regionaries," *Historia* 27 (1978), 129–68.

23. E. Gowers, *The Loaded Table: Representations of Food in Roman Literature* (Oxford: Oxford University Press, 1991).

24. Noted by J. Hopkins, "The 'Sacred Sewer': Tradition and Religion in the

Cloaca Maxima," in *Rome, Pollution, and Propriety: Dirt, Disease, and Hygiene in the Eternal City from Antiquity to Modernity*, ed. M. Bradley (Cambridge: Cambridge University Press, 2012), 81–102.

25. D. S. Barnes, "Confronting Sensory Crisis," in *Filth: Dirt, Disgust, and Modern Life*, ed. W. A. Cohen and S. Johnson (Minneapolis: University of Minneapolis Press, 2005), 103–50.

26. Scobie, "Slums, Sanitation, and Mortality in the Roman World."

27. Koloski-Ostrow, "Roman Urban Smells: The Archaeological Evidence."

28. On the diet of the poor, see Garnsey, *Food and Society in Classical Antiquity* (Cambridge: Cambridge University Press, 1999).

29. Potter, "Odor and Power in the Roman Empire," 169.

30. See Classen, Howes, and Synnott, *Aroma*; Cicero, *In Verrem* 5.27.

31. The suburban villa was a place of *salubritas* and *amoenitas* compared with the city; tis might imply that it was less smelly, but the sources don't state this explicitly in the way that they do emphasize the heat, noise, and general busyness of urban life. See E. Champlin, "The Suburbium of Rome," *American Journal of Ancient History* 7, no. 2 (1982/5), 97–117.

32. Engen, *Perception of Odors*, 61–63.

33. Excrement spread out in sunlight loses its smell more rapidly: Corbin, *The Foul and the Fragrant*, 27–34.

34. Engen, *Perception of Odors*, 63–77.

35. Engen, *Perception of Odors*, 169.

36. Corbin, *The Foul and the Fragrant*, 57; Jenner, "Follow Your Nose." Over the course of the nineteenth century, the threshold of tolerance, as Corbin calls it, does shift among the mass of the population as well— which tends to emphasize the role of culture in shaping response to smells.

Chapter 3

Medieval Smellscapes

C. M. Woolgar

Smell is unlike other senses in that we lack a specific vocabulary to describe many of the sensations that can be perceived through this faculty. Some can only be put into words by borrowing terms descriptive of other senses, particularly taste, for example sweet, bitter, or acrid, or by analogy: things "smell of something," such as roses or decay. This phenomenon was equally true of sensory language in the late medieval period. Like sound before the latter part of the nineteenth century or taste, there is no way of storing smell for long periods of time, which means that we are entirely dependent on written descriptions for our information about the sense and its operation; our understanding is further constrained by the inherent need to transfer descriptive terms to olfaction.

The sense of smell has a special emotional or psychological impact: it often provides a crucial dimension to a multisensory experience, even if it is not in the foreground of our perception. The smell of individuals, of objects, or of environments frequently makes a lasting impression that we can recollect or understand without words—and we should not underestimate the immediacy or importance of these associations in the past.[1] The range of smells and their impact are therefore of peculiar significance in understanding medieval sensory perception and its cultural impact.

Why did things smell? The medieval answer was not straightforward. In Salernitan problem literature, a series of questions address olfaction. Why do smells seem good to some but awful to others? How many things are necessary to make a good smell? Why can a dog perceive the smell of a far-off deer and no other nearby animal? Why does musk placed in a fetid place smell greatly but when with other odoriferous spices very little? Why do fruits of some plants smell good and the plant itself bad? Why can we see further than we can hear or smell?[2] The answers drew especially on humoral analysis. Similarity of makeup was an indication of those smells that would be well received by an individual; dissimilarity indicated what would be noisome. So men with a predominance of melancholy or of evil complexion avoided what smelled good and associated with places that smelled bad—"loveþ stynkeng place"—as did those who could not smell or who smelled bad themselves, such as lepers, who fitted both categories.[3]

Smell, like all other aspects of sensory perception in the Middle Ages, was charged with moral and spiritual dimensions. The association between good smells, holiness, and the divine was of very great antiquity. Moses was given instructions for the preparation of aromatic ointments, based on a mixture of myrrh, cinnamon, sweet calamus, cassia bark, and olive oil, for the tabernacle, the ark, and the sacred vessels, and of perfumes, based on myrrh, galbanum, and incense.[4] There is then a long history of divine manifestations, or of individuals of exceptional sanctity, both in Judaism and Christianity, associated with good smells.[5] These events were well established in clerical writing long before the twelfth century.

The appearance of the odor of sanctity coincided not uncommonly with the death of a saintly individual. The martyrdom of Becket was likened to the breaking of a perfume box, suddenly filling Christ Church, Canterbury, with the fragrance of ointment.[6] The account of the opening of the tomb of Saint Wulfstan in 1198 used almost exactly the same words to describe the fragrance, drawing on the descriptions of Mary Magdalene anointing the feet of Christ in Bethany.[7]

Where we have descriptions of the odor of sanctity, it was often categorized as similar to honey, flowers, or as a most sweet smell (*suavissimus*). The reputation of Saint Birinus spread as an odor wafting from a garden of lilies.[8] In 1144, Henry de Sprowston, burying the body of Saint William of Norwich, noted a smell like that from a great mass of odoriferous herbs and flowers. When Saint William's body was subsequently exhumed for reburial, no bad smell was sensed, but rather the fragrance of spring flowers and herbs, even though there were none around.[9]

Visions of paradise were similarly populated by sweet smells and a multitude of flowers.[10] In the closing years of the twelfth century, Roger, a Cistercian lay brother at Stratford Langthorne, recounted an extensive dialogue he had in a vision of his friend, Alexander, a monk who had died about a year earlier. Alexander told how he was in paradise and that there they lived off smell, which at the start of the day descended from heaven, satisfying and refreshing each according to his merits by a differential sweetness.[11]

Fragrant flowers and odors were generally accepted as signs of virtue and grace, sometimes considered a foretaste of paradise. Twelfth- and thirteenth-century descriptions of Cistercian monasteries, for example Meaux and Rievaulx, frequently equated them with paradise, redolent with the fragrances of flowers, trees, and spices.[12] The locations of others imply similar imagery, the foundation at Strata Florida literally located in the "floral way," and Dore Abbey in the Golden Valley.[13]

Just as these pleasant odors were redolent of good things, so the correspondence between bad smells and evil, hell and the devil, was equally ancient and widespread. Hell was frequently characterized as sulphurous or reeking of corruption.[14] Two accounts of the cure of Elias, a monk of Reading who suffered from leprosy, suggest either that he visited the thermal springs at Bath but was not cured or that he proposed or pretended to visit; he subsequently went to Canterbury and was cured there by the water of Thomas Becket.

The waters of Bath were not only of no merit in his case, but their designation as "sulphurous" tainted them with undesirable, otherworldly characteristics that were no match for Saint Thomas and his water.[15] The places of torment seen by the monk of Eynsham in his vision encompassed baths of pitch, sulfur, and other liquids with a revolting stench.[16] If the Savoyard origins of the bishop of Hereford, Peter of Aigueblanche, were not enough to earn him opprobrium, the ingenious idea he had in about 1255 for raising funds for the Crown made sure that he merited it. By getting the English bishops and major religious houses to seal blank charters of obligation—which he took to Rome where the charters were completed with promises to pay large sums of money and the documents handed over to the bankers of Florence—he ensured himself an ill-starred place in monastic chronicles. Matthew Paris, in his account of this *démarche*, had no doubt that Peter was, so to speak, taking a diabolical liberty: "The Bishop, whose memory exhales a sulphureous and very foul stench, went to the King."[17]

There was a strong association between anal imagery and evil, doubly diabolical in that breaking wind involved both a bad smell and a reprehensible sound. Saint Godric had a vision of two demons, and he confessed the details to Roger, prior of Durham (1137–1149). The following night, one of the same demons returned to the half-sleeping prior and addressed him: "Because you have not refrained from turning that stinking Godric against me and my sister, you will receive such a reward from us." He then broke wind—a most disgusting stench, which did not completely clear from the prior's nostrils for three days.[18] In Chaucer's "Summoner's Tale," Friar John, groping in search of lucre under the clothing of Thomas, a sick churl whom he had been canvassing for funds for his friary, received instead a fart, louder than that of any cart horse. The lord and lady, whose confessor the friar was, did not hesitate to suggest that the fart was the work of the devil and that "a cherl hath doon a cherles dede." The lord then posed the remarkable problem, readily solved by his carver, of how this savory contribution to the convent might be divided into twelve—parodying the division of the Pentecostal breath among the apostles.[19]

A bad smell, "stinking," might be both a characteristic of those whose activities were nefarious or hypocritical and was a term of abuse. In the N-town plays, the nature of characters is illustrated by the use of language. Cain, showing his true mold, calls his brother Abel a "stynkyng losel" who has God's love when he does not, and Lameth, in turn, who has killed Cain believing him to be a beast, turns on the accomplice who has induced him to shoot, a "stynkynge lurdeyn," words indicative of the evil intent that led to this death.[20] At Leverington, near Wisbech, in 1467–1469, William Freng was brought before the ecclesiastical court for calling John Sweyn a "stynkyng horysson," defamation that had a strong moral odor.[21]

Evil smells marked out bad things or those destined for Hell: the stench of bad breath or of those who had eaten onions, leeks, and garlic—with their sulphurous odor—was a sign that could not be ignored.[22] In 1307, Brother Robert of Saint Martin reported that for a period of three weeks he had not been able to raise his arm or celebrate mass and that he had been cured by Thomas Cantilupe's intervention, but not before he had tried fruitlessly—and not perhaps unsurprisingly, given the moral implications—a remedy that involved rubbing crushed garlic on the affected area.[23]

A bad stench, however, could have merits. The *Alphabet of Tales* noted the case of a laborer, Arsenius, who changed his clothes just once a year. He then told himself that it was necessary for him to feel their stench to balance the good smells he had encountered.[24] The soul could recover from the effects of the bad odor of sin. Cleansing the taint of original sin took place at baptism, and further sins might be washed away through contrition.[25] Medieval authors likened baptism to bathing. In a metrical life, written circa 1300, the conversion of Saint Katherine was completed when she had bathed:

in a medieval, aristocratic bath, richly curtained, which would have been replete with spices and good odor.[26]

The idea that one virtue or a smell might counteract another was widely held. A saint's goodness could protect him from the excesses of bad odor. In May 1198, Saint Hugh of Lincoln officiated the burial of Simon, abbot of Pershore, at Bermondsey. Hugh's biographer recorded a very unpleasant occasion. The swollen and rotting body produced an overpowering stench, and some made use of strong spices or incense to lessen the ill effect, but Hugh needed none of this, even though he was peculiarly sensitive to smell and often objected to bad smells, a sensory predilection that echoes the powers of a number of saints. Indeed, he was completely unaware of the problem: the sweet odor of Christ protected him from the stench of death.[27]

Good smells might be used to counteract bad, not just as one might use a perfumed disinfectant, but also to create or return something of the odor of sanctity. Wimarc, a woman taken as a hostage at Gainsborough during the reign of Stephen, had conspired with her fellow inmates to poison the jailer's drink, but he had forced them to drink it first. She was the only one to survive, though she became very unwell. She visited doctors and shrines but then came to the cathedral at Norwich, where she was cured at the tomb of Saint William. The cure was marked by her vomiting the poisonous discharge over the pavement of the cathedral; the sacrists hastened to clean up the area and strew it with fragrant herbs.[28] The complete absence of smell might also be counteracted: a most sweet smell filled the nostrils of Eilward of Tenham on his visit to the tomb of Becket, "that odoriferous flower of England," curing the anosmia from which he had suffered for some years.[29] Bad odor might be used to combat a false good scent. When in 1440 the Lollard Richard Wyche was burned at the stake in London and a makeshift shrine sprang up at his place of execution, the vicar of All Hallows, Barking, mixed spices with the ashes there in an attempt to promote Wyche's sanctity. The authorities responded by countering smell with smell and, in a deliberate act of pollution, established a dunghill on the spot.[30] A bad smell, such as garlic, could mitigate other foul smells. Encyclopedists noted that the stench of garlic would defeat the odor of the dunghill.[31]

These ideas about smell endured through the medieval period, particularly at a popular and uncomplicated level, for example in preaching, in visions and descriptions of heaven and hell, of saints and demons, and of bodily corruption. They might also transfer to support individual versions of sanctity.

The association of smell with moral qualities was not favored in some circles, especially among canon lawyers. The papal commissioners who came to England in 1307 to inquire into the miracles and sanctity of Thomas Cantilupe, as a prelude to the canonization process, asked each witness to a miracle how it had happened. Although there are references to smell, there are no instances of a divine smell accompanying the presence of the saint or the performance of a miracle or the translation of the body or of diabolical smell associated with demons. The closest a witness came to mentioning the association in the commissioners' account was in the testimony of Cantilupe's successor as bishop of Hereford, Richard de Swinfield, who reported that his predecessor had lived honestly, seriously, and in the odor of good repute and without any infamy.[32] On the other hand, the mysticism of sensory devotion preached by Richard Rolle among others and followed by Margery Kempe maintained and uplifted the divine link with smell. An extreme personal delight in the senses was probably what characterized both the devotion of Rolle and Kempe, but on the Continent, for example in the case of Saint Bridget, the sense of smell was used for establishing the character of individuals.[33]

A further, widely accepted dimension to smell was to be found in carnal pleasure. Monks were urged to confess both their delight in smells, such as the good-smelling herbs they might spread in places where they wanted to sleep, or the smell of spices, sauces, and foods, such as meat cooking, which might provoke a desire for a more luxurious diet, and at the same time their unreasonable turning away from bad smells, those of disease or the sickness of one of their colleagues.[34] A formula used by the Dominicans for secular confession from the mid-thirteenth century inquired whether musk or other perfume had been worn by women with a view to its odor attracting men.[35] In 1354, Henry of Lancaster recorded how he had sinned through the nose, delighting in the smells of flowers, herbs, fruits, women, and scarlet cloth.[36]

There was an enduring belief in the regenerative or debilitating effects of odors. If smell was a substance, a vapor, and if it was drawn directly into the brain—as we have seen, considered by some to be the sense organ in this case—it could have a direct effect on the body by cooling or heating it. There was therefore potential to use smells as a means of therapy and also a danger from misapplied smells. The effect of the smell varied with the humoral composition of both the odor and the person perceiving it: cold smells (such as roses) would benefit those whose nature was hot; warm or hot smells (for example, musk), those whose temperament was cooler.[37] Smell was held to have a powerful effect on the spirits: aromatics were a first line of therapy to bring the patient's humors back into balance or as a prophylactic to keep the body well adjusted.[38] The monk of Eynsham, lapsing into an unrousable state while he had his vision, caused great consternation. Potions of various spices and herbs were forced into his mouth by his fellow monks in an attempt to revive him, but all ran straight out.[39] In the late thirteenth century, the infirmarer at Barnwell Priory was rarely without ginger, cinnamon, peony, and similar substances so that he could readily assist if someone were suddenly taken ill.[40] Taking this idea one stage further, the smell of food was believed to be nourishing, rather than just appetizing.[41]

As smell passed directly into the body, it was widely believed it was the channel both for benefit and for the transmission of disease. The Middle Ages inherited the gynecological theories of Hippocrates, and many believed that the uterus might move around the body, causing cardiac and pulmonary disorders as well as those associated with the reproductive system. The use of odor, applied as ointments or as fumigants, was a standard element in the treatment. For "suffocation" of the uterus, strong and unpleasant smells, such as those of burned cloth and feathers, were placed near the woman's nose to drive the uterus downwards, and a "suffumigacion" of good-smelling spices and herbs was placed close to her genitalia, to attract the uterus. For "precipitation" (prolapse) of the uterus, the opposite course was employed, with one late medieval treatise placing "all wel savird thynges to hire nose and benethe all ill savyrd thynges."[42]

Disease might come from close contact with infected individuals or more generally through bad air.[43] The miasma of lingering odors suggested the transmission of particles by a smoke or vapor and characteristics from one body to another. Eleanor of Provence was exercising reasonable caution when she wrote to her husband advising him not to take their son, the future Edward I, to the north: "When we were there we could not avoid being ill, because of the bad air, so we beg you to arrange some place of sojourn for him in the south, where the air is good and temperate."[44]

Bad smells, however, were indicative of more than disease: at the start of the thirteenth century, they were considered as revealing the nature of the individual. Remedies might treat the symptoms, but they could not change the underlying state of the person. Physiognomy emphasized the link between these manifestations and the moral character of the individual. Unpleasant body odors displayed one's character as a person. There was a real concern about bad breath. Treatises on cosmetics therefore gave a high priority to ways of concealing these failings.[45] Malodorous breath could have severe consequences for the medical profession. John Arderne in his treatise on clysters noted how it was believed that air changed the body and in consequence the wound. He could demonstrate from experience that the breath of a menstruating woman irritated a wound if she came close or the breath of a physician if he had recently slept with a menstruating woman or if he had eaten garlic or onions.[46] From the end of the thirteenth century, however, physicians began to seek the underlying causes of bad odors, using smell itself as an indication of physical disease and the sense of smell increasingly as a tool of discrimination in their diagnoses.[47] This change in emphasis, however, was slow to make an impact on popular beliefs.

To control infection, the malodorous were set apart. Lepers were isolated, outcast by the Third Lateran Council of 1179 and stripped of their property, their dreadful stench marking them as spiritually deficient as well as physically afflicted. Many of the leper hospitals adopted strict regimes of mortification of the flesh, prayer, and abstinence to treat the spiritual causes of the disease.[48] The foods that were suitable for them also had a stench: when butchers in York were convicted of selling rotten or measled meat, that meat was then given to the lepers.[49] In a tale reputedly told to Henry I of England, the odor of sweet spices that greeted Theobald, count of Champagne, sent by Louis the Fat to visit a leper who was on the point of death, was a poignant way of demonstrating that his act of mercy was rewarded.[50]

According to Isidore of Seville, the sense of smell, beyond its spiritual abilities, was the judge between the sweet and the stinking. Neither was lacking in the terrestrial realm. The pleasure taken in the smell of flowers and the countryside was widespread and is particularly evident in English poetry from the fourteenth century onwards.[51] Herbs and flowers were a ready means of creating perfumes: gathered fresh, they would be hung around the house or in clothes, and flower-gathering expeditions must have been common.[52] Purchases of flowers for the royal household at the end of the Middle Ages are indicative of a small-scale trade, and flowers were among the many commodities considered appropriate gifts for a queen.[53]

The construction of enclosed gardens, possibly modeled on those of the Middle East or Muslim Spain, an epitome of paradise from Eden to the apocalypse, was a feature of upper-class horticulture in the Middle Ages. Here plants were grown for their smell as much as for their color.[54]

In the natural world, unpleasant smells indicated danger, corruption, and even death. Standing water, in puddles, became "corrupte and stynkynge," just as a man would unless he emulated the sea continually in movement in a constant quest to stir for good works.[55] Bad smells characterized industrial areas, slaughterhouses, tanneries, and the premises of fullers.[56] The atmosphere underground could be noxious. On September 13, 1337, John de Maldone, who had been hired to clean a well in London, descended into it and was overcome and killed there by foul air.[57] In Nottingham in 1551, a man who went down into a cellar by a rope was suddenly overcome by a suffocating damp that caused him to fall to his death.[58]

Kitchens, prisons, latrines, and dunghills featured prominently in the litany of evil-smelling places. As bad air was considered responsible for the transmission of disease, much attention was paid to mitigating its effects. Kitchens were moved or rebuilt. Innovations were made in the construction of garderobes, and rubbish pits were lined with stone. Regimes of latrine- and street-cleaning were the responsibility of conscientious municipal authorities.[59] Individuals might adopt their own remedies, combating bad smells with good. That musk might be placed in latrines is envisaged by at least one of the answers to the Salernitan prose questions, and John Russell's *Boke of Nurture* enjoined the aristocratic chamberlain to keep the privy "fayre, soote [sweet], & clene."[60]

Those engaged in occupations associated with dirt and bad smell were stigmatized and stereotyped, from the cook and scullion to the dyer and tanner. A demon, questioned by a master of the Dominicans, was asked why it delighted so greatly in the stench of sin. It replied noting that in towns there were those whose job it was to clean the latrines: they reeked of the most awful smell, yet they did their work freely because of the considerable financial rewards. Demons similarly rejoiced in the gain they made, as the soul of the sinner was their meat and drink.[61] In 1339, William Wombe, whose job it was to clean the public latrines in London, was found dead in the Thames. He had gone into the river about the time of curfew to wash himself—understandably—and had drowned.[62] These were degrading professions to be avoided for the sake both of honor and of physical contamination. Moreover, spiritual impurity was close to physical contamination and pollution.[63]

From this stereotyping, it was a small step to condemning whole groups of society on the basis of odor, moral as well as physical. There is an extensive literature about smell and gender, particularly in the use of smell to elevate or demean women. There were standard repertoires of bad smells to associate with prostitutes and old and ugly women.[64] Sensory epithets for the Virgin Mary indicated her place as queen of heaven. In the play *Mary Magdalen*, probably circa 1515–1525, Christ on the heavenly stage praises his mother, her good odor countering a series of bodily ailments.[65] Smell, however, might be a false indicator. Chaucer's host incorrectly suggests that odor confirms his notion that the parson, who has rebuked him for swearing by God's bones is of suspect orthodoxy: "Oure Host answerde, 'O Jankin, be ye there? / I smelle a Lollere in the wynd,' quod he."[66]

There is good anthropological evidence that different cultures regard each other as smelling unpleasant; there is not necessarily any pejorative connotation beyond the physical observation, but in some cases that is a concomitant. The notion that the Jews had a distinctive smell does not appeal in English sources before the expulsion of 1290, but it was current on the Continent. While the archetype for the blood libel (the allegation that Jews sacrificed Christian children to employ their blood in Passover rites, to rid themselves of this odor) is English—the murder of Saint William of Norwich in 1144—neither this example nor subsequent English cases involved the use of blood for ritual associated with odor or anything of a sacrificial nature.[67] In fact, some held that any odor associated with the Jews was good because of their devotion. A late fourteenth-century Wycliffite sermon argued that the prayers of many were not heard because their prelate was "so stynkyng afor God." This exclusivity could work in reverse. The devout who made offerings smelled good to God but bad to men: David desired that his prayer pass to God as incense but stink unto men, "as Godus children stonkon to Pharao."[68]

Although its purpose was to attain virtue, fasting could be a cause of bad breath. As a practice that was widely prevalent in medieval England, in differing degrees, it could nonetheless have inspired the opprobrium associated with bad odor.[69] The odor of the poor, with sickness from which Henry of Lancaster resiled, to his shame,[70] was matched in the *Castle of Perseverance* by mankind's determination in consultation with avarice, not to feed or clothe a beggar: instead, he should starve and stink.[71]

The odor of decay represented a striking example of the transitory nature of the flesh: Lazarus and the stench of the tomb were common literary motifs.[72] The embalming of the bodies of the upper classes, both lay and clerical, may have been designed not only to preserve them from putrefaction until burial but also to imbue them with an odor that might reflect the virtue of their lives. The body of Saint Hugh of Lincoln was treated with sweet spices before its journey from London, where he had died, to Lincoln, where he was to be buried.[73] Typically the viscera were removed—in the thirteenth century, sometimes for separate burial—followed by the application of spices and ointments. The body was then wrapped in waxed linen cloth. In the late fifteenth-century romance *The Squire of Low*

Degree, the body of Sir Maradose, the steward, mistaken by the king's daughter for her lover, the squire, was eviscerated by the daughter, who "sered that body with specery, wyth wyrgin waxe and commendry" (either cumin or prayers).[74]

The link between odor and morality, goodness, even authority on the one hand and iniquity on the other has a distinctive bearing on the creation and manipulation of smell. If sanctity was accompanied by a good smell, were those that smelled good saints or otherwise good people? Did groups of individuals therefore set out to be identified by smell, to be raised up by it or condemned by it? By looking at how odors were created or controlled, the regimes of washing and bathing, the sources of perfumes and scents, who had access to them, and when, we can provide some answers. The odor of the individual is only one aspect of this: the wider environment might also be perfumed—in the first instance goods, such as bed linen, the contents of wardrobes and chests, then whole rooms and buildings. This last was least effective in certain conditions, for example where there was already a dominant odor of smoke in a building, and the investment was unlikely to be worthwhile until buildings and lifestyles had reached a certain pattern.[75] In England, buildings were increasingly divided into separate chambers rather than communal, smoky rooms, especially from the fourteenth century. In the fifteenth century it was common for substantial buildings to have ranges of chambers, each with its own fireplace and chimney, for individuals or small groups. These arrangements had obtained earlier in other settings, particularly ecclesiastical buildings. Before this, most perfumery focused on the individual and personal objects.

Evidence for the odor of individuals is oblique. There are practices that tended to deodorization through washing and some record of the opposite process, the use of odor in washing, through the employment of herbs, spices, waters, and perfumes. The object of washing was not cleanliness for its own sake; washing was a mark of gentility, and dirt, conversely, a mark of denigration. Beyond that, there were a few personal objects associated with smell and few preparations for looking after clothing and linen that would have been used by the individual. In all cases the evidence is better for the upper classes, but some common practices can be discerned elsewhere.

In terms of basic washing arrangements, both men and women bathed in streams. This was principally a summer activity: tubs in houses were used at other times of year.[76] Bathing the whole body was less common than washing the exposed parts, overwhelmingly the face and hands. Washing, as opposed to bathing, was an activity done at specific times, especially at the start of the day. It was the custom of Saint Hugh of Lincoln, while at Witham, to wash his hands at dawn without an attendant to serve him and without a towel.[77] The general pattern is also apparent in the records of coroners: at sunrise on August 10, 1375, Roger Alwey of Loughton, near Milton Keynes, went to wash his hands and fell into a well and was drowned.[78] Washing at dawn was probably more widely current in northern Europe. A treatise on healthy living, composed in 1286 by a Savoyard probably for the royal foundation of Benedictine nuns of Maubuisson, near Pontoise, gave advice for summer: the nuns were to rise and comb their hair, then wash their face and hands with good, cold water from a spring.[79] A late fourteenth-century English sermon noted that Christ and his disciples washed their hands when they ate and always when they were dirty, as Christ was a "most honest man."[80]

The ewers, bowls, jugs, and aquamaniles employed in washing are common in inventories and in the archaeological record.[81] Aquamaniles—shaped vessels for pouring water over the hands— appeared in the twelfth century in metal and were copied in the thirteenth century in pottery. The elaborate forms found across Europe suggest that they were for use on occasions where they could be seen, for example in the washing of hands before eating that was a part of dining ritual both among the upper classes and more widely.[82] There are also references to brass bowls, which seem to have been used while washing the head. One, worth twopence, was among the goods of Alan de Hacford, a London chaplain, seized in 1345 after he killed a rival for his mistress. Even among the upper classes, bowls for this purpose might be of brass.[83] Moralists condemned the vanity of both sexes in attending to their hair "as in wasschyng, in kembynge, in tresyng, and lokyng in þe myrrour, wherfor God wraþþeþ hym ofte and many tyme."[84] Around 1200, a woman of Lynn who washed her hair one Saturday afternoon at a time when all work was commonly prohibited because of the Sabbath immediately went mad and remained so for eleven weeks until she was cured at Sempringham.[85] By the sixteenth century, washing the hair, as much as other parts of bathing, required spiced preparations. In September 1501, the third duke of Buckingham expected to use cinnamon, licorice, and cumin to this end.[86]

Washing the hands and feet was understood as preparation for a journey, although the ablutions undertaken by Thurkill in October 1206 may have been as much about removing the mire after a wet day digging drains in the field he had just sown as about purification before his celestial excursion with Saint Julian. In either case, it annoyed his wife, who believed he should not conduct himself in that way on a Friday.[87] The members of Winchester College who had been allocated rooms other than on the ground floor were forbidden by William Wykeham to wash their head, hands, feet, or anything else in these chambers, lest any water or any other liquid—wine, ale, or other substance—pass through the floor to the detriment of those quartered below.[88] The routine outlined in 1396 by a treatise teaching the Anglo-Norman language covered the dressing of the lord, after which he was to go to one side of the chamber near the windows to wash and dry his hands. His newlywed wife then combed his hair. He also did not go to table until he had washed his hands.[89]

References to washing other parts of the body are less common. Saint Hugh was assigned to look after Peter, the archbishop of Tarentaise, when he was at Chartreuse. He used to wash his feet and legs, but Peter, who believed his frailty received much benefit from this treatment, had to persuade him to wash further up his body.[90] Ranulf Higden, circa 1340, classed the daily washing of genitalia as a Jewish custom that, along with the practices of praying to the west (like the Jews) or the south (like the Saracens) or kneeling before trees, was not to be tolerated.[91]

Aside from cleanliness, there were two reasons closely connected with odor for taking baths. Bathing formed a part of certain purification rituals from which it was intended that a good odor—and moral benefit—would result. It was a part of the ritual undertaken by catechumens. From the twelfth century it might be included in the ceremony of knighthood, and the Order of the Bath preserves this important association.[92] At Darlington in 1292, the barber of Edward I prepared a bath for four new knights at a cost of twenty shillings, with a further three shillings for a cover for the baths.[93] Bathing may also have featured in the ritual of preparation for weddings. Eleanor, sister of Edward III, married Reynald II, count of Guelderland, in May 1332, and she bathed probably on the eve of her wedding: a valet of her chamber was paid 18 d. for herbs and other aids in making a bath for her at Nijmegen.[94]

Second, odor gave the bath a therapeutic character. There are some references to spas, but most medicinal baths made use of herbs, with the tub cocooned in sheets in a tentlike arrangement.[95] There are occasional references to public baths in England but little to parallel those on the Continent. In England, the association of the bathhouses was with prostitution, although the continental experience appears to have been more sensuous and involved bathing.[96]

Peripatetic bathtubs feature in royal accounts, but some establishments had permanent bathhouses, as at Easthampstead, Eltham, and King's Langley in the mid-fourteenth century.[97] Where there were permanent bathrooms, they might be tiled, as at Leeds Castle in 1291–1292 and at Sheen under Richard II,[98] and there might be hot and cold running water, as there was at Westminster under Edward III.[99] The sunken bath adjacent to Henry VIII's lodgings at Whitehall Palace indicates something of the character of the event. The presence of stove tiles here suggests that hot water and steam—perhaps like a Turkish bath—were significant.[100] The expectation of warm or hot water was common, even if it were not "on tap." An ampulla of Saint Wulfstan's water resuscitated a boy who had drowned in a bath while his nurse had gone out for wood to heat additional water.[101] In her metrical life of circa 1230, Saint Modwenna instructed Bishop Kevin to bathe: he used a spring that miraculously produced warm water.[102]

There is one ingredient we might expect that is missing from these descriptions of bathing: soap. Although there are references in accounts to soap, many were probably to soft soap, which was based on the potassium rich wood ash common in northern Europe. Wood ash from Mediterranean countries, where there was more salt in the soil, had a higher sodium content and produced a hard soap.[103] Mentions of "Spanish soap" refer to this product and it may have been perfumed: in 1273–1274, two pounds cost eightpence.[104] In June 1289, four loaves of soap—that is, hard soap—bought for Queen Eleanor of Castile while she was in France cost ten shillings in money of Tours, or about two shillings, threepence sterling.[105] The 122 pounds of white soap bought for Elizabeth Berkeley, countess of Warwick, and her three daughters, Margaret, Eleanor, and Elizabeth, in 1420–1421 was mainly purchased in London along with the household's spices and ranged between one and a half and threepence per pound. Again, this was probably a fine product,[106] and one that implied a much higher level of consumption than that of an elderly widow: Isabella, Lady Morley, managed in 1463–1464 with six pounds of black soap and one and a half pounds of white.[107] By the fifteenth century, elegant soaps were in much greater use in the washing routines of the upper classes.

For medieval England, the principal source of spices, ointments, perfumes, scented oils, and waters, as well as exotic soaps—in fact, anything beyond commonly found herbs and the produce of gardens—was the Mediterranean and what trade routes brought there from the East. At the same time, Middle Eastern and Arabic customs and literature influenced the way in which these materials were used, particularly in areas where there were points of common experience for Muslims, Jews, and Christians, for example in Spain. Here, from the eleventh to the thirteenth centuries, there was considerable knowledge of the methods of perfume-making: obtaining essential oils by washing, sublimation, alembic (by sweating), and by burning, to produce a smoke (*per fumum*). Odors were based on a range of substances, including musk, ambergris and yellow amber, and camphor. The most desirable ointments were designated by their dominant ingredient: violet, jasmine, cloves, narcissus, rose, iris, and chamomile. In addition, mousses of various compositions, soap, and washes composed of wood lye, honey, and syrup of figs were among the procedures described.[108]

As with cosmetics, from which perfumes are sometimes indistinguishable, there were two significant changes in the later medieval period. The first, from the late fourteenth to the late fifteenth centuries, was the wider availability of perfumes and an increase in the number of people using them in the countries bordering the northern shores of the western Mediterranean. For example, a spicer's shop in Perugia, inventoried in 1431, contained an extensive selection of ointments, waters, and sugars, leading on to syrups, cosmetics and electuaries, powders, and scented oils, besides flasks, vessels, and equipment for making these products.[109] The second change, between the late fifteenth century and about 1560, saw a development in the technology of perfumery and an expanded knowledge of its products.

There was an evolution in the practical use of odor and perfume, with more sophisticated preparations coming into wider use. Drawing on continental practice, perfumes and olfactory waters were created for the aristocracy in the thirteenth century by their apothecaries or from the ingredients they supplied. In the fourteenth century, high-quality perfumes were imported, again for a very limited market, but during the following century they became much more widely used and in much greater quantities. Aromatic fumigants also featured to a greater extent at this period, expanding their use into the sixteenth century. Inventories of apothecaries' shops from the sixteenth century show how widely available these products had become. Much less is known of the use of odor among the lower classes, though the traditional lore that applied to garden herbs and wild plants may have extended to a basic perfumery. Certainly, herbs, many of which must have been widely available, were used indoors by all groups within society. The use of plants to counteract the noxious effects of bad air was widespread.

NOTES

1. C. Classen, D. Howes, and A. Synnott, *Aroma: The Cultural History of Smell* (London: Routledge, 1994), 3, 16.
2. B. Lawn, *The Salernitan Questions: An Introduction to the History of Medieval and Renaissance Problem Literature* (Oxford, 1963); *The Prose Salernitan Questions Edited from a Bodleian Manuscript (Auct. F.3.10): An Anonymous Collection Dealing with Science and Medicine Written by an Englishman c. 1200 with an Appendix of Ten Related Collections*, ed. B. Lawn (ABMA, 5; 1979), 25, 165, 167, 331–34 (hereafter *PSQ*).
3. *On the Properties of Things: John Trevisa's Translation of Bartholomaeus Anglicus De Proprietatibus Rerum*, ed. Mc. C. Seymour (Oxford, 1975–88), 2:1298 (hereafter *BA*).
4. Ex 30:22–28.
5. Classen, Howes, and Synnott, *Aroma*, 52–54.
6. *Materials for the History of Thomas Becket, Archbishop of Canterbury*, ed. J. C. Robertson (RS, 1875–85), 2:37 (hereafter *Becket*).
7. Mc 14:3; Io 12:3; *The Vita Wulfstani of William of Malmesbury to which Are Added the Extant Abridgements of This Work and the Miracles and Translation of St. Wulfstan*, ed. R. R. Darolington (Camden, 3rd series, 40; 1928), 182 (hereafter *Wulfstan*).

8.   *Three Eleventh-Century Anglo-Latin Saints' Lives: Vita S. Birini, Vita Et Miracula S. Kenelmi and Vita S. Rumwoldi*, ed. and trans. R. C. Love (Oxford, 1996), 9.

9.   A. Jessopp and M. R. James, eds., *The Life and Miracles of St. William of Norwich by Thomas of Monmouth* (Cambridge, 1896), 37, 39 (hereafter *WN*).

10. Dronke, "Tradition and Innovation in Medieval Colour Imagery," in *The Realms of Colour*, ed. A. Portmann and R. Ritsema (Eranos 1972 Yearbook, 41: Leiden, 1974), 77–88; D. Pearsall and E. Salter, *Landscapes and Seasons of the Medieval World* (1973), 56–75; *BA*, 2:788–90; "Vision of the Monk Eynsham," in *Eynsham Cartulary*, ed. H. E. Salter (Oxford Historical Society, 1907–1908) 2:360 (hereafter "Eynsham"); R. Beadle, ed., *The York Plays* (1982), 62–63.

11. C. J. Holdsworth, "Eleven Visions Connected with the Cistercian Monastery of Stratford Langthorne," *Cîteaux* 13 (1962):185–204, esp. 191n31, 197–201.

12. M. Cassidy-Welch, *Monastic Spaces and Their Meanings: Thirteenth Century Cistercian Monasteries* (Turnhout, 2001), 65–67.

13. D. Robinson, ed., *The Cistercian Abbeys of Britain: Far from the Concourse of Men* (1998), 101–4, 176–79.

14. T. H. Seiler, "Filth and Stench as Aspects of the Iconography of Hell," in *The Iconography of Hell*, ed. C. Davidson and T. H. Seiler (Kalamazoo: Medieval Institute Publications, 1992), 132–40.

15. *Becket*, 1:416–17, 2:242–43.

16. "Eynsham," 305–23; *Thurlkill*, 28–29.

17. C. E. Woodruff, "The Will of Peter de Aqua Blanca Bishop of Hereford (1268)," in *Camden Miscellany XIV* (Camden, 1926), vii; Matthew Paris, *Chronica Majora*, ed. H. R. Luard (RS, 1872–1873), 5:510–11.

18. *Libellus de Vita et Miraculis S. Godrici*, ed. J. Stevenson (Surtees Society, 1845), 356–58.

19. Geoffrey Chaucer, *The Riverside Chaucer*, 3rd ed., ed. L. D. Benson (Oxford, 1988), 134–36, III (D)11, 2089–294; B. Taylor, "The Canon Yeoman's Breath: Emanations of a Metaphor," *English Studies* 60 (1979): 381.

20. S. Spector, ed., *The N-Town Play: Cotton MS Vespasian D 8* (EETS, SS 11–12, 1991), 39, 47 (hereafter *N-Town*).

21. L. R. Poos, ed., *Lower Ecclesiastical Jurisdiction in Late-Medieval England: The Courts of the Dean and Chapter of Lincoln, 1336–1349, and the Deanery of Wisbech, 1458–1484* (British Academy, Records of Social and Economic History, NS 32, 2001), 427 (hereafter *LEJ*).

22. *BA*, 1:369–70.

23. *Biblioteca Apostolica Vaticana* MS Lat. Vat. 4015, f. 51 r. (hereafter *BAV*).

24. M. M. Banks, ed., *An Alphabet of Tales: An English 15th Century Translation of the Alphabetum Narrationum of Etienne de Besançon from Additional*

MS. 25,719 of the British Museum (EETS, OS 126–27, 1904–1905), 2:389 (hereafter *Alphabet*).

25. E.g., M. Eccles, ed., *The Macro Plays: The Castle Perseverance; Wisdom; Mankind* (EETS, OS 262, 1969), 145 (hereafter *Macro*).

26. G. Hesketh, "A Unpublished Anglo-Norman Life of Saint Katherine of Alexandria from MS. London, BL, Add. 40143," *Romania* 118 (2000): 74–76.

27. D. L. Douie and D. H. Farmer, eds., *Magna Vita Santcti Hugonis: The Life of St. Hugh of Lincoln [by Adam Eynsham]* (Oxford, 1985), 2:82–83 (hereafter *Hugh*).

28. *WN*, 246–50.

29. *Becket*, 2:66–67.

30. J. A. F. Thomson, *The Later Lollards, 1414–1520* (Oxford, 1965), 148–50.

31. *BA*, 2:909–10, 1303–4.

32. *BAV* MS Lat. Vat. 4015, f. 118v.

33. S. B. Meech and H. E. Allen, eds., *The Book of Margery Kempe: The Text from the Unique MS. Owned by Colonel W. Butler Bowdon* (EETS, OS 212, 1940), 86–87, 301 (hereafter *MK*).

34. J. Goering and F. A. C. Mantello, "The 'Perambulauit Iudas' (Speculum Confessionis) attributed to Robert Grosseteste," *Revue Bénédictine* 96 (1986): 138, 151–52.

35. J. Goering and J. Payer, "The 'Summa Penitentie Fratrum Predicatorum': A Thirteenth-Century Confessional Formula," *Mediaeval Studies* 55 (1993): 37.

36. E. J. Arnould, ed., *Le Livre de Seyntz Medicines: The Unpublished Devotional Treatise of Henry of Lancaster* (ANTS, 2, 1940), 13–14, 47 (hereafter *Seyntz Medicines*).

37. R. Palmer, "In Bad Odour: Smell and Its Significance in Medicine from Antiquity to the Seventeenth Century," in *Medicine and the Five Senses*, ed. W. F. Bynum and R. Porter (Cambridge, 1993), 63–64.

38. C. Rawcliffe, *Medicine and Society in Later Medieval England* (Far Thrupp, 1995), 60, 62, 149.

39. "Eynsham," 291.

40. J. W. Clark, ed., *The Observances in Use at the Augustinian Priory of S. Giles and S. Andrew at Barnwell, Cambridgeshire* (Cambridge, 1897), 202 (hereafter *Barnwell*).

41. Palmer, "In Bad Odour," 63.

42. A. Barratt, ed., *The Knowing of a Woman's Kind in Childing* (Turnhout, 2001), 76–79, 94–97; Rawcliffe, *Medicine and Society*, 197; M. H. Green, ed., *The Trotula: A Medieval Compendium of Women's Medicine* (Philadelphia, 2001), 22–23, 31, 83–87, 104–5.

43. Rawcliffe, *Medicine and Society*, 40.

44. H. Johnstone, "The Queen's Household," in T. F. Tout, *Chapters in the*

Administrative History of Mediaeval England: The Wardrobe, the Chamber and the Small Seals (Manchester, 1920–33), 5:233n3.

45. For example, Tony Hunt, *Popular Medicine in Thirteenth-Century England* (Cambridge, 1990), 133, 207; Ruelle, *L'Ornement des Dames (Ornatus Melierum)* (Brussels, 1967), 68–69; T. Hunt, ed., with M. Benskin, *Three Receptaria from Medieval England* (Oxford, 2001), 17–18, 105, 166–67; M. S. Ogden, ed., *The Cyrurgie of Guy de Chauliac* (EETS, OS 265, 1971), 477–78.

46. D'A. Power, ed., *Treatises of Fistula in Ano, Haemorrhoids, and Clysters by John Aderne from an Early Fifteenth-Century Manuscript Translation* (EETS, OS 139), 88.

47. M. R. McVaugh, "Smells and the Medieval Surgeon," *Micrologus* 10 (2002): 113–32.

48. Rawcliffe, *Medicine and Society*, 14–17.

49. M. Prestwich, *York Civic Ordinances*, 1301 (Borthwick Papers, 49, 1976), 12–13.

50. Walter Map, *De Nugis Curialium: Courtiers' Trifles*, ed. M. R. James, rev. C. N. L. Brooke and R. A. B. Mynors (Oxford, 1983), 462–65.

51. Pearsall and Salter, *Landscapes and Seasons*, 161–77, 198; C. D'Evelyn, ed., *Peter Idley's Instructions to His Son* (Boston: Modern Language Association of America, 1935), 128–29; G. L. Brook, ed., *The Harley Lyrics: The Middle English Lyrics of Ms. Harley 2253*, 4th ed. (Manchester, 1968), 43–44, 54–55; J. Kail, ed., *Twenty-Six Political and Other Poems (including 'Petty Job') from the Oxford MSS Digby 102 and Douce 322* (EETS, OS 124, 1904), 143.

52. For example, R. F. Hunnisett, ed., *Calendar of Nottinghamshire Coroners' Inquests, 1485–1588* (Thoroton Society, 1969), 28.

53. N. H. Nicolas, ed., *Privy Purse Expenses of Elizabeth of York: Wardrobe Accounts of Edward the Fourth, with a Memoir of Elizabeth of York, and Notes* (1830), 4.

54. Pearsall and Salter, *Landscapes and Seasons*, 27, 56, 76–80.

55. W. O. Ross, ed., *Middle English Sermons Edited from British Museum MS. Royal 18 B. XXIII* (EETS, OS 209, 1940), 75.

56. M. Kowaleski, *Local Markets and Regional Trade in Medieval Exeter* (Cambridge, 1995), 190.

57. R. R. Sharpe, ed., *Calendar of Coroners' Rolls of the City of London, AD 1300–1378* (1913), 198–99.

58. *Nottinghamshire Coroners' Inquests*, 141.

59. *The History of the King's Works*, ed. H. M. Colvin et al. (1963–1982), 2:652; W. MacBain, ed., *The Life of St. Catherine by Clemence of Barking* (ANTS, 18, 1964), 47; Rawcliffe, *Medicine and Society*, 40; E. L. Sabine, "Latrines and Cesspools of Mediaeval London," *Speculum* 9 (1934): 303–21; L. Thorndike, "Sanitation, Baths, and Street-Cleaning in the Middle Ages and Renaissance," *Speculum* 3 (1928): 192–203; M. S. R.

Jenner, "Civilization and Deodorization?: Smell in Early Modern English Culture," in *Civil Histories: Essays Presented to Sir Keith Thomas*, ed. Burke, B. Harrison, and Slack (Oxford, 2000), 127–144; C. Platt, *Medieval Southampton: The Port and Trading Community, AD 1000–1600* (1973), 171; J. Steane, *The Archaeology of the Medieval English Monarchy* (1993), 116; A. M. Kristol, ed., *Manières de langage* (ANTS, 53, 1995), 30; Hodgson, ed., *The Cloud of Unknowing and the Book of Privy Counselling* (EETS, OS 218, 1944), 46, 191; *Peter Idley's Instructions*, 148.

60. *PSQ*, 190–91; F. J. Fuvrnivall, ed., *Manners and Meals in Olden Time* (EETS, OS 32, 1868), 179–80.

61. A. G. Little, ed., *Liber Exemplorum ad Usum Praedicantium Saeculo XIII Compostis a Quodam Fratre Minore Anglico de Provincia Hiberniae* (British Society of Franciscan Studies, 1908), 121.

62. *Calendar of Coroners' Rolls of London*, 221.

63. For example, J. E. Merceron, "Cooks, Social Status, and Stereotypes of Violence in Mediaeval French Literature and Society," *Romania* 116 (1988): 172–74.

64. E. O'Connor, "Hell's Pit and Heaven's Rose: The Typology of Female Sights and Smells in Panormita's *Hermaphroditus*," *Medievalia et Humanistica* NS 23 (1996): 25–51.

65. D. C. Baker, J. L. Murphy, and L. B. Hall Jr., eds., *The Late Medieval Religious Plays of Bodleian MSS Digby 133 and E Museo 160* (EETS, OS 283, 1982), xxx, 69, 212.

66. *Riverside Chaucer*, 103–4.

67. G. Largey and D. R. Watson, "The Sociology of Odors," *American Journal of Sociology* 77 (1972), 1021–34; L. Golding, *The Jewish Problem* (London, 1938), 59–60; Classen, Howes, and Synnott, *Aroma*, 161–79; C. Roth, *A History of the Jews in England*, 3rd ed. (Oxford, 1964), 9, 13.

68. A. Hudson and Gradon, eds., *English Wycliffite Sermons* (Oxford, 1983–1986), 2:137.

69. Classen, Howes, and Synnott, *Aroma*, 31.

70. *Seyntz Medicines*, 25.

71. *Macro*, 28–29.

72. William Langland, *The Vision of Piers Plowman: A Critical Edition of the B text*, ed. A. V. C Schmidt (London, 1987), 197; *N-Town*, 1:242; M. Stevens and A. C. Cawley, eds., *The Towneley Plays* (EETS, SS 13–14, 1994), 1:429.

73. *Hugh*, 2:219.

74. *The Squire of Low Degree*, in *Middle English Metrical Romances*, ed. W. H. French and C. B. Hale (New York, 1964), 2:742.

75. B. A. Hanawalt, *The Ties That Bound: Peasant Families in Medieval England* (Oxford, 1986), 50–51.

76. Ibid., 41, 43, 61.

77. *Hugh*, 2:49.

78. L. Boatwright, ed., *Inquests and Indictments from Late Fourteenth Century Buckinghamshire: The Superior Eyre of Michaelmas 1389 at High Wycombe* (Buckinghamshire Record Society, 1994), 21; *Nottinghamshire's Coroners' Inquests*, 128.

79. A. Collet, "*Traité d'hygiène* de Thomas le Bourguignon (1286)," *Romania* 112 (1991): 477.

80. *English Wycliffite Sermons*, 3:115.

81. A. G. Vince, "The Saxon and Medieval Pottery of London: A Review," *Medieval Archaeology* 29 (1985): 25–93; D. Gaimster and B. Nenk, "English Households in Transition, c. 1450–1550: The Ceramic Evidence" in *The Age of Transition: The Archaeology of English Culture 1400–1600*, ed. D. Gaimster and Stamper (Society for Medieval Archaeology, 1997), 171–95.

82. S. Vandenberghe, "Une Aquamanile Ornitomorphe Trouvée a Gistel (Flandre Occidentale) (An Ornithomorphic Aquamanile from Gistel)," in *Everyday and Exotic Pottery in Europe, c. 600–1900: Studies in Honor of J. G. Hurst*, ed. D. R. M. Gaimster and M. Rednap (Oxford, 1992), 336–39.

83. C. M. Woolgar, *The Great Household in Late Medieval England* (New Haven, 1999), 167 (hereafter *GH*); *Calendar of Coroners' Rolls of London*, 147–48.

84. W. Nelson Francis, ed., *The Book of Vices and Virtues: A Fourteenth Century English Translation of the Somme le Poi of Lorens d'Orléans* (EETS, OS 217, 1942), 179–80.

85. R. Foreville and G. Keir, eds., *The Book of St. Gilbert* (Oxford, 1987), 332–35.

86. *GH*, 167.

87. *Thurkill*, 5–6.

88. T. F. Kirby, *Annals of Winchester College from its Foundation in the year 1382 to the Present Time* (1892), 510.

89. *Manières de Language*, 4–34.

90. *Hugh*, 1:39.

91. G. R. Owst, "Sortilegium in English Homiletic Literature of the Fourteenth Century," in *Studies Presented to Sir Hilary Jenkinson*, ed. J. C. Davies (London, 1957), 287n5.

92. J. Lamart, "Les Bains dans la littérature française do Moyen Age," in *Les Soins de beauté* (Nice, 1987), 195–210; M. Bloch, *Feudal Society* (1965), 2:316; G. Kipling, ed., *The Receyt of the lady Kateryne* (EETS, OS 296, 1990), 50–51.

93. A. J. Taylor, "Count Amadeus of Savoy's Visit to England in 1292," *Archaeologia* 106 (1979): 123–32.

94. British Library, Add. MS 38006, f. 5r: bath on May 21; the date of the marriage is given as May 22 in E. W. Safford, "An Account of the Expenses

of Eleanor, sister of Edward III, on the Occasion of her Marriage to Reynald, Count of Guelders," *Archaeologia* 77 (1927): 111–40.

95. John Russell's *Boke of Nurture*, in *Manners and Meals*, 183–85. The tent-like arrangement was common, e.g. in the 1320s, BL Add. MS 60584, f. 24r.

96. Arrangements for bathing do not feature in J. B. Post, "A Fifteenth-Century Customary of the Southwark Stews," *Journal of the Society of Archivists* 5 (1974–77): 418–28; for the Continent, Paulino Iradiel, "Cuidar el cuerpo, cuidar la imagen: los paradigmas de la belleza femenina en la Valencia bajomedieval," in *Les Soins de beauté*, 72–73.

97. H. M. Colvin et al., eds., *The History of the King's Works* (6 vols., 1963–1982), 2:926, 934, 974 (hereafter *HKW*).

98. *HKW*, 2:697, 998.

99. *HKW*, 1:246.

100. Gaimster and Nenk, "English Households in Transition," 181–82; S. Thurley, *Whitehall Palace: An Architectural History of the Royal Apartments, 1240–1698* (New Haven, 1999), 49.

101. *Wulfstan*, 120.

102. A. T. Baker and A. Bell, eds., *St. Modwenna* (ANTS, 7, 1947), 50–51.

103. R. D. Berryman, *Use of the Woodlands in the Late Anglo-Saxon Period* (British Archaeological Reports, 1998), 35–37.

104. H. Johnstone, "The Wardrobe and the Household of Henry, Son of Edward I," *Bulletin of the John Rylands Library* 7 (1922–23): 384–420; Tony Hunt, *Popular Medicine in Thirteenth-Century England*, 206.

105. B. F. Byerly and C. R. Byerly, eds., *Records of the Wardrobe and Household, 1286–1289* (1986), 393n3238.

106. Longleat House MS Misc. IX, ff. 15r–16r.

107. C. M. Woolgar, ed., *Household Accounts from Medieval England* (British Academy, Records of Social and Economic History, NS 17–18, 1992–93), 2:578.

108. L. Bolens, "Les parfums et la beauté en Andalousie Médiévale," in *Les soins de beauté*, 145–69.

109. R. Staccini, "L'inventario di una Spezieria del Quattrocento," *Studi Medievali* 22 (1981): 377–420.

CHAPTER 4

Smelling the New World

Holly Dugan

Sir Humphrey Gilbert, knight, merchant adventurer, veteran of English wars in Ireland, and an important early proponent of English colonization of the Americas, argued strenuously that English success in the New World required blind faith in the endeavor. In his widely read *Discourse of a New Passage to Cataia*, which circulated in manuscript form for almost a decade before it was published without his permission in 1576 by George Gascoigne (and later republished in Richard Hakluyt's *Principal Navigations* in 1589), Gilbert argued that the bold would be separated from the brute by their ability to transcend their senses: "The diversity between brute beasts and men, or between the wise and the simple, is, that the one judgeth by sense only, and gathereth no surety of anything that he hath not seen, felt, heard, tasted, or smelled: and the other not so only, but also findeth the certainty of things, by reason, before they happen to be tried."[1]

In the transcendence of the senses lay Gilbert's prescient "certainty" of English colonialism. Although English endeavors in the New World hitherto had been unsuccessful, rendering only a profound sensory absence—things *not* seen, felt, heard, tasted, or smelled—Gilbert was sure that undetected riches would reward those who persevered despite such a lack of evidence. As the byline of the *Discourse* implies, no goal was impossible: "Sir Humphrey Gilbert, Knight, *Quid Non*?"[2]

Perhaps recognizing the temerity of such a motto and the need for broader support of English colonization, Gascoigne, in his introduction to the *Discourse*, supplemented Gilbert's stark insistence on reason with a plethora of sensory embellishments. Likening himself to a "huswife" who "is no lesse curious to decke her bees hive, to rub and perfume it with sweet herbes, to cover and defend it from raine with clay and boordes, and to place it in the warme Sunshine safe from the Northerly blastes," Gascoigne thought it "good (Allegorically) to write in behalfe of the right and worshipful and [his] very friend S. Humfrey Gilbert. . . . As a good Gardener doth cover his tender herbes in winter, and cherishe them also in summer: so have I thought my selfe bounded somewhat to . . . answere vnto the obiections that might bee made."[3] Redefining Gilbert's sensory dearth through allegorical perfumes, Gascoigne argues that, unlike other texts that describe things "already known," Gilbert's "doth tend to a very profitable and commendable practice of a thinge to be discouered."[4] Gilbert's emphasis on the absence of sensory data and Gascoigne's allegorical buzzing and perfuming in the wake of such a claim show the ways early English colonial endeavors hinged on desire for sensible proof of things yet "to be discouered."

Gilbert was poised for success. His goal was to claim Newfoundland, an area well known to English (and French, Portuguese, Spanish, and German) fishermen, for England.[5] As Gilbert prepared for his voyage, he petitioned alchemists, mathematicians, and natural philosophers for advice, reading extensively in the classical and contemporary accounts of the flora, fauna, navigational routes, and peoples in the New World.[6] In 1578, he secured a charter from the queen; he invested his entire fortune, along with his wife's, in the endeavor. In 1583, Gilbert set sail for Newfoundland with 260 men, including apothecarists, carpenters, masons, physicians, refiners, a band of musicians, and sundry "petty haberdasherie wares to barter with these simple people."[7]

Despite such extensive preparations, Gilbert's trip was brief. Early conflicts with fishing fleets off the coast near Saint John Bay, combined with short supplies, hastened his return to England.[8] And though one refiner purportedly discovered silver mines, all samples and notes were lost when Gilbert's ship sank off the cost of the Sable Islands. Gilbert headed back to England emptyhanded, determined that the reports alone could convince the queen to invest heavily in future endeavors.[9] On the return voyage, they encountered rough seas near the Azores. His ship, the *Squirrel*, sank, killing all onboard. Gilbert reportedly remained resolute in his conviction of England's divine manifest destiny until the very end. He was last seen on deck, holding a book in his hand, quoting Thomas More: "we are as neere to heaven by sea as by land."[10]

Gilbert's journey was a spectacular failure, but not in a way he or Gascoigne anticipated.[11] Gilbert had prepared for a dearth of sensory data, but he encountered its opposite—an overwhelmingly harsh and inhospitable sensory environment. One participant recorded an "impassable" wilderness, cluttered with undergrowth and fallen trees, with unbearable heat in summer, insurmountable "heapes and mountaynes" of ice in winter, and "ayres" riddled with mists and constant rain.[12] A later account corroborates this point: Newfoundland's air was thick, corrupted with the vapors of half-rotten trees; the roar of the sea so great it could drown out the sound of cannons; and its natives cunning and fierce, described as "wolves."[13] Worse still, it seemed devoid of merchandisable commodities. Southward, ever southward, lay English hopes in the New World.[14]

On Gilbert's death, his half-brother, Sir Walter Raleigh, inherited the charter.[15] Learning from Gilbert's mistakes, Raleigh abandoned Newfoundland for more temperate land.[16] In 1584, Raleigh sent two servants, masters Philip Amadas and Arthur Barlowe, on a four-month reconnaissance mission of new coasts, led by veteran captain Simon Ferdinando, a pilot under Gilbert's command during his first attempted voyage to Newfoundland in the 1570s. Perhaps wary of Gilbert's northern route, Ferdinando risked encountering the Spanish fleet and headed farther south, stopping briefly in a secluded harbor off a large island in Spanish-held West Indies (probably Puerto Rico), before heading north of Spanish territories in Florida toward the Carolina coast.

Such risk seemed to offer immediate reward. In June 1584, Amadas and Barlowe detected a scent wafting out to sea; it was a smell "so sweet and so strong . . . as if we had bene in the midst of some delicate garden abounding with all kinds of odoriferous flowers, by which we were assured, that land could not be farre distant."[17] Two days later, they reached land and discovered the origins of that smell: cedar, pine, Lentisk (or Mastic, which they erroneously identified as cinnamon), and sassafras, which made a "most plentifull, sweete, fruitfull and wholesome [soil] of all the worlde: there are above fourteene severall sweete smelling timber trees, and the most part of their underwoods are Bayes and such like: they have those Okes that we have, but farre greater and better."[18] The voyage was reported as a great success: in their accounts, Barlowe and Amadas describe the Carolina coast as a veritable paradise, peopled with peaceful natives, temperate climes, and abundant resources. More importantly, they returned with proof.[19] Based on their reports, Raleigh readied for the first English colony in the New World in Roanoke.[20]

Sensory Worlds

It is tempting to read these two accounts of the New World against one another: whereas Gilbert's is a tale of failure that requires Gascoigne's allegorical perfume, Barlowe and Amadas's account reports overwhelming New World material sensations, including a most fragrant terra firma. Gilbert hopes for sensations yet to be discovered; Amadas and Barlowe describe New World delights experienced firsthand. Gilbert's is a tale of northern failure; Barlowe and Amadas's opens Raleigh's southern plantation saga. However, both accounts approach the New World as sensory zones, describing overwhelming new environments through multisensorial data. Though Gilbert's impact at Newfoundland was ephemeral, it greatly affected how sixteenth-century English men and women understood America and its landscape, whether imagined as allegorically perfumed or experienced firsthand as cold, harsh, and vast. This was especially true for the explorers moving between the contact zones of Newfoundland, Roanoke, and Jamestown, who learned that successful colonization in the New World would require mastering such environs.

Describing these colonial failures as early lessons in "sensory warfare," historian Peter Hoffer argues that such encounters shaped English approaches to the colony in Virginia.[21] Faced with "oceans" of forests and the "roar" of the sea, explorers increasingly relied on sense of smell, which offered a proximate way through unfamiliar terrain. As the English searched for sensible and merchandisable matter in these realms, they learned that their failure and success depended on mastering new strategies of "discovery," including olfaction. One smell in particular symbolized for the English the potential for success in the New World—the smell of sassafras.

Sassafras may seem a rather surprising commodity for the English to have based their early endeavors in the New World, especially since its legacy has been eclipsed by tobacco. But for a brief period of time, before successful cultivation of tobacco at Jamestown in 1622, sassafras seemed to offer the English a way to excavate botanical riches from New World ecologies, just as the Spanish had a century before. Though a host of perfume ingredients fueled English commercial interest in the New World, sassafras in particular gripped English imagination. Between 1602 and 1607, six separate voyages went in search of it in the region south of Saint Lawrence and north of Roanoke in order to meet commercial demand.[22] Growing along the eastern shore of North America, in

Florida, Virginia, and New England, it galvanized European markets in New Spain, New England, and New France as a potential cure for those suffering from the pox or syphilis.[23] Even as smallpox decimated native populations in the New World, the great pox, believed to be an exogamous disease with origins in the New World, raged in Europe. Galenists believed that sassafras, or "ague-tree," could relieve ailments of the liver or spleen and, like tobacco and guaiacum, cure syphilis.

Yet the aromatic qualities of sassafras associated it with the "contagion" of luxury perfumes and the sensuality they connoted. In Ben Jonson's *Cynthia's Revels*, Amorphus and his perfumer (Signior Fig) discuss a price for Spanish scented leather gloves. When Mercury, disguised as a page for the courtier Amorphus, inquires of their value, the perfumer names no set price: "Give me what you will, sir: the *Signior* payes me two crownes a pair; you shall give me your love, sir" (5.4.400).[24] Mercury, outraged perhaps at the price and at the suggestion, exclaims, "My love? with a pox to you, goodman *sassafras*" (5.4.399). Love leads to the pox. The perfumer, formally an aphrodisiacal fig, becomes Goodman Sassafras. The joke here is multifold. Mercury was a rival cure for syphilis in the period, often prescribed by Paracelsians; Mercury allegorically haggles with sassafras, capturing the widespread cultural link between the pox and its cures. The perfumer, however, does not reject his status as Goodman Sassafras; he merely reconfigures his approach to making a sale. Shifting from gloves to pomanders, he playfully responds, "I come, sir. There's an excellent *diapasme* in a chain, too, if you like it." The perfumer sells both aromatic aphrodisiacs and cures, namely sassafras, for the diseases they inspire, namely syphilis.[25]

Such a joke may seem surprising to modern readers. Within modern sensory configurations, sassafras is most commonly identified as a taste rather than a smell, let alone a perfume ingredient.[26] As Jonson's play documents, however, sassafras was valued for its aromatic scent in early modern Europe. Like rose-water, sassafras was believed to have powerful medicinal, religious, and ornamental uses. Its bark was distilled into an essential oil that smelled like fennel; its leaves were also distilled, producing a citrusy essential oil; and medicinal teas made from crushed leaves offered their own scent, similar to bergamot.

During the last quarter of the sixteenth century, sassafras was a panacea; in some accounts, it was even reported to protect the wearer from aging. By the end of the first quarter of the seventeenth century, it was made into infant cribs and aromatic boxes to house English bibles, due to its purported ability to ward off evil spirits. Ships with large amounts of sassafras in their hulls were believed to be unsinkable. The scent of sassafras, described in early sixteenth-century sources as rivaling the scent of the Ceylon cinnamon tree, was thus one of hope, particularly for consumers in England. But, as I argue, for English explorers it was also a scent of hunger, failure, and loss, gesturing to the complicated ways in which the scent of the New World was experienced both in the contact zone and in Europe. Its varied smells underscore the seemingly limitless medicinal and ornamental uses for sassafras in Europe and the inherent difficulty in finding it in the New World.

What is most striking about the role of sassafras in shaping European encounters in the New World is that it was so ubiquitous. Christopher Columbus, in some myths, was drawn to terra firma by its scent. Samuel de Champlain recounts its succor and delightful smell in his explorations of Maine. Francisco Hernández describes it in his travels through Mexico. Nicolás Monardes publicizes its role as a panacea in his *Joyful Newes*. Jacques le Moyne de Morgues envisions it encircling Jean Ribault's column in eastern Florida. Thomas Harriot proclaims it one of three important commodities native to Roanoke. John White's watercolors depict natives literally covered in it. Ralph Lane claimed to survive famine by drinking a tea made with it. Martin Pring, under the guidance of a collaboration of Bristol merchants, led a trip to Newfoundland solely to collect it. Walter Raleigh was convicted of treason when his covert continental correspondence about offloading a stolen cargo of it was misinterpreted as part of the Wye rebellion. It is one of eleven commodities specifically mentioned in the Virginia Company's charter for Jamestown, and it was one of the first exports Captain John Smith sent back to England. By 1620, members of the Virginia Company complained that planters were too focused on cultivating tobacco and sassafras for private profit, at the expense of company lands.

Despite being so pervasive in early accounts, sassafras has faded from most scholarly accounts of the New World and Anglo-Indian contact. Of all the scent ingredients examined in this book, sassafras is perhaps the most ephemeral. Though a lucrative commodity, the difficulty of harvesting it made it an unreliable one on which to base permanent English colonies. At times, it was rare and valuable in English markets; at other times, it was plentiful and cheap. As such, it often failed to bring in the hoped-for profits, particularly as a perfume ingredient. It would not be until the end of the seventeenth century, with the introduction of jasmine, that a distinctively New World perfume would emerge in Europe for mass consumption. Rather, sassafras, as a perfume ingredient, documents only evaporated hope for early English voyages to the New World and would soon be replaced by the smoke of tobacco. As such, its ephemeral history gestures toward the lost sensory worlds of Anglo-Indian contact and the ways olfaction functioned within them.

English sassafras consumption may seem only a curious historical footnote until one considers its large role in shaping Anglo-Indian contact. In order to understand how the New World, repeatedly described in sixteenth-century sources as an overwhelmingly fragrant land—a veritable Eden—became, in seventeenth-century sources, a savage and hostile "wasteland" requiring deforestation in order to establish English tobacco plantations, we must grapple with the sensory worlds of the contact zone and the challenges they posed to European explorers.[27] In the nascent years

of English colonialism, before proofs of success were visible, sassafras represented a paradox of sensation for Europeans in the new
contact zones. When one switches from technologies of sight to
technologies of olfaction, the phenomenology of discovery becomes
proximate and dangerous.

Sassafras was not easy to find, nor was it easy to harvest. Early
reports sent back to Europe described only the plant's roots, making
it difficult to identify living specimens by sight alone. Most adventurers had only vague descriptions of the sassafras root to guide
them, with almost no description of the tree or flower.[28] Nicolás
Monardes's depiction of it was reprinted widely, but sassafras varies
greatly along the eastern seaboard. Small in the north, it could grow
to almost eighty feet in the south, with a trunk six feet wide.[29] The
leaves also change shape: old boughs have boat-shaped, smaller
leaves while new ones are large and mitten-shaped. As explorers
soon discovered, one of the only ways to identify it was through
the scent of its leaves, a method that sounds simple enough until
one factors in the dense "oceans" of forests (and their overwhelming collective scent) described in travel narratives. The experience
of searching for sassafras, along with other botanical matter, was
often frustrating. Francis Higginson wrote from Boston in 1629,
"This country abounds naturally with store of roots of great variety
. . . and other sweet herbs delightful to smell, whose name we know
not."[30] As such accounts document, harvesting sassafras required
a deep sensory engagement with a foreign ecology. English explorers seeking lucrative sassafras (of which there were many) had only
their noses, or native informants' noses, as guides.[31] Sassafras chal-
lenged English visual mapping of landscapes. Success of this crop
would require more than visual proofs; it would require olfactory
proof, rendering English bodies vulnerable to the new environs of
North America.

The first European reference to sassafras occurs in the second
part of Nicolás Monardes's influential three-volume catalog of New

World drugs, *Historia medicinal de las cosas que se traen de nuestras Indias Occidentales* (1569). Republished in an expanded version in 1574 and translated into Latin and English shortly thereafter, Monardes's text was influential and worked to connect New World ingredients to established European medical practices.[32] Arguing that the New World's vast riches were pharmacological rather than metallic, Monardes cited four drugs in particular: tobacco, guaiacum, sarsaparilla, and sassafras. Whereas scholars have examined the impact of tobacco and guaiacum on European medicine and consumerism in great detail, the impact of sarsaparilla and sassafras remain understudied.[33]

The value of both stemmed from their use as medicinal cures.[34] In his English translation of Monardes's book, John Frampton emphasized that the treatise on New World materia medica could also function as a kind of field guide for merchant adventurers. Renaming it *Joyfull Newes out of the Newe Founde Worlde*, and, more importantly, adding "portrature" of the "said hearbes, very aptly described," Frampton asserted in his title that Monardes's treatise "might bring in tyme rare profite, to my Countrie folks of England."[35] Frampton, an English merchant in Seville, turned translator on his return to Bristol after he was captured, imprisoned, and had his goods confiscated by the Inquisition.[36] He was notoriously reticent to discuss his time in Spain; his translations, some have suggested, represent an attempt at revenge, disseminating Spanish knowledge about the New World to English merchant adventurers like himself.[37] Frampton states in his introduction that medicines Monardes includes, like tobacco and sassafras, are already merchandisable: They are "now by Marchauntse and others, brought out of the West Indias into Spaine, and from Spain hether into England, and that the excellencie of these Hearbes, trees, oyles, plantes and stones, &c. hath been knowen to bee so precious a remedie for all maner of deseases, and hurtes, that maie happe unto Man, Woman, or child."[38] English profit lay in mastering Spanish trade networks and experience with New World materia medica, like sassafras.

After writing seven pages on the wonders of tobacco and two on the power of nicotine, Monardes begins his eleven-page description "of the Tree that is brought from the Florida, whiche is called Sassafras," by asserting its great "vertues" and "excellencies." These he corroborates through firsthand reports, citing sailors in Florida, doctors in Havana, and opportunists in Michoacán, all of whom confirm his assessment of the virtues of this "woodd and roote."[39] He also relies on his own experiential knowledge of the root, suggesting that he had specimens in his famous Seville garden: "It maie bee three yeres paste, that I had knowledge of this Tree, and a Frenche manne which had been in those partes, shewed me a peece of it, and tolde me merueiles of his vertues."[40] At first, Monardes remained skeptical of the Frenchman's claims, since "of these thynges of plantes, and hearbes, whiche is brought from other places, thei saie muche, and knoweth little," but he vouches for the efficacy of sassafras: "now I dooe finde to bee true, and haue seen by experience."[41] By emphasizing the visual nature of sassafras—"seeing" by experience—Monardes helps skeptical readers also "see" the "truth" of its efficacy through the circulation of print.

Such claims of experiential knowledge of New World botany bridged the sensory worlds of the contact zone and the metropole. Like rose attar, which extended the body's influence on an environment through aromatic self-presentation, the smell of sassafras extended the influence of the environment on the body. When the French Huguenots, led by Jean Ribault and René Goulaine de Laudonnière, were massacred near the Saint Johns River by the Spanish led by Pedro Menéndez de Avilés in 1565, only a few survived. Those who did warned the Spanish of a terrible disease—a tertian fever—with an efficacious local cure: sassafras, about which the Timucua of Florida (Outina) had informed them. Monardes writes, "after the Frenche menne were destroyed, our Spaniardes did

beginner to waxe sicke, as the Frenche menne had dooen, and some
which did remaine of them, did shewe it to our Spaniardes, and how
thei had cured them selues with the water of this merueilous Tree."[42]
Sassafras returned to Europe with the conquering Spaniards: "in
this tyme it was, when the Capitaine generall Peter Mellendis came
from the Florida, and brought with hym in common this wooded
of the *Sassafras*."[43]

Buried in Monardes's description of sassafras is a glimpse of the
conflict and exchange between the Timucua, French, and Spanish
in Florida—and, in Frampton's translation, between the English
and Spanish. Both a commodity to be harvested and a panacea that
underscored the dangers and diseases latent in new environments,
sassafras was a complicated symbol, useful in both New and Old
Worlds. From a modern perspective, it may seem emblematic of
European hysteria and greed, along with outmoded medical practices, but to early English explorers, it represented both the risk
and reward of the unfamiliar terrains, weather, flora, fauna, and
peoples of the New World.

A View of Virginia's Invisible Sensory Realms: White's Sketches of Sassafras

The English were slow to adapt to the frighteningly new sensory
realms of the Atlantic coastline. Like Newfoundland's inhospitable
frozen landscape, Roanoke's dark forests, thick fogs, noisy animals,
and sweet airs presented a difficult environment to master and control, particularly using visual technology. Later, near Jamestown
and in Martha's Vineyard, the English would learn from these
early mistakes and shift tactics, burning large portions of forests to
assert greater visual control over the areas surrounding their camps.
Though the goal was obviously to clear the land, the resulting smoke
from such fires also functioned as sensory warfare—a visual and
olfactory assault—upending the sensory hierarchy of the contact

zone that very much favored the natives. Natives would have been able to smell such smoke miles away. Its stench thus extended the colonists' presence far beyond their armed forts, sending a clear and menacing signal of impending violence to natives hidden nearby in the forest.

Such tactics reflect a profound adjustment in English approaches to the New World, shifting from discovery and exploration toward colonialism and plantations, from distant views of the New World toward proximate, intimate understanding of distinct realms. Theodor de Bry's engravings of le Moyne's watercolors, for example, offered visible proof of Floridian contact zones, yet they also shaped English views of other newly "found" lands like Virginia. In particular, the engravings emphasized technologies of sight as a strategy for navigation and control of unfamiliar terrains. Like Ribault, early English explorers sought to leave visible markers of their possession of the land. On August 3, 1583, Sir Humphrey Gilbert raised the arms of England, engraved in lead and set on wood, "claiming" Newfoundland for England. Ralph Lane, in his 1584 scouting expedition to Roanoke, defied native traditions—and religious beliefs—by erecting a large, visually imposing, permanent fortress on a spiritual landscape; when he left, the natives erased all traces of it. Its disappearance, like that of the later English colonists, shows that in these vast new realms the impact of the English was minimal at first. That 115 colonists could simply disappear into such an "ocean" of forests underscores the disjunction between European "views" of the New World and sensory experiences of them.

Thomas Harriot's *A Briefe and True Report of the New Found Land of Virginia* is at the center of both approaches. While previous accounts like Amadas and Barlowes's cite both the sweetly scented allure of New World forests and the dangers that lurked within them, Harriot's narrative offers a "view" of the contact zone. In it, Virginia is a peaceful and fertile zone. De Bry's engravings of John White's watercolors emphasize this pictorially, so much so that historians often describe *A Briefe and True Report* as propaganda. Such propaganda operates by distancing readers from the contact zone through sight. Although Harriot "touches" the diversity of relations and reports, seeking to settle them "firmly," particularly in dealing with "natural inhabitants," he encourages prospective "adventurers, favorers, and well willers" for the Virginia enterprise to "see" and "know" for themselves "what the country is." His treatise is divided into three parts to facilitate this "more readie view." He lists Virginia's "merchantable" goods and useful commodities, citing his own experience "hauing seen and knowne more then the ordinarie" and dismissing other reports as slanderous "trifles." Taking Harriot's visual emphasis one step further, Theodor de Bry, in the 1590 edition of the text, explains that he republished Harriot's narrative with his engravings of White's images because every man should "exert him-selfe for to *show* the benefits which they haue receeue of" the colony.[44]

But Harriot's hopeful framing of such explicit, visual proof failed spectacularly. Against such a vision unfolds the mystery of the colonists' disappearance at Roanoke. Harriot's narrative is one of the few we have of Anglo-Indian contact at Roanoke. As many critics have noted, his description of Virginia is biased toward English mercantilism, as are de Bry's engravings. By aligning English colonial desire with a mastery of technologies of sight, the narrative tells a story of English dominion of new lands, people, and especially new "merchantable" commodities. But the narrative, when read alongside White's watercolors that were turned into de Bry's engravings, also documents anxiety about the sensory realm of the contact zone, particularly about the invisible effects of bodily contact. Such anxiety focused on proximate, intimate, and olfactory contact with natives.

Harriot famously recounts native misinterpretation of English optical illusions—a lodestone, "a perspective glass whereby was shewed manie strange sightes . . . spring clocks that seem to goe of themselves"—as divine power.[45] This belief, in Harriot's view, leads the natives to declare the English once and future conquerors of the land. The English are ubiquitous, lurking in the air "without bodies," waiting to kill natives by "shooting inuisible bullets into them."[46] The phrase has perplexed literary critics and historians alike: what did Harriot mean to convey by such "invisibility"? Although his exact meaning remains a mystery, Harriot's account of native belief in invisible bullets seems to suggest that the English had an advantage due to their technologies of sight, while the natives relied on other sensory ways of knowing.

But such a conclusion reveals not only the ways vision structured English approaches to the New World, particularly at Roanoke, but also how vision has shaped our histories of contact. The implicit association of vision with science, technology, and modernity offers a view of Virginia deeply biased toward English colonial success in the New World, in spite of the spectacular failure at Roanoke. Harriot's "view" supplants the historical conclusion of the colony. Though it is possible to read against the grain, there is a danger that doing so implicitly shapes scholarly approaches to the history of contact, so much so that Alan Taylor warns that "scholars have recently become so sophisticated at detecting hidden bias and covert messages that we risk writing only about the construction of illusions."[47]

Sassafras, however, was hardly a hidden or covert message in these histories. And its presence in the text (as a merchantable commodity) and in both White's watercolors and de Bry's engravings indicates the important role of olfaction in the contact zone of Roanoke. In this zone, both the English and the natives struggled to understand the novelty of the effects of contact.[48] Whereas the Roanoke imagined a forest full of unseen English spirit-bodies attacking them, the English imagined a benevolent god protecting them. As Harriot describes, a few days after the English visited Roanoke towns and villages, the natives suffered from a strange and deadly disease. The disease only affected native populations; furthermore, Harriot asserts that it only occurred in towns where there had been native resistance. Yet the experience described is unsettling, resonating with colonists' fears about airborne environmental hazards, particularly the vulnerability of breathing in unfamiliar terrain.[49] Harriot emphasizes the novelty of this epidemic; religious men report no such occurrence for "time out of mind."[50]

The description of sassafras emphasizes the vulnerability of the English in unfamiliar terrain and the role of olfaction in navigating it successfully. Harriot's survey names sassafras as an important commodity for any potential colony at Roanoke since it was both "merchantable" in England and "most helpful" to planters in Virginia as a medical cure. Both values stemmed from its invisible, airborne qualities. Harriot notes its "most pleasant and sweet smell" and that it is "found by experience to be farre batter and of more uses than the wood which is called *Guaiacum,* or *Lignum vitæ.*" He concludes: "For the description, the manner of using and the manifolde vertues thereof, I referre you to the book of *Monardus,* translated and entitled in English, *The Joyfull newes from the West Indies.*[51] He does not elaborate on why planters might need to rely on sassafras as a medicinal cure, sidestepping any potential reference to the pox, to English vulnerability to airborne diseases, and to Spanish and French failures in the contact zone of New Spain. Instead, he focuses on its aromatic wood. Later explorers would discover new applications for it the hard way, boiling and eating its leaves to fend off starvation.

Harriot includes the native term for sassafras, *winauk,* which suggests not only that aromatics were a subject discussed in early Anglo-Indian exchanges but also that this particular one was plentiful. Unlike vision, olfaction offered proximate and sometimes inexact knowledge of these new realms. Explorers often falsely reported the presence of botanical matter. Orris root, for example, a popular aromatic ingredient used to scent cloth, hair, and tooth powders, was routinely reported as common to the New World, despite that it is not native to North America. Smell offered proof of a commodity's presence and potential value, even when unseen. Harriot includes civet cats in his list of merchantable goods, claiming that "good profites will rise" from them. Though no colonist saw a cat, he remained convinced of their presence. Colonists noted a distinctive smell, left "where one or more had lately been." The presence of civet cats was also corroborated "by relation of the people there are some in this country."[52] Similarly, Harriot suspected that there were many "sweet gummes and many other Apothecary drugs" in the area. But without an expert he could only hint at their usefulness.[53] He reports confidently, however, that Virginian winauk is the same described by Monardes, suggesting how native olfactory mapping of local terrain supplemented English visual ones.

Like the native echo of *winauk* resonating in Harriot's texts, de Bry's images contain their own phenomenological trace of the contact zone: John White's watercolor sketches. Though John White's watercolors supplement Harriot's narrative, they also function as a personal archive of sensation. As such, they participate in what Mary Fuller has described as the ways personal memory becomes historical memory. Sassafras was an important part of this process. Sent to Virginia to assist Harriot in mapping and cataloging the Virginian coast, John White was a gentleman limner.[54] He kept detailed notebooks of his journey and made copious sketches of native portraits, scenes of native life, details of flora and fauna, and intricate maps. Though most of these notebooks were lost, and the catalog of watercolors inspired from them were shown only to a very limited selection of people, de Bry's reproduction of them in his *America* series made them some of the most influential and widely disseminated images of the New World.

White's perspective is hardly unique (his watercolors reflect an amalgamation of travel narratives describing flora, fauna, and peoples from Turkey, Florida, Brazil, Newfoundland, and Virginia) or objective (they also reflect wildly optimistic view of temperate climate, peaceful people, and bountiful crops). Yet it reveals a struggle to objectify his firsthand experience of the New World and present it to others, particularly Walter Raleigh. That these images survived even after Roanoke colony disappeared emphasizes the ways subjective, phenomenological engagements in the contact zone could become spectacular and iconic representations of English colonialism.

Risking his own family and money, White invested everything in the success of English plantations in Roanoke. His granddaughter, Virginia Dare, was the first English child born in the New World; she remained in Roanoke with her parents, waiting with the other colonists for his return. Furthermore, he was a gifted limner, with powerful connections to Harriot and through him to Raleigh and the court; White traveled to Virginia six times in ten years, mostly to search for lost colonists. All of this, Kim Sloan suggests, "situates him perfectly as our Elizabethan interpreter of the New World."[55] His phenomenological engagement with Roanoke remains one of the more compelling aspects of its archive. How did Roanoke smell? What did it sound like? How did it feel? Do his visual images sketched in the field betray the broader sensory worlds in which they were engaged, or do they merely reflect illusory desires of the metropole?

Much has been made of the optimism that opened White's career and shaped his depictions of the Anglo-Indian contact zone. In his watercolors, he greatly extends the Virginia growing season (planting three successive crops), and his natives generously offer foodstuffs (despite that White and his colleagues arrived in the midst of a terrible drought, when natives were most likely anxious to preserve holds from strangers).[56] Less attention has been paid to his disillusionment and his framing of it in sensory terms. His final letter to Raleigh, before retiring to Ireland, expresses his own disappointment in the venture: "I would to God it had been as

prosperous to all, as *noysome* to the planters" (emphasis added).[57]
His use of *noisome* had olfactory connotations: it signaled not only
annoying, disagreeable, or troubling hazards but also, increasingly
in the sixteenth century, stench.[58] What was once so sweetly allur-
ing has become cloying. White's disappointment is palpable; he
describes himself as "lucklesse" and "froward" in his early hopes.[59]
Though he concludes that he has been content with the "sight" of
the New World, his concern for the planter's noisome struggles
gesture toward other sensory experiences in the New World, experiences both good and bad that could not easily be represented in
travel narratives.

De Bry embellishes the environmental backgrounds but retains
White's focus on the smiling, naked natives, who function as important visual clues to wary investors in the Virginia plantations. Their
scantily clad bodies signal a temperate (and potentially fruitful) climate, and their gestures convey their status as helpful (and hopefully peaceful) native neighbors. Against a stark white background,
in White's original drawings the figures of the natives and individual details—tattoos, jewelry, hairstyles, clothing, postures, and
gestures—are clearly visible. If such details signal an illustrious
future for English plantations in Harriot's published treatise, then
they also point toward a not-so-distant past: the artistic moment of
production, when John White was in the field sketching. As such,
they function as an archive of the ecology of contact and, perhaps,
a trace of White's phenomenological experience of it.

Consider, for example, White's depiction of "a festive danse,"
which de Bry engraves and includes under the label "their danses
which they use att theigr hyghe feastes." Harriot's narrative recounts
a great and solemn feast that occurs at a "certayne tyme of the
yere," "in a broad playne," "after the sunne is sett," which included
neighbors from nearby towns. In this feast, men, "attired in the
most strange fashion they can deuise," dance and sing around
three "fayre virgins," who embrace in the center, "abowt which are

planted in the grownde certayne posts caured with heads like to the faces of Nonnes couered with theyr vayles."[60] So important is this feast that White includes two images of it: one in detail and one placed on the map of the Secotan village.

In his watercolor of the town of Secotan, White offers a snapshot of life there. Along with images of their tomb, their place of solemn prayer, and their fields of "ripe corn," "green corn," and "corn newly sprung," the dance is an integral part of the landscape. White describes it as "a ceremony in their prayers with strange iestures and songs dansing abowt posts carued on the topps lyke mens faces."[61] The dancing men hold rattles while others rest, waiting to join the dance, or guard the corn crops in the distance. In his detail of the festive dance, White seeks to represent the dance as motion, elaborating on such strange gestures. Each figure is surrounded by light shadowing, which demonstrates the shape of the dance. White also includes light shadows of branches of leaves, which seem to be passed to each participant as he enters the circle. These shadowy branches resemble sassafras leaves. It is as if White seeks to represent not only the figures of the body but also the sensory effects of their ritualized motions. The smell of sassafras is captured by representing the branches in motion. Given that the dance occurred after sunset, such a scent would undoubtedly be an important component of the colonists' experience of it.

The men are painted holding rattles and wearing feathers and pouches. Some scholars argue that both represent tobacco, which Harriot describes as an important part of native rituals (although Harriot mentions only powdered ceremonial uses).[62] Indeed, de Bry's engravings interpolate tobacco and corn into these scenes. He adds fields of tobacco (along with giant sunflowers) to the depiction of the Secotan town, and though he eliminates the shadowy steps of the dance, de Bry emphasizes the use of branches in the dance, filling them in and supplementing them in with husks of corn. These embellishments are consistent with others he makes; he translates

White's blank backgrounds into specific environments, even if they
are generic. The effect is to translate White's sensory record into a
discrete narrative. The dancers are frozen in time, and the sassafras
no longer represents a smell but a visual symbol of future monetary
success. Both White's and DeBry's representations of Secotan town
life purport to offer an "objectification" of sensory data, rendered
through an imagined aerial perspective.[63] But as critics note, there
are hints of a counternarrative embedded within them. John White's
watercolor of the dance, with its shadowy aromatic branches and
vivid movement, are one such clue, suggesting that the English were
just as captivated with the natives' rituals and invisible, aromatic
technologies as the natives purportedly were with theirs.

The English settlement at Roanoke, like Gilbert's journey, was a
spectacular failure. By 1586, the natives and English were involved
in armed struggles. The natives had the distinct advantage of stealth,
whereas the English were armed with matchlock muskets, which
required that one strike a dry match and ignite the gunpowder to
fire the weapon. The scent of a struck match alerted the natives,
armed with bows and arrows and hiding in trees, of their presence. Though the guns were loud and smoky, they were ineffectual
against the natives' guerrilla tactics. The English built a large, vis-
ibly imposing, permanent fort on the settlement. The natives retali-
ated by withdrawing their support, allowing the English to starve.
Lane reported to English investors that he and his men survived by
eating sassafras leaves alone, which again testifies to the ubiquity
of the plant. When Lane and his men returned to England in 1586,
the natives destroyed all evidence of an English settlement. White,
along with 150 colonists, returned to Roanoke in 1587, rebuilding
the abandoned and destroyed settlement. Conditions soon wors-
ened, and White returned to England to secure additional supplies,
leaving approximately 115 colonists behind. When he returned in
1590, all traces of them and their settlement had vanished into the
thick, dense forest air.

The disturbing disappearance of the colony presented Raleigh with a challenge not unlike Gilbert's twenty years prior: how to inspire English colonists in the wake of such tragic news. Sassafras, as both a luxury perfume commodity and as a potential medicinal cure, was one possibility. Its value in Europe provided an incentive to mitigate the failures at Roanoke. In sixteenth-century accounts of the contact zone, sassafras served as an important symbol of potential English success in the New World, despite that phenomenological descriptions of its smell in those same accounts underscore English vulnerability to native attack and hostile environments. By the start of the seventeenth century, however, it also functioned as a symbol of the failure at Roanoke, its ephemeral scent in English markets a troubling reminder of what remained elusive. In published accounts of return voyages, Raleigh cites greed as the reason the colony remained lost; rather than searching for the colonists, the voyagers collected sassafras.

As Raleigh's men continued to search the Carolina and Virginia coasts for signs of the settlers, Sir Humphrey Gilbert's nephew, Captain Bartholomew Gilbert, along with Captain Bartholomew Gosnold, sailed (without Raleigh's knowledge) to the "north part of Virginia," a region now known as New England. Gosnold's and Gilbert's voyage was strategic, short, and profitable, if not entirely successful. Planning to retrace Giovanni da Verrazzano's route to Narragansett Bay, Gilbert and Gosnold sailed west to Maine, down the coast toward Provincetown, around Cape Cod, and into Buzzard's Bay, near Martha's Vineyard. There, they established a small fort on the western part of Elizabeth Island and commenced trading with the Wampanoag people. They had hoped that such a settlement would be permanent; Gosnold was to remain in command of the settlement while Gilbert navigated the *Concord* back to England. Due to a dramatic miscalculation in supplies in which the proposed settlers would be left with six weeks' worth of supplies rather than six months' worth, the settlement plan was abandoned.

The *Concord* returned home to Bristol with her entire crew and 2,200 pounds of sassafras, which was almost a ton.[64]

Raleigh discovered Gilbert and Gosnold's endeavor surreptitiously, only after their profitable cargo saturated England's sassafras market.[65] Furious, he worked to impound the *Concord* and confiscate their remaining cargo; he even sent Harriot from London to Southampton to seize a cartload of sassafras that had been sent ahead.[66] Raleigh's goals for such seizures were twofold: to protect his own financial interests in sassafras and to secure his charter. He addressed his financial interests first, arguing that any additional importation of sassafras would "cloy" England's markets.[67] Raleigh quickly recognized, however, that he could parlay their success into his. Recasting their voyage as part of his New World endeavors, he published an account of the voyage alongside of reports of his searches for the lost colony.

Repackaged as "Northern Virginia" rather than harsh Newfoundland, the north again seemed economically promising. Gilbert and Gosnold's lucrative journey revived English colonial endeavors, and their haul of sassafras helped to transform the failures of Newfoundland and Roanoke into a promising future that would coalesce around a different "Virginia." John Brereton's widely read *A Briefe and True Relation of the Discoverie of the North Part of Virginia*, published in 1602, represents this new approach, suturing together Brereton's account of Gilbert and Gosnold's journey and a brief description of Captain Samuel Mace's search for the lost colonists of Roanoke.[68] In combining these two distinct journeys, Brereton conflates Gilbert and Gosnold's sassafras collection in the north in 1602 with Captain Mace's failure to find the lost colony of Roanoke in the south the same year. Mace fails to find the colonists because of his greed; he searches for sassafras rather than colonists.

Perfume was an important part of this political repackaging, its ephemeral scent linked to the lost colony of Roanoke. In Brereton's account, Mace chased the wrong scents. Brereton reports that Mace was "a very sufficient Mariner, an honest sober man, who had been at Virginia twice before," suggesting his knowledge of the terrain. In this way, Mace was like others that had searched for the lost colony. As Brereton notes, Raleigh "hath sent fiue seuerall times at his owne charges," concluding that "some of them follow[ed] their own profit elsewhere; others return[ed] with friuolous allegations."[69] He then reports that the ship returned loaded only with lucrative scent ingredients. The "brief note" on the voyage disregards the difficult navigation conditions along Cape Hatteras, blames Mace for failing to find the colonists, and catalogs the tremendous merchandise available for harvesting.[70] That sassafras could conflate disparate journeys to North Carolina and New England demonstrates its important role and the role of olfaction in shaping the representational history of Anglo-Indian contact.

Brereton's condemnation of Mace was political. Gabriel Archer's account of the same journey, published in 1625 after the success of Jamestown, reports the experience of collecting sassafras in the north very differently from Brereton, particularly the phenomenological experience of vulnerability and fear experienced by the English in these zones. Archer was a chaplain on Gosnold and Gilbert's voyage. Like Brereton's, his narrative highlights the prosperity of the voyage from the start. Even the multiple signs of landfall were portentous: the water turned to a "yellowish greene," the ground became "sandie" with "glittering stones . . . which might promise some Minerall matter," weeds and woods floated by, and finally, "we had a smelling of the shore, such as the from the Southerne Cape and Andaluazia in Spaine."[71] The natives were comely, tall, and surprisingly adept at trade, undoubtedly due to previous participation in the fishing trade to the north. Newfoundland, in this account, is hardly a failed encounter in an empty, harsh landscape but rather an important first step in Anglo-Indian contact. Its history emerges through native familiarity with "Christian" language. As a result, in Archer's view, the natives were altogether more knowledgeable about the English than the English were of them.[72] Brereton corroborates Archer's conclusion, but deemphasizes its implications, noting only that "they pronounce our language with great facilitie."[73]

Brereton's narrative describes the landfall at Maine as an encounter with a veritable paradise. The environment is so lush that the sailors, "when coming ashore . . . stood a while like men rauished at the beautie and delicacie of this sweet soile," marveling that "nature would shew herself aboue her power artificiall."[74] Despite such a spectacular setting, Brereton remains focused on profits, noting that sassafras trees are "great plenty all the Island ouer" and that they are "a tree of high price and profit."[75] The first listing, and the only one to include European values, is "Sassafras trees, the roots whereof at 3 s. the pound are 336.1 the tunne."[76] Archer's account offers a different perspective, narrating difficult labor and harsh working conditions. Though the trees were plentiful, the labor of collecting sassafras was difficult. For sixteen days, the labor of collecting sassafras and of building a permanent settlement consumed the crew, interrupted only by native encounters or foul weather.[77] Archer's narrative also documents that the Mi'kmaqs, Massachusetts, and Wampanoags offered assistance with the collection of sassafras, perhaps using this as an opportunity to examine the English and their defenses.[78]

Though he emphasized the ease with which sassafras might be culled from the landscape, Brereton also claimed that England's sassafras market was limited, suggesting that any subsequent voyages and attempts to harvest such merchandise would need supervision under Raleigh's charter.[79] Though it is tempting to trust Raleigh's conservative and self-interested assessment of Europe's sassafras market, sassafras continued to buoy English investments in the New World, culminating in the Virginia Company's stakes at Jamestown. Despite Raleigh's warnings about a glut in the market, the success of Gilbert and Gosnold's voyage, along with the popularity of

Brereton's narrative, increased demand for sassafras. Raleigh himself chartered two more voyages to the Chesapeake region to search for it. These voyages were important precursors to the permanent settlement at Jamestown, sharpening the sensory lessons learned at Roanoke and providing explorers with opportunities to apply them to new realms.[80]

Sensory Substitutions: Jamestown, Tobacco, and the Colony of Virginia

After reading early accounts of Amadas and Barlowes's early reports of the Virginia coast, and perhaps inspired by the impending departure of the Jamestown expedition, Michael Drayton wrote his ode "To the Virginian Voyage" (1606). In it, he commands the brave to "go and subdue" the newfound land. Virginia is a paradise, where "nature hath in store Fowl, venison, and fish / And the fruitful'st soil, / Without your toil, / three harvests more."[81] Chief among these resources are cedar, cypress, pine, and sassafras. Indeed, sassafras was written into the charter for Jamestown. The irony, of course, is that Virginia's success depended not on these fragrant resources but rather on a different kind of crop: tobacco.

In his analysis of the sensory worlds of early America, Peter Hoffer argues that when the English renewed their attempts to colonize southern Virginia, they applied the lessons learned at Roanoke, namely the importance of sensory manipulation of the environment.[82] Though the first two decades of the plantation would be marked by crises, by the late 1620s, the English secured a permanent settlement in the New World through their success at what Hoffer terms "sensory imperialism."[83] Tobacco was a large part of such imperialism. The successful planting of tobacco crops after 1622 enabled Jamestown to emerge as a powerful and stable settlement and allowed the English to forever alter the landscape of Virginia.

If tobacco marks English success in Virginia, then sassafras represents its failures. Tobacco defined the English presence in the New World; as Hoffer concludes, "the plough was the pen with which the English husbandman wrote his name on the land."[84] Sassafras, however, could only be collected; it could not be cultivated. Any English presence associated with it was ephemeral as its scent. Since its roots were the source of its value, a sassafras tree, once collected, was forever destroyed. Thus, the colonists' early survival in Jamestown depended largely on sassafras's overwhelmingly abundant presence in the surrounding areas; settlers could collect it even while under attack from native forces. In 1610, sassafras's fragrant wood was one of the first commodities Smith sent back to the Virginia Company as proof of the settlement's viability. Yet sassafras was a commodity better suited to raiding missions than to permanent settlements.[85] As the Jamestown settlers attempted a more permanent presence on the landscape, they destroyed the surrounding stores of sassafras. By 1622, the settlement failed to make its quota of thirty pounds of sassafras, and the Virginia Company penalized tobacco planters for failing to meet their share.

Though such deforestation undoubtedly left an impact on the landscape, it was nowhere near the scale of tobacco plantations. And, despite that the English used sassafras to survive those early hardships, sassafras remained resoundingly under native control. English struggles to permanently inhabit Virginia emphasize this point. The territory to the north of the valley of Powhatan was known as Winauk or Wynaoke, a term that connoted both "roundabout way" and, as Harriot noted in his *Briefe and True Report*, a land of sassafras.[86] Its name reverberated with the English experience of the space and undoubtedly led the English to equate the landscape with odoriferous qualities of native realms.[87]

Thus, a wholesale shift in the landscape, both in terms of its name and its sensory worlds, was required for the English to inhabit such a space. To do so, they would revive Humphrey Gilbert's dichotomous distinction between sensuous, brute animality and English reason, locating sensory experiences of space—olfactory ones in particular—firmly in the former. Whereas up to this moment English success in the New World required olfaction, after 1622, and after what Peter Hoffer terms John Smith's successful "sensory warfare" against Opechancanough and the Powhatan confederacy, the smell of the contact zone was associated with natives' brute physicality rather than English humanity. In 1622, the Jamestown settlers, struggling to meet their sassafras quotas while planting fledgling crops of tobacco, suffered a vicious attack from the Powhatan confederacy. Peacefully entering the homes of the English unarmed, the natives used English tools as weapons against them (and their animals). A quarter of the settlers were tortured, killed, decapitated, and hung in plain sight; such violence was meant to demonstrate native control over the realm, even those spaces purportedly under English control.

The English, however, answered such violence with sensory warfare tactics described in accounts like Pring's and Archer's. Rather than attack the natives directly, the English sought to change the landscape in which they dwelled. For Governor Francis Wyatt, writing to defend his leadership of the colony in the wake of the attack, the solution lay in deforestation. The English must seat "the whole colony upon the forest." Deforestation would enable the landscape to become more hospitable for the English; it would make the climate drier, warmer, louder, less diseased (due to fewer mosquitoes), and more arable for tobacco planters and their animals. John Smith, of course, had called for such measures from the beginning, particularly for "carpenters, husbandmen, gardeners, fishermen, blacksmiths, masons, and diggers up of trees, roots well provided, than a thousand of such we have."[88]

Though his first encounter with the Powhatan Valley was characterized through olfaction, Smith quickly derided the natives through their association with smell. Sassafras, and its smell, was

a profit to be harvested from the landscape, but the natives would
have to be evacuated from it. Later, Smith derided the natives as
mere "brutes, vile and stinking in their customs," despite his noting
of the foul stench of the English and their deplorable living conditions.[89] His description of the natives as stinking brutes demonstrates how smell participated in the violence of early Anglo-Indian
contact. Preserving the role of olfaction in the terrain of the New
World by associating it with English perception of bodies rather
than landscapes, Smith transforms the natives and their brute physicality into objects, rather than subjects, who smell.

The English success in Virginia ultimately depended on visual
mastery of new landscapes. With the successful cultivation of
tobacco, the English were able to rework the landscape so that
it mimicked the sensory worlds of England. Such a distinction
between subjects and objects and between bodies and environments was never as stable as the English hoped, for the nose prominently displayed how ephemeral contact with other sensory worlds
could permanently reshape bodies. In her reading of how technology and science shaped the Anglo-Indian contact, Joyce Chaplin
begins with two tales of diseased noses—one native, one English.
Both document how the nose, as an organ of smell, represented
"the tip of the problem" in navigating the sensory worlds of the
contact zone. The first, a Santee tale told in the Carolinas in the
early 1700s, relates two natives who emerge noseless from a remote
forest, having survived a terrible illness. When asked about the loss
of their noses, they reply that they had conversed with the "Great
Being" who "had promis'd to make their Capacities equal with the
white People in making Guns, Ammunition &c." in return for their
noses.[90] In such a tale, the natives demonstrate a profoundly sar-
donic awareness at how the history of contact would be told: sagacious, native knowledge would succumb to English weaponry. As
Chaplin argues, noses represent the "tip of the problem" if one seeks
to understand why "the inhabitants of colonial America, Indian

and English, dwelled so obsessively, and ultimately, so decisively on bodies and technologies."[91]

The Santee story demonstrates how olfaction bears the cultural trace of a brief moment in which the environment of the contact zone absorbed, affected, and transformed the bodies within it. A story about Thomas Harriot tells the story the other way around. After returning to England, Harriot, mathematician, famous surveyor of Virginia, and enthusiastic proponent of smoking, suffered from an ulcer on his face, which slowly consumed his entire nose and ultimately killed him. It was most likely a nicotine-induced cancer. Harriot's colleague, mocking his mathematical belief in atomism, described his death as the ultimate "nihilium" or triumph of nothingness: "for in the top of his nose came a little red speck, which grew bigger and bigger and at last killed him."[92] Though the joke pokes fun at Harriot's mathematical beliefs, it gains teeth through its invocation of deadly nothings, whether they be atoms, tobacco smoke, invisible bullets, or exogamous disease. Harriot's ghastly and painful condition would have registered as a symptom of the pox, a pox conflated with the effects of the New World on English bodies, which made visible how vulnerable English bodies were in New World environs.

Though artificial noses could mitigate the cosmetic effects of the disease, such prosthetics, usually made of silver or of grafted skin, in some ways functioned like sassafras: an important visible sign of the invisible hazards of breathing dangerous air. Prosthetic noses, after all, hindered one's ability to smell. They functioned as brute bodily material rather than as organs of sense. Prosthetic noses also had visual associations with plague beaks used in continental Europe. Those elongated beaks, stuffed to the brim with potent herbs and spices, isolated the nose as a very vulnerable sensory organ in diseased spaces. Olfaction's association with transmission of disease would galvanize new kinds of fears about bodily contact, especially with those ravaged by plague in urban spaces.

NOTES

1.   See "A Discourse Written by Sir Humphrey Gilbert, Knight" in *Voyages in Search of the North-west Passage: From the Collection of Richard Hakluyt*, ed. Henry Morley (London: Cassell and Company, 1886), 41.

2.   Gilbert's motto takes on a sinister air when considered alongside his actions as military commander in Ulster during the Irish wars. Gilbert reported in a letter to Sir Henry Sydney that "I slew all those from time to time that did belong to, feed, accompany, or maintain any outlaws or traitors; and after my first summoning of any castle or fort, if they would not presently yield it I would not afterwards take it of their gift, but won it perforce, how many lives so ever it cost, putting man, woman and child of them to the sword"; quoted in Ben Kiernan, *Blood and Soil: A World History of Genocide from Sparta to Darfur* (New Haven, CT: Yale University Press, 2007), 47. As David Quinn concluded, Gilbert's "method of waging war was to devastate the country, killing every living creature encountered"; *Voyages and Colonising Enterprises of Sir Humphrey Gilbert* (London: Hakluyt Society, 1940), 1:17, also cited in Kiernan, *Blood and Soil*, 47.

3.   George Gascoigne, "The Epistle to the Reader," in Sir Humphrey Gilbert, *A Discourse of a Discouerie for a New Passage to Cataia* (London, 1576), sig. qiiij r.

4.   Ibid., sig. qqiiij v.

5.   In 1497, Henry VII granted a patent to explore westward lands, including Ireland. John Cabot, hoping to discover China, discovered Newfoundland and its early fishing colonies.

6.   Gilbert got as far as Ireland, engaging in acts of piracy against Spain. This was Gilbert's second endeavor to the New World; the first ended disastrously. See Kim Sloan, "Setting the Stage for John White, A Gentleman in Virginia," in *A New World: England's First View of America*, ed. Kim Sloan (Chapel Hill: University of North Carolina Press, 2007), 17, 19. The reward for such expertise included large tracts of land in the Saint Lawrence area, including one granted to John Dee. See Gillian Cell, *English Enterprise in Newfoundland* (Toronto: University of Toronto Press, 1969), 41.

7.   See Sloan, "Setting the Stage," 21.

8.   When Gilbert arrived in Saint John Bay, Newfoundland, sixteen Spanish, Portuguese, and French fishing ships were already in the harbor. Nevertheless, on August 5, 1583, Gilbert formally took possession of Newfoundland for the English. See Cell, *English Enterprise*, 23, and Sloan, "Setting the Stage," 21. For more on the early European fishing industry in Newfoundland, see Peter Edward Pope, *Fish into Wine: The Newfoundland Plantation in the Seventeenth Century* (Chapel Hill: University of North Carolina Press, 2004).

9. Based on reports by Frobisher and by Anthony Parkhurst, including his reported discovery of copper in Newfoundland, Gilbert brought along a Saxon refiner who collected sample ores, purportedly of copper, iron, lead, and silver. See Carlos Slafter, *Sir Humphrey Gylberte and His Enterprise of Colonization in America* (Boston: Prince Society, 1903), 41.

10. Andrew Hadfield, *Amazons, Savages, and Machiavels: Travel and Colonial Writing in English, 1550–1630: An Anthology* (New York: Oxford University Press, 2001), 237.

11. Contemporaneous accounts, such as Hayes's, blamed his irascible temper, avarice, and poor judgment. Sir William Alexander similarly identifies Gilbert's poor judgment, describing his desperation and "needlesse bravery," which led to his death; *An Encouragement to Colonies* (London, 1624), sig. D4 v–E r.

12. See Richard Hakluyt, *The Principal Navigations, Voyages, Traffiques, and Discoveries of the English Nation,* ed. Edmund Goldsmid (Edinburgh: E. and G. Goldsmid, 1887), 8:81–84, cited in Cell, *English Enterprise*, 43.

13. See Marc Lescarbot, *Noua Francia: or The Description of that Part of New France Which Is One Continent with Virginia* (London, 1609), sig. E3 r. The overwhelming effect of these sensations was sickness and disease, which was not aided by the seafaring conditions. "I would adde willingly to all the foresaid causes the bad foode of the sea, which in a long voyage brings much curroption in mans bodie. For one must of necessity, after foure or fie daies, luie of salt meate, or to bring sheepe aliue, and store of poultry . . . and the waters stinking" (sig E3 v).

14. As Henry Wadsworth Longfellow wrote in a poetic tribute, "By the Seaside," Gilbert's colonial endeavors ended tragically: "southward, for ever southward, / They drift through dark and day; / And like a dream, in the Gulf-stream, / Sinking, vanish all away"; *Poetical Works* (London: Houghton Mifflin, 1891), 46.

15. See Alan Taylor, *Writing Early American History* (Philadelphia: University of Pennsylvania Press, 2006), 108.

16. As Mary C. Fuller has argued, Newfoundland shaped how most Englishmen imagined "America" in the sixteenth century. Despite that Newfoundland "was probably England's earliest landfall, and certainly its earliest land claim in North America," England's lessons in colonization there remain "startlingly unremembered and unrecorded"; *Remembering the Early Modern Voyage: English Narratives in the Age of European Expansion* (Houndsmill, UK: Palgrave Macmillan, 2008), 118.

17. Henry S. Burrage, ed., *Early English and French Voyages, Chiefly from Hakluyt, 1534–1608* (New York: Charles Scribner's Sons, 1906), 228.

18. Virginia's potent scent is a trope echoed in later voyages. Strachey recorded that "before we come in sight of yt thirty leages, we smell a

sweet savour as is usually from off Cape Vincent, the South Cape of Spayne, if the wynde come from the Shoare." Captain Devries is more specific about the origins of this scent, reporting in 1630 that "The 2nd December, threw the lead in 14 fathoms sandy bottom and smelt the land, which gave a sweet perfume as the wind came from the northwest, which blew off land and caused these sweet odors. This comes from the Indians setting fires at this time of year to the woods and thickets, in order to hunt, and the land is full of sweet smelling herbs as sassafras, which has a sweet smell. When the wind blows out of the north west and the smoke too is driven to sea, it happens that the land is smelt before it is seen"; quoted in Philip Bruce, *Economic History of Virginia in the Seventeenth Century* (New York: Macmillan, 1896), 88.

19. See Alden T. Vaughan, "Sir Walter Raleigh's Indian Interpreters, 1584–1618," *William and Mary Quarterly* 59 (2002): 343–57.

20. Though Raleigh seems to have intended the natives to act as interpreters, learning English, Thomas Harriot, and perhaps also John White, studied Algonquin. See David Quinn, *Explorers and Colonies: America, 1500–1625* (London: Hambledon, 1990), 243–44.

21. Peter Hoffer, *Sensory Worlds in Early America* (Baltimore: Johns Hopkins University Press, 2003), 19.

22. See David B. Quinn and Alison M. Quinn, eds., *The English New England Voyages, 1602–1608* (London: Hakluyt Society, 1983), 31.

23. On the pox, and its association with exogamous, foreign diseases (particularly in the New World), see Jonathan Gil Harris, *Foreign Bodies and the Body Politic: Discourses of Social Pathology in Early Modern England* (New York: Cambridge University Press, 1998), 14.

24. All quotations are from *Ben Jonson: "Cynthia's Revels," "Poetaster," "Sejanus," "Eastward Ho,"* ed. C. H. Herford, Percy Simpson, Evelyn Simpson, and Evelyn Mary Spearing Simpson (New York: Oxford University Press, 1986).

25. Jordan Goodman argues that Galenists prescribed guaiacum and sassafras as a cure for syphilis, while Parcelsians prescribed mercury; see *Tobacco in History: The Cultures of Dependence* (London: Routledge, 1993), 43.

26. Once commonly used in the production of root beer soda and in tea, sassafras connotes a unique taste rather than scent. Sassafras is now banned by both the FDA and the IFA for use in either drinks or perfumes due to its carcinogenicity. Interestingly, it is surmised that native collection practices avoided the poisonous white-stemmed sassafras leaves, which are carcinogenic, collecting only red-stemmed leaves. See Maurice M. Iwu and Jacqueline C. Wooton, eds., *Ethnomedicine and Drug Discovery* (New York: Elsevier Science, 2002), 131.

27. For more on the ways in which the New World became a "wasteland," see Patricia Seed, *American Pentimento: The Invention of Indians and the*

Pursuit of Riches (Minneapolis: University of Minnesota Press, 2001), chap. 2.

28. See Quinn and Quinn, *English New England Voyages*, 87.

29. See Donald Culross Peattie, *A Natural History of North American Trees* (New York: Houghton Mifflin, 2007), 276–77.

30. Francis Higginson, *New-Englands Plantation* (London, 1630), sig. B3 r. For example, orris root, a popular aromatic ingredient used to scent cloth, hair, and tooth powders, was difficult to cultivate commercially; it was routinely reported as common to the New World, despite the fact that it is not native to North America. Other aromatic ingredients thought to be discovered include benzoin (probably North American spicebush), cassia (perhaps dogwood, though *cassia* was often a generic term for aromatic wood), and china root (probably a smilax). Such confusions suggest that smell was an inexact sensory guide in unfamiliar environments. Discovery of new kinds of aromatic ingredients, such as sweet flag, or *Acorocus calamus*, and sarsaparilla, resulted from contact with natives. Of the numerous aromatic properties discovered in the New World, sassafras was the most prominent and the most elusive; it was also one of the few native medicines that explorers and colonists preferred to their own. See Charlotte Erichson-Brown, *Medicinal and Other Uses of North American Plants: A Historical Survey with Special Reference to the Eastern Indian Tribes* (Mineola, NY: Dover Publications, 1989), xi.

31. For example, Master Robert Meriton in the Archer expedition, Robert Salterne and Thomas Bridges in the Pring expedition, and James Roseier in the Waymouth expedition are listed as identifying sassafras (and other New World plants), yet no explanation of their expertise is listed, though perhaps previous experience in southern trips aided in the discovery of this difficult specimen. See Quinn and Quinn, *English New England Voyages*, 16. *Sagacity*, Susan Scott Parish argues, was the word most often used by English naturalists to describe their native informants, a term that emphasized their "animal acumen," particularly their sense of smell; *American Curiosity: Cultures of Natural History in the Colonial British Atlantic World* (Chapel Hill: University of North Carolina Press, 2005), 239.

32. Goodman, *Tobacco in History*, 44.

33. For more on tobacco, see Marcy Norton's *Sacred Gifts, Profane Pleasures: A History of Chocolate and Tobacco in the Atlantic World* (Ithaca, NY: Cornell University Press, 2008), which examines both pre- and post-Hispanic culture in the new world; Jordan Goodman's *Tobacco in History*, which examines the commodity history of tobacco in Enlightenment Europe; and Jeffrey Knapp's "Elizabethan Tobacco," *Representations* 21 (1988): 26–66. One exception is Charles Manning and Merrill Moore's "Sassafras and Syphilis," in *New England Quarterly* 9, no. 3 (1936): 473–75.

34. John Frampton, *Ioyfull Newes out of the Newe Founde Worlde* (London, 1577), sig. Mij r.

35. Ibid.

36. See Donald Beecher, "John Frampton of Bristol, Trader and Translator," in *Travel and Translation in the Early Modern Period*, ed. Carmine G. Di Biase (New York: Rodopi, 2006), 103–22.

37. Frampton was connected with influential Bristol merchants, many of whom founded the Spanish Company in 1577. All six of Frampton's influential translations deal with trade, including two navigational texts, three on China, and one on Portuguese trade.

38. See Frampton, *Ioyfull Newes*, sig. Mij r.

39. Ibid., sig. Mii r, Nii r, Nii v, Niv r.

40. Ibid., sig. Mij r.

41. Ibid.

42. Ibid., sig. Nii r.

43. Ibid. Lawrence C. Wroth describes Monardes as "an eager investigator haunting the Seville docks in order to meet the ships which would bring him new plants or new regimes for those already growing in his garden"; "An Elizabethan Merchant and Man of Letters," *Huntington Library Quarterly* 17, no. 4 (August 1954): 306.

44. Thomas Harriot, *A Briefe and True Report of the New Found Land of Virginia* [1590], ed. Paul Hulton (New York: Dover, 1972), sig. A2 r.

45. Harriot writes: "Most thinges they sawe with vs, as Mathematicall instruments, sea compasses, the vertue of the loadstone in drawing yron, a perspectiue glasse whereby was shewed manie strange sightes, burning glasses, wildefire woorkes, gunnes, bookes, writing and reading, spring clocks that seeme to goe of themselues, and manie other thinges that wee had, were so straunge vnto them, and so farre exceeded their capacities to comprehend the reason and meanes how they should be made and done, that they thought they were rather the works of gods then of men, or at the leastwise they had bin giuen and taught vs of the gods"; ibid., sig. C4 r.

46. Ibid., sig. D r.

47. Taylor, *Writing Early American History*, 23.

48. Karen Ordahl Kupperman, *Indians and English: Facing Off in Early America* (Ithaca, NY: Cornell University Press, 2000), 178.

49. Harriot, *Briefe and True Report*, sig. C4 v.

50. Ibid.

51. Ibid., sig. B r.

52. Ibid.

53. Ibid., sig. B2 r.

54. See Ute Kuhlemann, "Between Reproduction, Invention, and Propaganda: Theodor de Bry's Engravings after John White's Watercolours," in Sloan, *New World*, 79.

55. Sloan, *New World*, 6.
56. Joyce Chaplin argues that John White's watercolors are a theatrical view of the New World. "They dance. They wave to each other. They prepare food. They smile. . . . In a very real sense, White introduced Virginia's natives to the English as if he were displaying them in a theatre"; "Roanoke 'Counterfeited' According to the Truth," in Sloan, *New World*, 51, 59.
57. Hakluyt, *Principal Navigations*, vol. 8 (New York: Macmillan, 1906), 406.
58. Oxford English Dictionary, 2nd ed., s.v. "noisome," n. 4. For more, see Holly Dugan, "Coriolanus and 'the Rank-Scented Mienie': Smelling Rank in Early Modern London," in *Masculinity and the Metropolis of Vice, 1550–3750*, ed. Amanda Bailey and Roze Hentschell (Houndsmill, UK: Palgrave Macmillan, 2010), 139–59.
59. John White, "To Master Richard Hakluyt, written from my house at Newton, in Kilmore, the 4th of February, 1593," in *History of North Carolina: With Maps and Illustrations*, ed. Francis Lister Hawks (Fayetteville, NC: E. J. Hale and Son, 1857), 214–15.
60. Harriot, *Briefe and True Report*, sig. C2 v.
61. Ibid.
62. "This Vppówoc is of so precious estimation amongst then, that they thinke their gods are maruelously delighted therwith: Whereupon sometime they make hallowed fires & cast some of the pouder therein for a sacrifice . . . also after an escape of danger, they cast some into the aire likewise: but all done with strange gestures, stamping, some-time dauncing, clapping of hands, holding up of hands, & staring up into the heauens, uttering therewithal and chattering words & noises"; ibid., sig. B4 v.
63. See Hoffer, *Sensory Worlds*, 29.
64. See Quinn and Quinn, *English New England Voyages*, 206. Though it is impossible to say for certain how much an early modern "ton" weighed, Raleigh's reference to the *Concord*'s cargo as both a "tunne" and as 2,200 pounds comport to a long ton, a common weight of measurement used in early modern shipping pounds to connote 2,240 pounds. See Frederic C. Lane, "Tonnages, Medieval and Modern," *Economic History Review* 17, no. 2 (1964): 213–33.
65. In 1602, sassafras was priced at about twenty shillings a pound, until its price dropped rapidly. Raleigh, investigating the drop, discovered reports of sassafras sales in England's southern ports, all from a recent voyage to northern Virginia.
66. See Quinn and Quinn, *English New England Voyages*, 204.
67. In a letter to Cecil dated August 21, 1602, Raleigh charges that Gilbert has destroyed the sassafras market: "whereas sarsephraze was worth 10s, 12s, & 20s apound before Gilbert returned his cloying of the market will overthrow all myne & his also /he is contented to have all stayed,

not only for this present, butt being to go agayne others will also go &
destroy the trade, which otherwise would yield 8, or 10, for on certenty,
& a returne in xx weekes"; Quinn and Quinn, *English New England
Voyages*, 206.

68. Gosnold was the captain and Brereton the shipmaster.
69. Quinn and Quinn, *English New England Voyages*, 206.
70. Brereton is explicit in this accusation: "When they came along the
coast to seeke the people, they did not pretending that the extremitie of
weather and losse of some principall ground-tackle, forced and feared
them from searching the port of Hatarask, to which they were sent.
From that place where they abode, they brought aboard Sassafras, Radix
Chinae or the Chinae root, Beniamin, Cassia lignea, a rinde of a tree
more strong than any spice as yet knowen [most likely sweet bay]"; M.
John Brereton, *A Briefe and True Relation of the Discouerie of the North
Part of Virginia, Being a Most Pleasant, Fruitfull and Commodious Soile*
(London, 1602), sig. B4 v.
71. Quinn and Quinn, *English New England Voyages*, 115–16.
72. The account makes this connection explicitly: "With a piece of Chalke
described the Coast there abouts, and could name Placentia of the
New-found-land, they spake divers Christian words and seemed to
understand much more than we, for want of Language could comprehend." Archer focuses on visual recognition through clothing: "One
that seemed to be their Commander wore a Wastecoate of black worke,
a paire of breeches, cloth Stockings, Shooes, Hat, and Band, one of the
two more had also a few things made by some Christians." Some scholars
interpret the "Placentia of the New-found-land" to be a Basque reference.
Quinn and Quinn, *English New England Voyages*, 117.
73. Brereton, *Briefe and True Relation*, sig. B2 r–v.
74. Ibid., sig. B v.
75. Ibid., sig. A4 r.
76. Ibid., sig. B3 r.
77. After describing the fair conditioned people and the activities of trade,
Archer again records that on "the first of June, we employed our selves
in getting Sassafrage and the building of our Fort. . . . [O]n the fifth
we continued our labor . . . the company with me only eight persons."
Approached by fifty "Indians in hasite manner," among them a leader of
"authority," Archer "mooued my selfe towards him seuen or eight steps,
and clapt my hands first on the sides of mine head, then on my breast,
and after presented my Musket with a threatening countenance, thereby
to signifie unto them I either a choice of Peace or Warre." According to
Archer, such motions worked: "Hee vsing me with mine owne signes of
Peace, I stept forth and imbraced him, his company then all sate downe
in manner like Grey-hounds upon their heeles with whom my company
fell a bartering." Here, the narrative emphasizes their "maruelling" at

"bright and sharpe" knives. Quinn and Quinn, *English New England Voyages*, 134.

78. The crises avoided, the natives then labor with the English: "Our dinner ended, the Seignior first took leaue and departed, next all the rest sauing foure that stayed and went into the Wood to helpe vs digge Sassafrage, whom we desired to goe aboord vs, which they refused and departed." Archer does not comment on the natives' reluctance to board the native ship, nor their motives in extending the offer. He only continues to chronicle the labor of collecting sassafras: "the fourteenth, fifteenth, and sixteen wee spent in getting Sasafrage and fire-wood of Cedar, . . . the seuenteenth, we set sayle"; ibid., 133–38.

79. Not surprisingly, when he returned to England, Gosnold corroborated Raleigh's assessment of England's sassafras market. In a letter to his father dated September 7, 1602, Gosnold describes that sassafras was easily procured from Elizabeth Island, with "little disturbance" was "reasonable plenty," but he reports that the bulk of their labor was not spent on collecting sassafras since "we were informed before our going forth that a tunne was sufficient to cloy England"; ibid., 210. Gosnold's assessment of England's sassafras market sounds suspiciously like Raleigh's; the *Concord*, after all, brought back just short of a long ton.

80. In Martin Pring's narrative, smell provides a proximate and shared experience of the environment, which sometimes facilitates trade and sometimes facilitates violence. For example, although the sailors were struck by the size of native boats, it was the sweet-scented rosin that captivated their narrative description: "Their Boats . . . were in proportion like a Wherrie of the Riuer of Thames, seventeen foot long and four foot broad, made of the Barke of a Birch-tree, farre exceeding in bignesse those of England: it was sowed together with strong and tough Oziers or twigs, and the seames couered over with Rozen or Turpentine little inferiour in sweetness to Frankincense"; ibid., 223.

81. Michael Drayton, "To the Virginian Voyage," *Poems* (London, 1620), sig. Pp 5 r–v.

82. Hoffer, *Sensory Worlds*, 19.

83. Ibid., 49.

84. Ibid., 72.

85. Philip Boucher makes this point about sassafras in relationship to the Huguenots' presence in Florida; "Revisioning the 'French Atlantic': or, How to Think about the French Presence in the Atlantic, 1550–1625," in *The Atlantic World and Virginia*, ed. Peter C. Mancall (Chapel Hill: University of North Carolina Press, 2007), 274–306.

86. Philip Alexander Bruce, *Economic History of Virginia in the Seventeenth Century: An Inquiry into the Material Condition of the People, Based upon Original and Contemporaneous Records* (New York: Macmillan, 1907), 1:92–93.

87. William Wallace Tooker, "Some More about Virginia Names," *American Anthropologist* 7 (1910): 524–28.

88. Hoffer, *Sensory Worlds*, 72.

89. John Smith, "A True Relation" [1608] in *Jamestown Voyages under the First Charter: 1606–1609*, ed. Philip Barbour (New York: Cambridge University Press, 1969), 1:170, 172.

90. John Lawson, *A New Voyage to Carolina* [1709], ed. Hugh Talmage Lefler (Chapel Hill: University of North Carolina Press, 1967), cited in Joyce Chaplin, *Subject Matter: Technology, the Body, and Science on the Anglo-American Frontier, 1500–1676* (Cambridge, MA: Harvard University Press, 2001), 3.

91. Chaplin, *Subject Matter*, 3.

92. Jean Jacquot, "Thomas Harriot's Reputation for Impiety," *Notes and Records of the Royal Society* 9 (1952): 164–87, cited in ibid., 31.

CHAPTER 5

Gender, Medicine, and Smell in Seventeenth-Century England

Jennifer Evans

Across the seventeenth century writers in several medical self-help manuals noted that aromatic substances, in the form of fumes, suffumigations, gloves, and ointments, were a suitable remedy for female barrenness. In particular the use of musk, civet, and ambergris was thought to stimulate the reproductive organs, encouraging sexual desire and fertility. Many traditional histories of early modern medicine have suggested that physicians did not touch their patients, except to take a pulse, instead relying upon patient narrative and in some cases urine analysis to diagnose and treat the sick body.[1] Similar comments were also made about the male practice of gynecological and obstetric medicine.[2] Yet it would appear from the language of medical texts, as will be seen, that not all physicians diagnosed and cured at a physical distance from their patients; they, like other medical practitioners, could and did touch the body when necessary. Accordingly, several scholars have modified and nuanced our understanding of how medical practitioners negotiated access to their patient's bodies. Lianne McTavish, for example, has demonstrated the ways in which patients resisted the gaze and touch of man-midwives and male practitioners structured their practice in response to these concerns, by presenting touch as a method of viewing.[3]

Thus, it is possible to understand some of the occasions when it was allowable for practitioners, predominantly surgeons, midwives and man-midwives, to view and touch a woman's body. Nonetheless, much of what has been uncovered relates to the perhaps unique circumstances of parturition.[4] It has been noted, however, that "tactility was always suspect because of its potential to incite erotic feeling."[5] Winfried Schleiner has argued that Renaissance male practitioners became increasingly concerned about the potential erotic results of the medical manipulation of the female genitals.[6] Similarly, McTavish has shown in her work on midwifery in early modern France that royal midwife Louise Bourgeois was concerned that her patients may have experienced shame at having their bodies exposed to the visual and tactile scrutiny of a surgeon.[7] Shame was an important part, therefore, of the complexities of gendered bodily access at this time. It has been argued for the medieval world, though, that "women's shame was merely an unfortunate obstacle to male medical practice, not an absolute impediment to it."[8] Similarly, Wendy Churchill has argued that even though female modesty was unquestionably a social custom espoused in early modern society, it should not be assumed that this was a pervasive element of all patient-practitioner interactions.[9] It is therefore no longer simply enough to state that physicians did or did not touch their patients. It is necessary to consider in more detail the multisensory nature of early modern medicine. In doing so a much more nuanced understanding of medical practice and gendered patient-practitioner interactions in early modern England may be found. This chapter adds to this understanding and in particular to the discussion about the potentially sexual nature of medical contact with patients by investigating the ways in which male physicians could negotiate access to the female body through smell in cases of infertility, a disorder that was invested with concerns about modesty, appropriate bodily comportment, and access to the sexual organs.

In a recent introduction to a special issue of the American Historical Review, Martin Jay noted that "exploring the infinite variety of sensual experience has become a staple of contemporary historical analysis"; in particular, it has become a common phenomenon not simply to investigate the interactions with the natural world in the past but to explore in detail the meanings attributed to those interactions.[10] The increased interest in the study of the history of the senses was also demonstrated by a similar special edition of the *Journal of American History*.[11] The articles presented in these editions show that from its traditional beginnings, exploring the importance attributed to each of the senses and their hierarchical ordering—and in particular the ascension of sight as the primary sensory tool of human intellect and development—the history of the senses has expanded to encompass a wealth of topics and historical eras.[12] In terms of the history of smell, this has included investigations into the relationship between smell, tourism, and environmental history and the social use of smell to create racial divisions.[13] Studies of the senses in the early modern and eighteenth-century world have also become increasingly popular and varied, including examinations of the strong smells and loud noises of urban life, the way smell was used in political and travel literature, and the centrality of smells to religious belief and ritual and to the Reformation.[14]

Studies in the history of medieval and early modern medicine have also utilized smell as a lens through which to assess aspects of medical practice and intellectual development. Michael McVaugh's innovative study of thirteenth-century surgery, for example, has shown that smell could be used in the identification of certain skin diseases such as ulcers and leprosy.[15] Nonetheless, much of the scholarship on the early modern period has focused on the medical theory of miasma, which outlined that dangerous and noxious fumes and smells created by putrefaction would enter the body, causing corruption and disease. Most frequently this topic has been addressed by anthropologists and historians in relation to the causation and cure of plague.[16] Classen, Howes, and Synnott have explored the common use of fumigations and pomanders during plague and asserted that virtually any pungent odor was thought to be good for this purpose.[17] Nonetheless, as this chapter shows, the use of smells was not always this indiscriminate: certain smells were believed to be more relevant for the treatment of barrenness because they were considered to be sexually stimulating and heating. This article will expand upon the existing historiography of smells in early modern medical treatments to demonstrate that they were not only used to combat miasmatic infections and pestilence. It will also bring together the discussions of medicinal smells with the relatively few studies that have assessed smells and perfume within eroticism and sexuality. These works have shown that in literature that dealt with sex and conception as a matter of eroticism, rather than a medical process, smell was relatively maligned and is perhaps conspicuous by its absence.[18] This is particularly puzzling given the ways in which erotic literature and pornography readily incorporated medical ideas about the body and focused on the reproductive potential of sex as a key measure of its ability to provide pleasure.[19] However, there were several pungent substances that were overtly accepted as arousing in the medical literature and beyond.

The need to investigate the use of aromatic diagnostics and cures for barrenness is further highlighted by the importance of sight and touch in the diagnosis of early modern pregnancy. Many scholars have examined the experiences of single women, illegitimate pregnancies, potential infanticides, and unusual pregnancies—such as those occurring in prisons—and have shown that identifying a pregnancy in these cases relied heavily upon touch and sight: the breasts and abdomen would be squeezed, and visual markers, such as the inflation and deflation of the abdomen, would be sought.[20] In this situation the woman's body was open and exposed to the senses of her community. Examining the relationship between physicians and barren patients enables us to broaden and nuance our understanding of the multisensory experience of conception and the potentially pregnant body. It will also begin to reveal the experience of married women whose reproductive bodies were the least likely to be exposed to the senses of the community. Olivia Weisser has suggested that early modern patients relied upon a "range of sensory perceptions and observations to read and treat their bodily ailments."[21] Thus, by moving beyond the senses of sight and touch, it will be demonstrated that odoriferous substances provided a means for penetrating the internal cavity of the body and illuminating the reproductive potential of the generative organs. This, moreover, was not limited to use by physicians: women themselves could employ these diagnostic tools to establish their own fertility. Smells provided an alternative treatment option for physicians who may have been refused access to the female body. Although surgeons and midwives may have been allowed to assess the genitalia through touch, it was potentially necessary for practitioners to utilize all of the senses to assess and repair the health of the internal generative organs. In advocating the use of fumes it is apparent that medical men could circumvent the dictates of modesty that may have prevented them from directly applying a sexually stimulating remedy to a female patient's genitals. More than this, medical men also expected the patients themselves and their husbands to administer these treatments, allowing a remedy to reach the internal cavity of the womb without practitioner interference.

This chapter examines medical treatises published in the seventeenth century, including one or two that were originally produced in the sixteenth century but continued to sell and be of intellectual significance into the seventeenth century (where sixteenth-century texts have been consulted, every effort has been made to use the earliest available edition from the seventeenth century). The period between 1650 and 1750 was characterized by stagnant population growth caused by late marriage and reduced fertility.[22] This started to change around 1701, when the age of marriage began to fall, yet as Tim Hitchcock has noted, a subsequent increase in fertility did not become apparent until after 1750.[23] The characteristically low fertility of the seventeenth century was reflected in the interest shown by medical writers and the broader populace about the causes and cures of infertility. Although early modern men and women were unaware of these demographic trends, barrenness was a matter of concern for most medical writers, who discussed the diagnosis, prognosis, and cure of the many types of infertility in their works.[24] Other disorders that could lead to barrenness were also discussed in these treatises, including dropsy, tumors, inflammations, ulcers, and diseases affecting women's "stones" (ovaries).[25] Indeed, historians such as Patricia Crawford, Laura Gowing, and Amanda Capern have identified that laypeople in the early modern period were equally concerned about the reproductive potential of the body and expressed anxiety when faced with barrenness and impotence.[26] This widespread apprehension was reflected in popular and ephemeral literature from this period. Ballads including *The Sorrowful Bride* and *The Lamenting Lady* emphasized to a diverse audience the necessity of healthy fertile sexuality in both men and women for a successful and stable marriage.[27] In *The Lamenting Lady*, a barren woman who scorned a female beggar who had borne twins was punished by God to deliver "forth in feare, As many children at one time, as daies were in the yeare."[28]

The seventeenth century is also of particular interest because at this time there was an explosion of print culture. Printed materials were produced in much greater quantities and covered a wider range of topics and ideas than ever before. The production of medical texts was very popular, particularly following the collapse of censorship and the critique of elite knowledge by radicals during the English Civil War. As Laura Gowing has suggested, one of the central topics of these works was "the greatest mystery of all"—generation or reproduction.[29] These texts ranged from costly folios to cheaper works, and, as Mary Fissell has shown, medical texts could also be bought secondhand at auctions, making them available to artisans and others.[30] The ideas perpetuated in these treatises are suggestive of the understandings of the wider populace. Many were reprinted and ran into several editions, indicating some measure of popularity. Numerous medical treatises were presented as self-help manuals designed to provide consumers with useful and relevant information for seeking medical help or attending to their own ailments. The seventeenth century consequently provides a distinct and clear body of literature through which to assess the understanding and use of medical treatments for barrenness. This chapter does not, however, propose that concerns about modesty or the potential use of smell therapies as a strategy for negotiating these tensions were unique to the seventeenth century.[31] The use of aromatics for diagnostic purposes and therapeutics was part of the classical medical inheritance utilized throughout the medieval period and the Renaissance. Yet this does not mean that the role of aromatics should not be thoroughly investigated as a part of early modern medical practices. Even though the use of these substances might not be culturally specific, examining the ways in which aromatics may have been used can add substantially to our understanding of early modern medical practices and patient-practitioner interactions at this time.

In particular, this chapter uses printed treatises that fit into three broad categories. First, there are the general medical treatises that provided readers with information about the range of diseases that could afflict the body of man. These were often arranged in a head-to-toe format and dealt with diseases in both the male and female bodies. They were also aimed at both male and female readers. Conversely, the second category, midwifery manuals such as Jane Sharp's *The Midwives Book* or Nicholas Culpeper's *Directory for Midwives*, were addressed to an ostensibly female audience of midwives.[32] Although these books were read by both sexes, these treatises suggest how those directly involved in the care of the female

reproductive system, including female medical practitioners and
midwives, may have understood barrenness and its treatment.
Finally, books aimed at laywomen rather than midwives, like *The
Compleat Doctoress* and *The Sicke Womans Private Looking-glasse*,
were produced throughout the seventeenth century.[33] Again, as
Monica Green has argued, producing vernacular texts aimed at
women did not mean that they passed into a solely feminine medical community, but they do reflect a tendency to consider more
specifically the female body and the potential responses of female
readers.[34] These texts explored a range of women's diseases, though
they often discussed similar material to the midwifery manuals. Texts like these can be used to glean an idea of how women
themselves may have understood these problems and remedies.
Examined together these three genres, all predominantly written and published by men, will illuminate the ways in which male
medical practitioners sought to deal with a disorder that was intimate to the female body and constrained by the dictates of modesty
and shame. It may also be possible to highlight whether the advice
and types of remedy offered, particularly the use of aromatics and
fumes, were altered depending on the perceived audience of the text.

Several of the treatises utilized here were originally written or
produced on the Continent. Their origin, however, does not make
them irrelevant to a study of medical ideas in England. At this
time many medical writers and practitioners shared in a broader
European medical culture. A number of texts by writers across
Europe were published in the medical lingua franca, Latin, to
reach a wide audience and were then translated into the vernacular languages of different countries. This European medical culture
extended beyond the written word, with many English medical students traveling to study at the major European centers of medical
learning like Padua, Bologna, and Leiden. Thus, although not everything found in these texts was absorbed and adopted by English
audiences, the belief of the translators and publishers of such works

was that they would find an English readership and that the information they conveyed was of relevance to English understandings of health and disease.

Richard Palmer has charted in detail the ways in which the sense of smell was understood in early modern medicine.[35] This understanding was predominantly based upon the writings of the ancient medical authorities Hippocrates, Galen, and Aristotle. Palmer has suggested that most medical writers and practitioners subscribed to the theory that the two small porous membranes protruding from the brain into the naval cavity were the organs of smell.[36] Despite this general agreement on the organ of smell, the way in which odors were perceived and indeed what odors actually were was much more uncertain. One consequence of this uncertainty was that smells were thought to exist in many different forms, including smokes, fumes, balms, waters, and powders.[37] In terms of their medical properties, many early modern medical writers, including Helkiah Crooke, believed that smells were invisible particles that penetrated the organs in the nasal cavity and touched the brain.[38] By touching the brain these substances were therefore able to transfer their humoral properties to the body; as material particles, smells contained the humoral properties of the substances from which they originated. Importantly, smells created by decay and corruption could cause the body to decay and corrupt, linking them with the spread of diseases like plague. The use of sweet and refreshing smells was believed to prevent bad odors from reaching the body, and so fumigations were used to correct pestilential rooms and environments. More than this, as will be seen, sweet and refreshing smells could also be thought to affect the body directly, heating and provoking sexual desire.

The uncertainty around the ways in which smells were understood to work in the body becomes even more apparent in discussions of the womb. Many writers reiterated, from a long pedigree of

ancient and medieval medical knowledge, that smells were known
to affect the womb, causing it to move around the internal cavity of
the body.[39] It was explained that these peculiar sensations resulted
from the womb's superficial similarity to the brain. Although it is
not always apparent in medical treatises why the brain and womb
were considered to share qualities, by the latter part of the seventeenth century some writers were attempting to explain this connection. William Salmon, while describing the virtues of "hystericals"
(substances that were used as treatments for the womb) in *Synopsis
Medicinae* (1671), declared that "These are known chiefly by their
scent: for sweet scents draw the Womb that way they are applyed;
stinking scents the contrary: and the reason is, because it sympa-
thizes with the head and brain, from whence the nervous parts take
their beginning."[40] Nicholas Culpeper agreed in *Select Aphorismes*
that "The Womb, thus resembles the Brain and Ventricle, that it
manifestly draws to Cephalicks and Aromaticks, and flies from
their contraries."[41] Yet even in these descriptions it is not clear how
aromatic medicines caused these effects; it may have been that the
similarity to the brain meant that the womb could also be touched
by the particles of an odor. This confusion was apparent to some
writers at the time who attempted to rationalize this phenomenon:
Daniel Sennert asserted in *Practical Physick* that "it is probable to
me that the womb is not delighted with Scents as Scents, for the
Privities have no smelling, and the sense of smelling doth not reach
so far; but the quality by which it is well or ill, is occult, and not to
be explained, and not to be separated from the Odors."[42] As will be
seen, this ambiguity allowed for the idea that certain odors could
impart heat and could sexually stimulate the womb, thus enhancing its fertility.

The potent effect that smells appeared to have upon the womb
had long been used to explain and cure several diseases, predominantly the suffocation of the mother, or mother fits, and a prolapsed
uterus.[43] The suffocation of the mother, in which the womb rose

toward the diaphragm and induced breathlessness, was thought to be caused by numerous aromatic substances. Additionally, it was believed that the womb would be drawn toward sweet smells, so placing them at different points on the body would return the womb to its correct position. In the seventeenth century, Nicholas Culpeper explained in the most basic terms that "in the fits of the Mother, which is the Womb turned upwards, stinking things applied to the Nose, and sweet things to the Matrix, reduce it, but sweet things applyed to the Nose, and stinking things to the Matrixe produce it."[44] The aromatic substances utilized in this instance could be quite diverse, including burnt partridge feathers, leather, asafoetida, galbanum, rue, civet, musk, and cloves.[45] Similar remedies were also offered to correct a prolapsed uterus, where placing foul-smelling substances at the genitals was thought to encourage the womb to rise back into its correct position.[46] Yet Eccles noted that the best surgeons, in cases such as this, still reduced the prolapse using their hands, a candle, or a blunt stick padded with rags.[47] Despite the widespread recommendation of treatments of this kind for these hysteric disorders, not all authors were convinced that the womb was affected by aromatics in this way. Even Culpeper, who recited these treatments and in general asserted that they worked, criticized those "Sots" who believed that the womb contained a sense of smell.[48] Despite these controversies, recommending the use of aromatic substances to manipulate the position of the womb within the body and restore health was a consistent part of medical treatises throughout the medieval and early modern periods. This was not, however, the only function that smells could serve; they were also discussed by medical writers as a means of diagnosing barrenness in women and often recommended as treatments for this disorder.

Each of the three genres examined in this research included the use of odors as a means of testing a woman's fertility. To do so, garlic, red storax, or another smelly substance was placed beneath or within the woman's genitals; if the smell from this substance moved through the woman's body to her head it indicated fertility. These tests were consistently described as having been recommended by Hippocrates, and authors appealed to this pedigree to assert the test's authority.[49] The use of odoriferous substances to diagnose barrenness not only demonstrates that smells were utilized in reproductive medicine to manipulate the womb's position but also illuminates the ways in which smells could be used to gain access to the internal cavity of the body without the use of touch and sight. It has been widely suggested that physicians in the early modern period did not touch their patients except to take a pulse, while surgeons and midwives and irregular practitioners engaged in a much more tactile form of practice.[50] It has also been assumed that much gynecological medicine was provided by midwives and surgeons, who in particular were known to treat venereal disease.[51] Yet several scholars have noted that the boundaries between different forms of medical practice were blurred in this period and that it is difficult to make definitive statements about the practices employed by specific groups of practitioners.[52] Access to the female barren body was therefore a complex issue. Patricia Crawford has suggested that this issue was heightened during the 1670s as fears about fraudulent "Groaping Doctors" developed.[53] These practitioners claimed that they could not discover the cause of a woman's disorder without feeling and touching a woman's genitalia.[54] Winfried Schleiner has also shown that Renaissance medical practitioners were concerned about manipulating the female genitals, in cases of suffocation of the mother, and so found it necessary to call for a midwife who could touch the organs instead.[55] Moreover, he has shown that even when these men called upon the mediating touch of the female hand, they could still express anxieties about the potentially shameful nature of that touch if it was needlessly titillating.[56] These aromatic tests, however, demonstrate that physicians and other medical practitioners could utilize a range of multisensory techniques to assess and penetrate the female reproductive organs in order to diagnose barrenness and could similarly use smells to treat these disorders. These tests could thus have been employed to safeguard a male practitioner's reputation.[57] They could also be utilized by women themselves to avoid the unwanted gaze and touch of a male practitioner.

Before examining these tests more fully, it is worth highlighting that they were unique to the female body. Male infertility, which along with impotence was recognized in the early modern period, was also tested for but without using materials that penetrated the reproductive organs and body. Men's bodies were most frequently described as being tested alongside women's bodies through their urine: each partner had to urinate into a pot that had been planted with barley or another grain, and the seed that sprouted first demonstrated the fertility of the person who had watered it.[58] A similar test was also suggested where both parties urinated on a lettuce leaf and the person whose urine dried away (evaporated) from the leaf first was thought to be infertile.[59] As far as this research has shown, only one text recorded a test for male infertility that was not conducted in conjunction with the woman: Christopher Wirtzung's general medical treatise suggested, "let him pisse in a pot, and let the urine stand awhile, if wormes grow therein, then is that urine barren."[60] It would thus seem from these tests that male fertility could be established externally, without any need for accessing or assessing the internal structure of the reproductive organs.

In general medical compendiums, written for both a male and a female audience, there appears to be little consensus about who should carry out these tests or on whose authority the final diagnosis rested. In some treatises the suggestion is made that they will be carried out by someone other than the female patient. Daniel Sennert wrote that "*Hippocrates* proves Barrenness thus. *Put a Fume*

(Saith he) *under the Coats of a woman, and let her be close clothed about, and if the scent come to the Nose, she is not barren, and he bids you put Garlick clensed into the wombe, and if she smell of it at the Mouth, she is fruitful.*[61] This extract does not exclude the possibility of a female reader doing this test herself, but the suggestion is perhaps that the physician will be conducting it. In particular, it is apparent that it is someone other than the woman who is detecting the outcome of the test: it is the ability of a physician to detect the smell of garlic on a woman's breath that dictates whether or not she is diagnosed as barren.[62] Lazarus Riverius was more explicit in avowing that it was physicians who employed these tests, stating *"cover her with blankets, and burn some perfume under her,"* but he noted that they were used in cases that were "of a certain hidden disposition" and usually at the instigation of those outside the medical profession: "yet are Physicians necessitated sometimes to make use of them, in favour of Princes and Nobles, who are permitted to divorce their Wives in case of Barrenness."[63] Although Riverius's text suggested that these tests "carry no great certainty," it was again implied that it was the physician's sensory perception that made the final diagnosis, smelling the woman's breath and head.[64] These physicians may have described these tests both to show their familiarity with Hippocratic medicine and to access a female body with which they had been denied visual and tactile contact.

Conversely, several medical treatises expected physicians to be granted access to the female body and suggested that assessing fertility rested on the symptoms that would be detected visually and by touch during a consultation. At the very start of the seventeenth century, an edition of Philip Barrough's sixteenth-century text listed the many signs of barrenness to which a physician should pay attention, noting that "the rest of the causes may be knowne, partly by sight, and partly by the telling of the partie or other about her."[65] Most of the signs Barrough noted were physical aspects of the body, including the hairiness of the genitalia, and behavioral traits, such as a loss of sexual desire.[66] In other examples the authors go further in proposing that the tests, including those that utilized smell, were only relevant for nonphysicians who were not expert enough to detect barrenness without them. In the 1659 treatise *The Hidden Treasures of the Art of Physick*, John Tanner explained that most of the signs of barrenness were "evident to the Senses. . . . He who cannot discover hath not a Head befitting a Physitian: therefore, to abbreviate the work, I shall leav[e] it to the search of the Ingenious, and trouble the Reader with a few Rules, left by the Ancients, to try whether a Woman be naturally barren or no."[67] William Salmon concurred with this opinion in his own late seventeenth-century tract, which argued that "Antiquity has proposed several ridiculous things [for diagnosing barrenness]. . . . But it may far better be knowne, by the cold temperature of the Woman, her strait Loins, defect of hair on her *Pubes* and other Parts, and by the Whites."[68] Salmon did not recite the perfume/odor test but instead thought that feeling the temperature of the woman and visually examining her genital region would suffice.

It was perhaps this assumption of male access to the female body that encouraged some writers to include perfume-based tests that would have allowed women a measure of control over who saw and handled their genitalia. Indeed Tanner included the garlic/galbanum test for his readers to try.[69] More explicitly, Christopher Wirtzung's treatise, an English edition of which was published in 1605, described these tests as relying completely on the woman's sensory perception of the results: "if the woman finde that this smoke go through the body, and feeleth it in her nose, then is she fruitful."[70] In this text the garlic test was slightly altered in that it involved no direct contact with the reproductive organs; instead the garlic was placed beneath the woman's back. Yet here it was the woman's sensory perception that created the diagnosis; if "she feele the smell in her nose, then is it a token of fruitfulnesse."[71] In these instances, the physician appears distanced from the actual diagnosis or entirely absent from the process. This may, of course, reflect the fact that many of these texts were designed as self-help guides intended to educate readers about their bodies, ailments, and cures.[72] Nonetheless, the authors of these texts often aimed to create a knowledgeable audience who would seek the appropriate help from a physician when necessary. These books advertised the knowledge, reputation, and efficacy of a physician's practice and sought to secure his role in the medical marketplace.

In several texts addressed to midwives there is an absence altogether of much diagnostic information.[73] This may imply that for midwives, and perhaps trusted man-midwives, access to the female body was not problematic, and a diagnosis could be made through sight or touch or both. Only a few midwifery treatises included the use of fumes to test for barrenness. Again there is little coherence about who should be conducting these tests. In an early seventeenth-century edition of Jakob Rueff's *The Expert Midwife*, the identity of the person conducting the test is ambiguous: "so that if a fume being used underneath, be perceived above by smelling" it is a sign of fruitfulness.[74] However, Rueff did go on to comment that "some old women likewise have their signes by which they observe whether the greater sterility of unfruitfulnesse be in the husband, or in his wife," which suggests that he did draw distinctions between which types of practitioners utilized particular diagnostic tools.[75] Hugh Chamberlen's translation of François Mauriceau's original French text was similarly unclear. It included a description of the test in both Latin and in English, in which the woman was wrapped in clothes, suggesting the involvement of at least one other person. Despite the potential presence of the midwife, the diagnosis rested upon whether "she perceive the sent to pass through her body to her nose and mouth."[76] Even more obscurely, James MacMath's *The Expert Midwife*, published in Edinburgh in 1694, only noted that "the Vent of *Perfumes* up through the *Womb*, to the Mouth and Nostrils, is made a sure *Sign of Fecundity.*"[77] The suggestion made in this genre of medical text is thus that the midwife would usually make the diagnosis but that the potential existed for a woman either to conduct the test herself or to use her own sensory authority to assert that she was fertile. Similarly, books addressed to laywomen, rather than midwives, did not always include these tests.[78] Again this may reflect the ability of women to know their own bodies and assess their own symptoms and so have no need to conduct a test that probed the internal cavity of the womb. Moreover, the tone of these works, when the test was included, placed the woman at the center of the diagnostic process: "but if shee feeles not the fume in her mouth and nose, it argues barrennesse"; "if the woman feel the smoke ascend through her Body to her Nose, then she is fruitful."[79]

Thus, diagnosing barrenness could be a multisensory endeavor involving a variety of people, including physicians, surgeons, and midwives. In early modern medical treatises, the use of laudanum, garlic, and red storax was often considered an aspect of this diagnosis. In many cases, it is evident that the female patient was a central figure in confirming a diagnosis of infertility. Additionally, it is plausible that as well as serving to demonstrate learned knowledge of Hippocratic medicine, these tests were also recounted because they allowed a variety of people access to the female body. For male physicians who relied upon visual and tactile interaction with the female genitalia for diagnostic purposes, the use of fumes allowed access to the bodies of modest patients who refused examination. Odoriferous fumes were particularly pertinent in this instance, as they were associated with truth and knowledge because of their ability to move beneath the skin and penetrate the internal body.[80] Conversely, for those women who had not yet sought the advice of a physician or who were reluctant to allow any access to their bodies, it was a test they could do themselves, knowing that often it was the woman's own interpretation of the results that assured a diagnosis.

As noted above, early modern medical writers frequently advocated the use of smells in cases of suffocation of the mother to move the womb back into its correct position. Aromatic substances were also widely recommended for the treatment of barrenness. At least one medical author suggested that this treatment for barrenness would move the womb back into a healthy position, thereby improving the chances of conception.[81] However, for most medical writers it was the ability of certain smells to heat and stimulate the womb that made them applicable. Odors and fumes could penetrate the body and carried the humoral and occult (hidden) qualities of the substance they were taken from into the womb. The odors that were most frequently recommended were thought to be aphrodisiacs: they warmed the body, creating sexual desire, and through sympathy (sometimes called the doctrine of signatures) they sexually stimulated the womb. Thus, they encouraged a woman to engage in intercourse, which was clearly necessary for conceiving a child. Certain remedies were recommended for use immediately before engaging in intercourse to stimulate the reproductive organs and increase sexual desire. Modern approaches tend to polarize sensual arousal and medical understanding of fertility and conception, but this does not accurately reflect the complexities of early modern understandings of these issues. Sexual pleasure and desire and fertility were inherently connected facets of the same medical process; to stimulate desire was to improve the fertility of the body, and fertile sex was more pleasurable.

Heat was a fundamental element of the sexual and reproductive capabilities of an early modern body. A fertile body was believed to be warm and moderately moist; a body that was cold was frigid. Frigidity caused the body to lack sexual desire, be unresponsive to sexual pleasure, and consequently be unable to conceive.[82] Early modern medical practitioners mostly seem to have subscribed to the idea that male and female bodies were analogous, so that both men and women produced a seed that was released at orgasm to create a conception. Thus, without female sexual desire and pleasure there could be no conception. An overly cold disposition of the womb was further thought to quench the heat of the male seed, which was vital for imparting new life to the conception. Many infertility remedies were offered in early modern medical treatises, not all of which were designed to stimulate sexual desire. Nonetheless, those substances that did provoke sexual desire and encouraged sexual pleasure were ubiquitously understood to be beneficial for aiding conception and promoting fertility.[83] Hot foods, including spices and meats, that stimulated sensations of warmth when consumed or applied externally to the body were often considered to be sexual stimulants because they combated frigidity and promoted sexual desire.[84]

It is apparent that heat was perceived to be integral to the efficacy of many remedies using aromatics. Medical writers did not explain fully how these substances were supposed to act upon the body but did inform their readers that it was the heat of these substances that was important. The general medical text by Theophile Bonet, a Swiss physician practicing in Geneva, suggested that fumes and steams in general were good for women suffering from types of barrenness caused by cold.[85] Here Bonet suggested that no matter what ingredients were used, all fumes were to some extent warming. More explicitly, when describing a pessary made from the gall of a goat or wolf combined with musk and civet, it was noted that "for all these things lax, draw the Womb downwards, heat, and stimulate *Venus*."[86] Other texts also advised that certain smells were inherently warming. The 1662 English translation of Felix Platter's *Practice of Physick*, produced by Abdiah Cole and Nicholas Culpeper, included many references to the personal practice of both Cole and Platter and so provides a good indication of what medical practitioners believed about their medicines.[87] Within the chapter on absence of copulation, the text explained to readers that "sweet scents provoke not only by refreshing, but by heating and piercing, as Amber-greece, Musk, Civet."[88] As will be seen throughout the rest of this article these were three of the most commonly recommended aromatic substances for the treatment of barrenness.

In addition to humoral/constitutional explanations of medicines provided in the seventeenth century, medical practitioners believed that certain medicinal substances worked through sympathy or through occult (hidden) qualities. As Daniel Sennert explained, when describing diseases of the womb caused by smells: "There are many Qualities in Nature that are hid from our Senses, and yet we cannot deny them, because we see their Effects."[89] The presence of these virtues was made manifest by the outward appearance or behaviors of the plant or animal from which they were taken. Medical writers described a plethora of substances that were believed to encourage sexual desire and improve reproductive ability in this way. In particular, phallic plants, such as certain orchis species, and the genitalia or brains of potent, vigorous, or lascivious animals were believed to pass sexual vitality to the consumer.[90] It is thus very plausible that musk and civet, as the glandular secretions of the musk deer and civet cat, were believed to be sexually stimulating and thus particularly relevant for the treatment of barrenness.[91] A similar substance, castoreum, the testicular secretion of the beaver, was also often described as an aphrodisiac in medical texts. The use of musk, civet, ambergris, and other aromatic substances was therefore not simply a means of moving the womb into the correct position: they were intended to stimulate sexually and heat the reproductive organs of the woman, making her both more fertile and more inclined to engage in intercourse and thus conceive a child.

Having diagnosed barrenness, medical writers proffered a vast range of medicines and treatments in their texts, including internal medicinal compounds, fomentations, lotions, and pessaries. Many general medical compendiums also included aromatic treatments for barrenness, which contained a range of ingredients but often

featured musk, civet, storax, sage, alipta moschata, and frankincense.[92] As already noted, some of these remedies were designed to
stimulate sexual desire and encourage sexual pleasure, including
some smells and fumes. The aphrodisiac qualities of these medica-
ments potentially complicated the nature of treatment for barrenness. The involvement of the male physician or practitioner may
have been viewed as inappropriate in a situation where the intended
outcome was sexual arousal. Smells could therefore have provided a
means of applying sexual stimulants to the genitals and reproductive organs without direct contact, though it is not always clear who
was meant to apply fragrant lotions. Medical writers described the
application of pungent remedies with a range of terms that allowed
for the removal of the medical practitioner. Although I do not suggest that male practitioners never applied these remedies, nor that
they were always recommended as a way of avoiding patient/prac-
titioner contact, it is possible that the use of smells was one part of a
multisensory approach to the treatment of barrenness that provided
a range of options for the patient.

It is not always apparent who administered a particular remedy.
It may be that the use of fumes was just another means of dis-
pensing the appropriate remedy and that the author did not consider the question of access to the patient's body. Daniel Sennert's
Practical Physick merely asserted that fumes and baths were also
relevant and recited the receipt for the appropriate fume.[93] Similarly
Culpeper's edition of Riverius's *The Practice of Physick* explained
only that "before or after the Injection," which was strongly scented,
containing musk, ambergris, alipta moschata, and civet, "this following Fumigation may be used."[94] After listing the ingredients,
the text only directed the reader to *"let one or two [troches] be laid
upon burning coals, and let the smoak be received by a Funnel into
the Patients Womb."*[95] A more pressing concern for Riverius was the
wealth of the potential patient: "The poorer sort may be smoaked
with Mirrh, Frankincense, Lignum Aloes, Storax, Benjamin,
Cinnamon and Cloves, of each a like quantity."[96] Although this

language is ambiguous, some general texts were more explicit in stating that women themselves should administer fumigations: the 1650 edition of *The General Practice of Physicke*, originally compiled in German by Christopher Wirtzung, told readers: "It were also very good that whe[n] such women arise a mornings, they do gird about them a lo[n]g garment, and set some fire under them, and to strew therein this powder following, that she may receive the vapour thereof, and use a little at once."[97] This fume contained musk and amber, among other pungent substances. In this instance, the medical practitioner was entirely removed from the treatment process.

Although it was not always clear who was supposed to perform these cures, it is evident that many physicians offered a range of remedies including pills, drinks, topical applications, and fumigations. Therefore, it is possible that the readers of these texts may have selected only those medications that allowed them to restrict access to their reproductive bodies. Moreover, it may be that one of the reasons why medical writers included such a variety of medicinal types was to highlight their ability to provide treatment in all circumstances. If a woman did not want direct physical contact and intervention, these books make it clear that the physician could still treat the patient without visual or physical contact. As John Sadler lamented in the introduction to his medical treatise *The Sick Womans Private Looking-Glasse*, women were likely to suffer needlessly in cases of "hysteric" diseases because of ignorance and because "*through her modestie, being loth to divulge and publish the same unto the Physitian to implore his aide, shee conceals her griefe and so encreaseth her sorrow.*"[98]

In midwifery manuals, again, fumigations were featured, potentially allowing practitioners to utilize aromatics to enter into the womb and provide relief without direct tactile interaction. Indeed, Jakob Rueff's treatise stated that "it is certaine, that the Fumes or Suffumigations before prescribed, to be the most approved of many later Physicians."[99] This praise may reflect the fact that smells could directly enter the womb and so perhaps provided a fast form of relief. Rueff's instructions for fertility treatments also suggested liniments, ointments, and pessaries. Yet the descriptions he provided suggest that fumes were the main form of treatment that could be supplemented by pessaries if desired. For example, the treatise explained, "let Trochisks be made with a hot Pestle, of which being cast upon the coales, let a fume be made underneath thorow a Tunnell: Likewise Pessaries may be made of the Masse or Lumpe of them."[100] Thomas Raynalde's translation of Roesslin's midwifery text *The Birth of Mankinde* was clear in its instructions that this method was one enacted by the woman herself: "seeth these [the ingredients] together in faire water, and when they be perfectly sodden, then let the woman set her selfe over the vapour thereof, sitting groveling, other els set on a cover made for the nonce with a tunnell or conduite, thorow the which the vapour may be directed into the womans privie passage, the neere thereby, that the vertue thereof may approach unto the wombe or wombe port."[101] Similar to Rueff's text, Raynalde's continued by suggesting that the mixture could also be applied to wool or linen and inserted into the vagina.[102] Books for women also included a range of medicines that could be used together or individually: *The Sicke Womans Private Looking-Glasse* included a complex mixture of ingredients that was to be split into several parts, each of which was to be made into a "pomum odoratum," pills, a pessary, and a suffumigation.[103] However, it appears that it was less common for these writers to recommend a range of fumigations. The marginalization of fumes and odors in these books may reflect the fact that women had easy access to their own bodies. This interpretation is perhaps reinforced by the absence of fumes designed specifically to address female barrenness found in domestic recipe books. While certain female recipe collectors did include fumes, these were often directed at nonreproductive health problems including gout and cold and wind in the body.[104]

As suggested above, in addition to the use of a tunnel or funnel, which may have been partially inserted into the vagina, many midwifery texts described the use of a stool for fumigating. The midwifery treatise of William Sermon (1671) offered three fumigations for the correction of barrenness. To administer these remedies, Sermon directed, "put the pot under some stool, having a hole in the midst thereof: through which let the woman receive the fume up into her privy parts."[105] John Pechey likewise explained that a fumigation for barrenness should be made in the following way: "Take juyce of Bistort, Schoenanth, Cypress nuts, red Storax, and Mastick, one ounce, Hares-dung; mix them, and pound them well together, and make a Fumigation; let the patient receive it sitting on a stool with a hole in it."[106] It is apparent in these texts, that even when midwives might have access to the body, male writers still offered a range of options for introducing medicinal substances to the womb. In some cases they favored fumigations, and presented them as a means for women to enact their own treatment.

A second method of introducing the scent of musk and civet into the womb was to apply it directly to the genitalia.[107] In this instance it is evident that the medical practitioner was not involved in the treatment; instead the musk or civet was applied by the woman herself or her husband.[108] Application to the husband's penis acted as a form of pessary allowing the remedy direct contact with the internal cavity of the reproductive organs. The *Practice of Physick* explained, "*let the Man smear his Yard with Civit immediately before he joyn himself.*"[109] Alternatively, following a lengthy description of strong-smelling baths, injections, and pessaries designed to improve female fertility, Riverius suggested that a mixture containing civet, musk, ambergris, and liquid storax should be applied to the woman's perineum.[110] In this treatise it is very clear that the man himself was to apply this remedy, yet for women the tone was more ambiguous: "let her be nointed with."[111] This ambiguity would potentially have allowed the husband to anoint his wife, if these two prescriptions were read together, or the woman to anoint herself, or for her to be anointed by a third party such as a midwife. However, the context within which this remedy was intended for use, just before intercourse, is likely to have limited the involvement of other parties. Although sex was not always a private affair, it is not explicitly suggested in any of the medical texts examined here that medical practitioners would be present at this moment, but neither is their presence explicitly rejected.

Many other medical writers repeated the recommendation for the man to anoint his penis with civet just before intercourse. The seventeenth-century edition of Felix Platter's medical treatise stated that "privately before Copulation, let the man anoynt his Yard wit Civet or the Gall of a Hen."[112] Here it is clear that the man alone was involved in the application of this medication. It is also implied that this remedy could be enacted without the woman's knowledge. The treatise further tried to explain why this was a successful remedy: "If a man afore Copulation anoynt his Yard with Civet, in regard the Womb is delighted with the scent thereof, some think the Seed will be sooner received."[113] Although at first glance this explanation does not indicate how the smell was thought to act, one possible interpretation would be that it had to do with the sexually stimulating nature of civet. Medical texts explained that sexual desire and pleasure were necessary to ensure that the neck of the womb opened during intercourse, so allowing the man's seed access to it.[114] Without this opening, conception would inevitably fail as the passage of the seed would be blocked, preventing it from reaching its final destination—the womb. In this instance the sexually stimulating nature of civet was intended to "delight" the womb, ensuring it was open and amenable to conception.

It was not only in medical texts for a general audience that this method of introducing smells to the womb was advocated. The texts ostensibly addressed to a female audience also repeated these recommendations. The 1652 English edition of Nicholas Fontanus's

The Womans Doctour was explicit that it was the husband and wife themselves who should administer this remedy: "when the man and the woman intend conjunction, let him anoint his yard with oyle of *mastick*, and *wormewood* mingled with a few graines of *musk* and *civet*; and let the woman also anoynt her privie parts therewith, as well within as without; for by this meanes there is raised mutuall inclination to *Venery*, and the seed is received with a greater pleasure, and is more duely retained and elaborated."[115] The treatise suggested clearly that this means of improving fertility did not involve anyone beyond the female patient accessing and touching her reproductive organs, not even her husband. In addition the author explicitly stated that the aim of this particular remedy was to improve sexual desire and pleasure; the smell acted as an aphrodisiac in order to improve the chances of conception.

Other authors also suggested that musk and civet should be applied to "the mouth and necke of the wombe" immediately before conception.[116] Although it might be expected that these remedies would be addressed to the woman herself, as the intended reader of the text, it is notable that in the *Compleat Doctoress* other remedies are described as being made for and given to the woman, rather than depicting her as an active participant in the treatment. Overtly addressing male physicians and describing a course of treatment, the author explained, "When you have thoroughly purged the body, and taken away the cause, the parts must be strengthened, and the distemper must be corrected with these pills."[117] Thus, the woman's role in the application of this treatment is intentionally emphasized. Midwifery books do not appear to offer this recommendation as readily as the other types of texts. This may have been because the remedy had to be applied to the male reproductive organs, again raising issues about the gender of the patient and the practitioner. Although not an aromatic treatment, the recipe book of Jane Jackson included a fertility enhancing remedy that had to be applied to the male genitalia: "Take the braine of a crane and medle it with ganders grease and fox grease and keepe it in a vessell of silver or of gould and at what time thou wold have knowledge annoynt therewith thy yard and shee shall conceave.'[118] It is apparent in this context that even for women practicing medicine in the home, the issue of gendered access to the sexual body was important. The female practitioner here did not administer the remedy but encouraged the husband to do so himself. Jackson also included a recipe that was applied to both the male and female genitalia, and again she documented that the husband would apply this remedy to both parties.[119]

Nevertheless, it is apparent that men and women in the early modern period were being advised to use strong-smelling, sexually stimulating remedies immediately before intercourse to improve the chances of conception. This method of treatment was usually conducted by the husband and occasionally by the woman as well but excluded the medical practitioner by omission. The stimulation of sexual desire at that moment was a personal matter or was at least bound by the constraints of modesty. The presence of the physician in applying these types of medications might have resulted in speculation about their role in encouraging intercourse and conception and about their own moral character; some man-midwives and physicians were already being tainted by suggestions of immodest behavior, some of which were well justified.[120] It is also noteworthy that it was rare for the husband and wife to be directed to apply the remedies to each other. The stimulating and heating effects created in the body were thus directly attributed to the remedy itself, not to the rubbing and touching of the patient's sexual partner. Medical writers probably did not allude to the possibility that sexual arousal could be obtained through the application of the remedy in this way to avoid connotations of obscenity and to retain a sense of professionalism. Conversely, Jane Jackson and other domestic writers were not constrained by the need to appear professional or by concerns about publishing obscene material and so could include remedies that were applied by the husband or wife to their spouse.

One treatment option suggested by a few medical writers circumvented the entire issue of access to the genitals and internal reproductive organs. In these recommendations the aromatics were directed to the head and the nasal passages through scented pillows or were worn on the body in perfumed gloves. This reflects the medical understanding seen in the discussion of diagnosing barrenness, where fumes and smells moved through the body. The use of smells in this way raises further questions about the necessity of directing smells into the body and whether they were also effective when in the general atmosphere of the sick body—as was the case in plague and pestilence treatments. In this way perfumed rooms or gloves that carried scent close to the body could create a sexually simulating environment without being directly applied to the genitals. Holly Dugan has suggested that scents could be a powerful component of sensual and sexual pleasure, particularly through the creation of erotic perfumed environments.[121] Again the presence of a physician in this situation would have been inappropriate as the environment created could have affected both the patient and the practitioner, creating the potential for illicit sexual encounters. In these instances women were again foregrounded as the principal agent in curing barrenness, allowing them a means of remedying an intimate sexual disorder without male interference: as the *Mercurius Compitalitius* argued, "They that are not propense to *Venus* may wear Amber or Musk about them and perfumed Gloves, and they may lay them at Night especially under their Pillows."[122] Other authors were not necessarily as explicit in removing the physician from this treatment. The *Golden Practice of Physick* ambiguously stated that "they report that the smel of Civet, Amber greese, Musk, in Baths, or [G]loves, or Pillows, especially at night, maketh Women apt to Conception."[123] The *they* spoken of here may have been patients or other physicians. Perfumed gloves were a fashionable item in the early modern period, and many household recipe books offered receipts for preparing them in the home.[124] However, it is not apparent that any of the perfumed gloves listed in these manuscript collections are explicitly for medical purposes, and no indication is given that they were relevant to or used for the treatment of barrenness.[125] This may suggest that women knew of the effects these gloves were thought to have and discounted their efficacy or that they simply did not need to record this virtue of the gloves as it was well recognized. Yet it is likely that medical writers were aware that women could possess the skills required to produce these items in the home.

The treatment of barrenness in early modern England was affected by concerns of modesty and access to the female reproductive body. In this respect it was merely one of a range of reproductive disorders that were framed in this way. As John Sadler complained in the introduction to *The Sick Womans Private Looking-Glasse*, there were "*manifold distempers of body; which yee Women are subject unto through your ignorance & modestie.*"[126] Beyond the patient, social anxieties existed about the access that male physicians could have to the female body. Although these concerns were not culturally specific to the early modern period, it would appear, as Schleiner and Crawford have suggested, that this was a matter at the forefront of the practice of gynecological and obstetric medicine at this time. It was feared that male medical practitioners would exploit the access they gained to the female genitals for their own sexual gratification and in the process would corrupt innocent maids and wives: one early modern joke played upon this theme, suggesting that a "Petulant Doctor of Physick" convinced a girl that he needed to have sex with her in order to break the eggs that she was breeding, which were causing her to be unwell, in order to satisfy his own sexual desire for her.[127] The issue of visual and tactile contact with the female reproductive body was thus one of importance. As this article has suggested, by examining the ways in which medical writers discussed and utilized smells, fumes, and aromatics, we can begin to move beyond a straightforward assertion that physicians either did not touch their patients or did so at the risk of their reputation. Although we know that male practitioners did indeed treat and touch female patients, and it is impossible to understand fully the motivation behind using smells to diagnose and treat barrenness, it is evident that practitioners engaged a diverse multisensory range of treatments for this purpose. These treatments utilized the aphrodisiac qualities of strong smells, such as musk, civet, and ambergris, directly to stimulate the female reproductive organs. They also allowed physicians to recommend treatments that could be carried out either in their presence—without the physicians needing to see or touch the female patient—or could be administered by the woman herself. Thus, the presence of fumigations and fumes allowed women to restrict access to the sexual parts of their bodies while still seeking a cure for infertility. Similarly, they allowed physicians to remain a useful source of prescriptions and cures even when the woman was not willing to undergo an intimate examination or treatment. It is therefore evident that both physicians and patients could employ treatments that relied upon a range of senses to treat the sick body and that the remedies themselves could be used to negotiate the difficult issue of bodily access.

NOTES

The research for this article was made possible by a postdoctoral research fellowship provided by the Society for Renaissance Studies. The author would also like to thank Alexandra Walsham, Sarah Toulalan and Catherine Rider, along with the anonymous reviewers, whose generous comments and suggestions helped to shape the final version of this article.

1. See, e.g., A. Wear, *Knowledge and Practice in English Medicine, 1550–1680* (Cambridge, 2000), 120–22; S. Cavallo, *Artisans of the Body in Early Modern Italy: Identities, Families and Masculinities* (Manchester, 2007), 26; E. Keller, "The Subject of Touch: Medical Authority in Early Modern Midwifery," in *Sensible Flesh: On Touch in Early Modern Culture*, ed. E. D. Harvey (Philadelphia, 2002), 69–70; B. Duden, *The Woman beneath the Skin: A Doctor's Patients in 18th-Century Germany* (Cambridge,

Mass., 1991), 83; C. Bicks, *Midwiving Subjects in Shakespeare's England* (Aldershot, 2003), 64 (Bicks noted that Simon Forman treated 830 women for gynecological problems in 1597 but rarely described manual examinations); M. MacDonald, *Mystical Bedlam: Madness, Anxiety and Healing in 17th-Century England* (Cambridge, 1981), 26–28 (MacDonald did not state explicitly that physicians did not touch their patients but described the process Richard Napier went through with his patients, relying on both questions and patient narrative); J. Lane, *John Hall and His Patients: the Medical Practice of Shakespeare's Son-in-Law* (Stratford-upon-Avon, 1996), xl. See also L. McCray Beier, *Sufferers and Healers: The Experience of Illness in 17th-Century England* (1987), 108–9. Beier did not specifically address the issue of touch in treatment but shows that medical practitioners used a range of methods for treatment.

2. L. Tatlock, "Speculum Feminarum: Gendered Perspectives on Obstetrics and Gynecology in Early Modern Germany," *Signs* 17 (1992): 733, 757–59; Beier, *Sufferers and Healers*, 44. Other works did not address this topic explicitly (A. Eccles, *Obstetrics and Gynaecology in Tudor and Stuart England* [1982]; Eccles did note at one point that an instrument could be used to help physicians view the internal cavity of the neck of the womb [84]).

3. L. McTavish, *Childbirth and the Display of Authority in Early Modern France* (Aldershot, 2005), 60–62; W. D. Churchill, *Female Patients in Early Modern Britain: Gender, Diagnosis and Treatment* (Aldershot, 2012), 64–73, 76–79. Churchill's analysis demonstrated clearly the complexities of physician access to the female body and highlights that physicians did touch female patients, who did not feel shame or fear about exposing their bodies to a male practitioner. Importantly, Churchill also considered issues of consent and permission in these cases.

4. Eccles, *Obstetrics and Gynaecology*, 87–88; McTavish, *Childbirth*, 63. For examples of touching the female body outside parturition, see Bicks, *Midwiving Subjects*, 61–62; W. Schleiner, *Medical Ethics in the Renaissance* (Washington, DC, 1995), 115–16. O. Weisser, "Boils, Pushes and Wheals: Reading Bumps on the Body in Early Modern England," *Social History of Medicine* 22 (2009): 330; see also Tatlock, "Speculum Feminarum," 757–59, who argued that male midwives used the speculum in order to gain visual access to the interior of women's bodies without touch.

5. E. D. Harvey, "Introduction: the 'Sense of All Senses,'" in Harvey, *Sensible Flesh*, 17.

6. Schleiner, *Medical Ethics*, 109.

7. McTavish, *Childbirth*, 57.

8. M. H. Green, *Making Women's Medicine Masculine: the Rise of Male Authority in Pre-Modern Gynaecology* (Oxford, 2008), 200; see also Beier,

Sufferers and Healers, 145–46. Elizabeth Pepys was concerned about the shame of having her private parts operated on by a surgeon and urged her husband to stay with her while the operation was performed. Pepys was thankful that the operation was eventually deemed unnecessary.

9.   Churchill, *Female Patients*, 64.

10.   M. Jay, "In the Realm of the Senses: An Introduction," *American Historical Review* 116 (2011): 307.

11.   *Journal of American History* 95, no. 2 (2008).

12.   *Journal of American History* 95, no. 2 (2008); *American Historical Review* 116, no. 2 (2011). Outlines of the historiography of the history of the senses can be found in these issues. For a discussion of the differences between history of the senses and sensory history, see M. M. Smith, "Producing Sense, Consuming Sense, Making Sense: Perils and Prospects for Sensory History," *Journal of Social History* 40 (2007): 842.

13.   C. Y. Chiang, "The Nose Knows: The Sense of Smell in American History," *Journal of American History* 95 (2008): 405–16; J. Parr, "Smells Like?: Sources of Uncertainty in the History of the Great Lakes Environment," *Environmental History* 11 (2006): 269–99; M. Smith, *How Race Is Made: Slavery, Segregation and the Senses* (Chapel Hill, NC, 2006).

14.   E. Cockayne, *Hubbub: Filth, Noise and Stench in England, 1600–1770* (New Haven, CT, 2007); C. Brandt, "Fume and Perfume: Some Eighteenth-Century Uses of Smell," *Journal of British Studies* 42 (2004): 444–63; M. M. Smith, *Sensory History* (Oxford, 2007); H. Dugan, *The Ephemeral History of Perfume: Scent and Sense in Early Modern England* (Baltimore, 2011); H. Dugan, "Scent of a Woman: Performing the Politics of Smell in Late Medieval and Early Modern England," *Journal of Medieval and Early Modern Studies* 38 (2008): 229–52; M. Milner, *The Senses and the English Reformation* (Farnham, 2011); "Special Issue: The Senses," ed. J. Reinarz and L. Schwarz, *Journal of 18th-Century Studies* 35 (2012): 463–627.

15.   M. McVaugh, "Smells and the Medieval Surgeon," *Micrologus* 10 (2002): 114–15.

16.   C. Classen, D. Howes, and A. Synnott, *Aroma: The Cultural History of Smell* (London: Routledge, 1994), 58–62. See, e.g., Wear, *Knowledge and Practice*, 327.

17.   Classen, Howes, and Synnott, *Aroma*, 60–62.

18.   K. Harvey, *Reading Sex in the 18th Century: Bodies and Gender in English Erotic Literature* (Cambridge, 2004), 205–8; S. Toulalan, *Imagining Sex: Pornography and Bodies in the 17th Century* (Oxford, 2007), 68–72. Toulalan highlighted the focus in erotic literature upon sight as a means of arousal.

19.   Harvey, *Reading Sex*, 78–101; Toulalan, *Imagining Sex*, 62–91.

20.   See, e.g., C. McClive, "The Hidden Truths of the Belly: The Uncertainties of Pregnancy in Early Modern Europe," *Social History of Medicine* 15

(2002): 209–27; L. Cowing, "Secret Births and Infanticide in 17th-Century England," *Past and Present* 156 (1997): 87–115.

21. Weisser, "Boils, Pushes and Wheals," 324.

22. T. Hitchcock, *English Sexualities, 1700–1800* (Basingstoke, 1997), 25.

23. Hitchcock, *English Sexualities*, 26.

24. This anxiety lasted into the eighteenth century (see R. Ganev, "Milkmaids, Ploughmen, and Sex in 18th-Century Britain," *Journal of the History of Sexuality* 16 (2007), 46).

25. Nicholas Culpeper, *Culpeper's Directory for Midwives* (1676), sig. A3v–A4r.

26. P. Crawford, *Blood, Bodies and Families in Early Modern England* (Harlow, 2004), 38–40; L. Gowing, *Common Bodies: Women, Touch and Power in 17th-Century England* (2003), 115; A. Capern, *The Historical Study of Women: England 1500–1700* (Basingstoke, 2008), 24.

27. *The Sorrowful Bride; Or, The London Lasses Lamentation for Her Husbands Insufficiency* (1682–94); *The Lamenting Lady* (1620).

28. *The Lamenting Lady.*

29. Gowing, *Common Bodies*, 17.

30. M. E. Fissell, "The Marketplace of Print," in *Medicine and the Market in England and Its Colonies, c. 1450–1850*, ed. M. S. R. Jenner and Wallis (Basingstoke, 2007), 112.

31. The terms *smell therapy* and *scent therapy* are not used extensively in this article because the author is discussing both aromatic diagnosis and treatment, and because these are not terms found in the early modern sources.

32. Jane Sharp, *The Midwives Book, Or the Whole Art of Midwifery Discovered* (1671); Culpeper, *Culpeper's Directory for Midwives.*

33. *The Compleat Doctoress: Or A Choice Treatise of All Diseases Incident to Women* (1656); John Sadler, *The Sick Womans Private Looking-Glasse: Wherein Methodically Are Handled All Uterine Affects, or Diseases Arising from the Wombe* (1636).

34. Green, *Making Women's Medicine Masculine*, 163.

35. R. Palmer, "In Bad Odor: Smell and Its Significance in Medicine from Antiquity to the 17th Century," in *Medicine and the Five Senses*, ed. W. Bynum and R. Porter (Cambridge, 1993), 61; see also Milner, *Senses and the English.*

36. Palmer, "In Bad Odor," 62.

37. Dugan, *Ephemeral History of Perfume*, 5.

38. Cited in ibid., 12.

39. Aromatic substances were used as treatment for the suffocation and descent of the womb in the medieval text the Trotula (see M. H. Green, *The Trotula: An English Translation of the Medieval Compendium of Women's Medicine* [Philadelphia, 2001], 71–73).

40. William Salmon, *Synopsis Medicinae, or, A Compendium of Astrological, Galenical and Chymical Physick* (1671), 359.

41. Nicholas Culpeper, *Select Aphorismes: Concerning the Operation of Medicines According to Place in the Body of Fraile Man* (1655), 77.

42. D. Sennert, *Practical Physick; The Fourth Book . . . By Daniel Sennertus, N. Culpeper, and Abdiah Cole . . .* (1664), 63.

43. Green, *Trotula*, 71–73.

44. Culpeper, *Select Aphorismes*, 77.

45. These examples were taken from a list that is fairly representative (Sennert, *Practical Physick*, 110–11).

46. See, e.g., Nicholas Culpeper, *A Directory for Midwives: Or, A Guide for Women in Their Conception, Bearing, and Suckling Their Children* (1668), 76. Eccles discusses these treatments but with little consideration for concerns about access to the female body (*Obstetrics and Gynaecology*, 80).

47. Eccles, *Obstetrics and Gynaecology*, 80–81.

48. Culpeper, *Select Aphorismes*, 77.

49. See H. King, *Hippocrates' Women: Reading the Female Body in Ancient Greece* (1998), 31. L. Totelin, *Hippocratic Recipes: Oral and Written Transmission of Pharmacological Knowledge in 5th- and 4th-Century Greece* (Leiden, 2009), 103. The test attributed to Aristotle in this book is different than those recited in the early modern period—the smell is intended to color the eyes and saliva.

50. M. Pelling, *Medical Conflicts in Early Modern London: Patronage, Physicians and Irregular Practitioners, 1550–1640* (Oxford, 2003), 220; Cavallo, *Artisans of the Body*, 26.

51. Pelling, *Medical Conflicts*, 210–16.

52. R. Porter and D. Porter, *Patient's Progress: Doctors and Doctoring in 18th-Century England* (Stanford, CA, 1989), 17–18.

53. Crawford, *Blood, Bodies*, 34.

54. Crawford, *Blood, Bodies*, 34; see also Churchill, *Female Patients*, 88.

55. Schleiner, *Medical Ethics*, 115–16. This concern also related to the status of the woman. It was thought to be less acceptable to touch virgins, as the therapy might spoil their virginity; this was perhaps less of a concern in a discussion of fertility where medical writers assumed that their patients were married (see also Eccles, *Obstetrics and Gynaecology*, 79, 83).

56. Schleiner, *Medical Ethics*, 115–16; see also Bicks, *Midwiving Subjects*, 77–79.

57. Churchill noted that practitioners were aware of the importance of sexual trust and propriety in maintaining their own reputations and that male practitioners took steps to maintain this (Churchill, *Female Patients*, 89).

58. Thomas Raynalde, *The Birth of Mankinde* (1604), 191; Sharp, *Midwives Book*, 164; Culpeper, *A Directory for Midwives*, 74.

59. Christopher Wirtzung, *The General Practise of Physicke . . . Translated*

into English, in Divers Places Corrected, and with Many Additions Illustrated and Augmented, by Jacob Mosan (1605), 296.

60. Wirtzung, *General Practise of Physicke*, 296.

61. Sennert, *Practical Physick*, 136 (original emphasis).

62. See also Robert Johnston, *Praxis Medicinae Reformata* (1700), 246.

63. Lazarus Riverius, *The Practice of Physick in Seventeen Several Books . . . By Nicholas Culpeper, Physitian and Astrologer, Abdiah Cole, Doctor of Physick, and William Rowland, Physitian* (1655), 505 (original emphasis). Repeated verbatim in the 1668 and 1678 editions.

64. Ibid.

65. Philip Barrough, *The Method of Phisick* (1601), 202.

66. Ibid.

67. John Tanner, *The Hidden Treasures of the Art of Physick Fully Discovered in Four Books* (1659), 345.

68. William Salmon, *Systema Medicinale, A Compleat System of Physick Theorical and Practical* (1686), 5:237.

69. Tanner, *Hidden Treasures*, 345.

70. Wirtzung, *General Practise of Physicke*, 296.

71. Ibid.

72. M. Solomon, *Fictions of Well-Being: Sickly Readers and Vernacular Medical Writing in Late Medieval and Early Modern Spain* (Philadelphia, 2010), 26–32.

73. The following texts do not contain the test: *The English Midwife Enlarged Containing Directions to Midwives* (1682); Peter Chamberlen, *Dr. Chamberlain's Midwifes Practice: Or, A Guide for Women in that High Concern of Conception, Breeding, and Nursing Children* (1665); William Sermon, *The Ladies Companion, Or, English Midwife Wherein is Demonstrated the Manner and Order of How Women Ought to Govern Themselves* (1671); Nicholas Fontanus, *The Womans Doctour, Or, An Exact and Distinct Explanation of All Such Diseases as are Peculiar to that Sex* (1652).

74. Jakob Rueff, *The Expert Midwife: Or, An Excellent and Most Necessary Treatise of the Generation and Birth of Man* (1637), 17, irregular pagination; see also Raynalde, *Birth of Mankinde*, 192.

75. Rueff, *Expert Midwife*, 18.

76. Francis Mauriceau, *The Diseases of Women with Child, and In Child-bed* (1672), 5.

77. James MacMath, *The Expert Midwife: A Treatise of the Diseases of Women with Child and in Child-Bed* (Edinburgh, 1694), 5 (original emphasis).

78. See *Compleat Doctoress*; Richard Bunworth, *The Doctresse: A Plain and Easie Method of Curing Those Diseases Which Are Peculiar to Women* (1656); Fontanus, *Womans Doctour*; John Pechey, *General Treatise of the Diseases of Maids, Bigbellied Women, Child-Bed-Women, and Widows* (1696).

79. Sadler, *Sick Womans*, 111; Alessandro Massaria, *De Morbis Foemineis, The Womans Counsellour: Or the Feminine Physitian* (1657), 120.
80. Smith, *Sensory History*, 60.
81. Sermon, *Ladies Companion*, 12–13.
82. For a discussion of frigidity and infertility, see J. Evans, "Procreation, Pleasure and Provokers of Lust in Early Modern England, 1550–1780" (PhD thesis, University of Exeter, 2010).
83. Ibid., 183–96.
84. Ibid., 180–96.
85. Theophile Bonet, *Mercurius Compitalitius: A Guide to the Practical Physician* (1684), 569; see also Walter Charleton, *Physiologia Epicuro-Gassendo-Charltoniana* (1654), 239.
86. Bonet, *Mercurius Compitalitius*, 570 (original emphasis).
87. A. Cunningham, "The Bartholins, the Platters and Laurentius Gryllus: The *Peregrinatio Medica* in the 16th and 17th Centuries," in *Centres of Medical Excellence?: Medical Travel and Education in Europe, 1550–1789*, ed. O. Grell, A. Cunningham, and J. Arrizabalga (Farnham, 2010), 10.
88. Felix Platter, *A Golden Practice of Physick in Five Books* (1662), 171. The heating qualities of these drugs are also related in Jacques Ferrand, *Erotomania: Or A Treatise Discoursing of the Essence, Causes, Symptomes, Prognosticks, and Cure of Love, or Erotique Melancholy* (Oxford, 1640), 238.
89. Sennert, *Practical Physick*, 63.
90. For a discussion of aphrodisiacs, see Evans, "Procreation, Pleasure and Provokers," 221–31.
91. The aphrodisiac qualities of these substances are noted in Classen, Howes, and Synnott, *Aroma*, 72.
92. Storax is a fragrant resin of the tree *styrax officinalis* (see *Oxford English Dictionary* Online at oed.com [accessed 24 July 2012]).
93. Sennert, *Practical Physick*, 138.
94. Riverius, *Practice of Physick*, 509.
95. Ibid. (original emphasis).
96. Ibid. This advice was repeated in John Pechey, *The Store-House of Physical Practice: Being a General Treatise of the Causes and Signs of All Diseases Afflicting Human Bodies* (1695), 399.
97. Wirtzung, *General Practise of Physicke*, 300.
98. Sadler, *Sick Womans*, sig. A5V (original emphasis). This was part of a traditional topos of shame seen in medieval texts (Green, *Making Women's Medicine Masculine*, 167–69).
99. Rueff, *Expert Midwife*, 55.
100. Ibid., 53.
101. Raynalde, *Birth of Mankinde*, 195.
102. Ibid., 196.
103. Sadler, *Sick Womans*, 114–15.

104. British Library, Additional MS. 72619, Trumbull Papers, vol. 378, f. 79r, 89r; Wellcome Library, MS. 373, Jane Jackson, f. 47r; Wellcome Libr., MS. 751, Elizabeth Sleigh and Felicia Whitfeld, f. 22.

105. Sermon, *Ladies Companion*, 8.

106. John Pechey, *The Compleat Midwife's Practice Enlarged in the Most Weighty and High Concernments of the Birth of Man* (1698), 319.

107. Nonaromatic ointments were also applied in this way. Sir William Wentworth recorded that his father had an ointment applied to his genitals by an angel (William Wentworth, *Wentworth Papers, 1597–1628*, ed. J. P. Cooper [Camden, 1973], 28).

108. Beier noted that Samuel Pepys applied a tent to his wife's genital swelling or abscess, showing that husbands could be involved in gynecological treatments (Beier, *Sufferers and Healers*, 145).

109. Riverius, *Practice of Physick*, 509 (original emphasis).

110. Ibid.

111. Ibid.

112. Platter, *Golden Practice of Physick*, 171.

113. Ibid., 177.

114. See, e.g., MacMath, *Expert Midwife*, 7.

115. Fontanus, *Womans Doctour*, 145.

116. See, e.g., Sadler, *Sick Womans*, 119; or *Compleat Doctoress*, 145.

117. *Compleat Doctoress*, 144.

118. Wellcome Libr., MS. 373 f. 73v–74r.

119. Ibid., f. 74r.

120. D. Harley, "Provincial Midwives in England: Lancashire and Cheshire, 1660–1760," in *The Art of Midwifery: Early Modern Midwives in Europe*, ed. H. Marland (1993), 40; R. Porter, "A Touch of Danger: The Man-Midwife as Sexual Predator," in *Sexual Underworlds of the Enlightenment*, ed. R. Porter and G. S. Rousseau (Manchester, 1987), 206–32; Churchill, *Female Patients*, 86–89. For medieval context, see Green, *Making Women's Medicine Masculine*, 201–2.

121. Dugan, *Ephemeral History of Perfume*, 180–81.

122. Bonet, *Mercurius Compitalitius*, 570.

123. Platter, *Golden Practice of Physick*, 177. In the original text *gloves* is misspelled as *cloves*.

124. Dugan, *Ephemeral History of Perfume*, 126–53.

125. In my further research on infertility, a range of domestic recipe books from the sixteenth and seventeenth centuries were examined, none of which explicitly described medical gloves.

126. Sadler, *Sick Womans*, sig. A4r (original emphasis).

127. *Nugae Venales: Or, A Complaisant Companion: Being New Jests, Domestick and Foreign* (1675), 99–100.

Chapter 6

Smell and Victorian England

Jonathan Reinarz

In historical studies, smell is a frequently forgotten though particularly fertile field of inquiry. Although very little has been written on the sense, that which exists has been both imaginative and inspirational. This particular study was commenced shortly after an initial reading of Alain Corbin's *The Foul and the Fragrant* (1982) and has developed following subsequent and more critical rereadings of this unique piece of historiography. When *The Foul and the Fragrant* was first written two decades ago, Corbin clearly filled an important gap in our understanding of the social imagination of the past. Since then, other studies have followed. Nevertheless, most contain a substantial gap, as a binary model is used when conceiving of smells. As a result, these works tend to be studies of extremes, documenting primarily pleasant scents and bad odors. As the English translation of Corbin's title states, his work is essentially a list of the most foul and fragrant odors of eighteenth- and nineteenth-century France. A history of sound or hearing based on a similar model might have been entitled "Shouts and Whispers" and not *Village Bells*, as Corbin's subsequent study of the auditory became known and, while documenting the most noticeable outbursts and episodes of seduction and intrigue, would risk overlooking normal conversation entirely. In just this way, histories of smell have documented those odors considered most threatening to the social order in the past and those fragrances that promised a more stable society but very rarely discuss more subtle scents encountered daily and on a regular basis. This study is an attempt to list a few of these neglected scenes.

It also has a secondary aim, which is less concerned with smell than with smelling. Although recent histories of smell deal with those years that coincided with early industrialization, the nose appears out of place in an age of manufacture and more suited to an era of leisure or period of breakdown as occurred in Messina in 1908 or Kobe and New York more recently. Rarely do studies of smell suggest the nose was used for productive purposes. While the laboring classes appear to have driven economic growth, this appears to have been the result of visually aided manual labor. In terms of smell, only the noses of the middle classes, which had grown sensitive with their rise in status, could productively serve their communities, as those of the masses remained largely untrained and indelicate. In making this assertion, I am aware that criticism of a groundbreaking work such as Corbin's will hardly seem justified, given the new terrain opened by his unique study. It must also appear unfair to assume that Corbin could have considered all aspects of the history of smell in a single text. It is, however, sufficient to instigate further study of a neglected topic, especially as subsequent works have also concentrated primarily on the extremes of the olfactory spectrum. While sections of this chapter cover many of the same topics addressed in Corbin's study, only applying his categories to Victorian England, it is equally an attempt to examine the productive proboscis. As such, it will begin with the example of Joseph Bazalgette, the Victorian engineer, whose recent biography reads much like that of Jean-Noël Hallé, the disease hunter and chair of public hygiene whose memoirs inspired Corbin's study. This study will, however, also discuss the dismissive way in which the lower classes have been incorporated into histories of smell. For example, while medical officers seem sufficiently able to smell, laborers are unable to smell and merely stink. In general, research only seems

to confirm their status as the great unwashed. In order to challenge this notion, a final section will discuss some workers who
clearly relied on their sense of smell to fulfill key branches of the
production process in a variety of industries. More interestingly,
perhaps, an attempt is made to concentrate on those industries in
which workers were required to respond to very subtle scents and
not simply the foulest odors, which in most cases would have been
noticeable to even the untrained nose.

As already mentioned, it would be unfair to suggest that Corbin's
work does not describe the way smell has been used historically to
achieve a productive end. Most often, however, he demonstrates
the sense to have been used in the isolation of offensive and pathogenic odors by engineers and medical practitioners or members of
the middle classes in general. These not surprisingly are also the
skills that appear to have been exercised by Sir Joseph Bazalgette
in order to "create a sanitation system of unprecedented scale and
complexity which changed London forever and turned the Thames
from the filthiest to the cleanest metropolitan river in the world,"
the subject of Steven Halliday's recent work entitled *The Great Stink
of London*.[1] Despite its intriguing title, the work surprisingly does
not really deal with the history of smell. In fact, it only really contains two references to smell. Once again, these are memorable episodes because they deal with extremes but for the purposes of this
study they effectively highlight two interesting characteristics. The
first involves Benjamin Disraeli, who is described as having fled the
Parliamentary Chamber in 1858, handkerchief to nose, complain-
ing loudly of the "Stygian Pool" that the Thames had become.[2] The
other involves Michael Faraday, occurred three years earlier, and
is recreated in a cartoon from *Punch*. This particular image refers
to a boat trip Faraday made on the Thames between London and
Hungerford Bridges, the events of which led him to write to the
Times and complain of the river's filthy state. While traveling to
Hungerford, Faraday found the river water to resemble "an opaque,

pale brown fluid."[3] He then went on to test its opacity by drop-ping business cards into the water at every pier he reached. To his surprise, Faraday noticed that the lower part of each card disap-peared from view even before the upper portion had reached the surface of the water. Interestingly, for the purposes of this study, he never really attempted to describe the smell of the water and instead used a visual test to assess its contaminated state. A sole attempt at characterizing the water's smell on that day resulted in the vague description "Very bad." It is unlikely that he would have noticed any other specific properties of the smell, for, as Disraeli had, he spent most of the time holding his nose, as depicted in the now well-known image. Though said to be more sensitive to smell, many of the Victorian middle classes when facing similar situations are always shown or said to have held their noses. Despite appar-ently possessing more sensitive senses of smell, they were unable to describe scents more accurately than anyone else. More often they simply refused to smell. In any case, three years later, inspired by the Great Stink of 1858, the result of a long and dry summer that greatly reduced the Thames, Bazalgette eventually rebuilt the capital's sewers, which had so offended Faraday, thereby purifying a river and protecting a city from disease.

As the medical historian Lindsay Granshaw reminds us, such missions were common throughout the nineteenth century and were reenacted on more modest scales at most institutions, includ-ing prisons and hospitals.[4] Moreover, as one might expect, not all of such investigations were conducted by trained medical practi-tioners, as offensive smells were as likely to be uncovered by any member of the middle classes, a group whose services in most cases were valued by voluntary hospitals during this age of reform. For example, on February 8, 1876, a committee of such respectable visitors appointed to the Queen's Hospital, one of Birmingham's primary teaching hospitals, reported bad smells arising from the water closets and suggested pipes be laid to carry sewage outside the building.[5] Due to the bad smells emanating from waste pipes from both baths and sinks, they were to be disconnected and carried outside the building. The same had been recommended for the water closets, the cost having been defrayed by Thomas Heslop, one of the hospital's physicians and founder of several local medical institutions. The ledgers of each of these, incidentally, are filled with many similar episodes representative of a pre–germ theory era in which a number of presumed disease-causing miasma were carefully surveyed.

Besides having created a more pleasing environment, the institution's middle-class benefactors can also be credited with having allowed smell to be used more productively by medical practitioners. For example, by purifying the hospital of all offensive odors, doctors, it can be argued, could now concentrate on those odors directly linked to illness, even if discovered after the death of a patient. Predictably, references to smells and vapors in hospital records are often associated with the mortuary or postmortem room, where members of staff attempted to determine or confirm causes of death. Here, doctors relied on smell to locate lesions, which living patients might ordinarily have helped practitioners to locate. One case illustrative of this process comes from the Birmingham Children's Hospital from postmortem notes made on May 15, 1868, by the house surgeon, Henry Wood. The entry concerns six-year-old Ellen Lloyd, who had been admitted to the hospital on April 11 with scarlatina and caries of the temporal bone and remained there as an inpatient for approximately a month before succumbing to her illness. As was common, the postmortem was performed within twenty-four hours of death and produced nothing unusual, even after Wood opened the young girl's skull. However, "on attempting to remove the brain a most fetid stench gave evidence that there was something materially wrong."[6] The cerebellum on the right side "was at once seen to be hollowed out into one immense abscess, + from this the pus escaped which was the cause of the smell." The dura mater in contact with this was 'perfectly black + putrescent, the whole cavity of the tympanum filled with pus.'[7] Having located the disease, only now did Wood commence a more detailed investigation using tools such as a microscope, a weigh scale, and a rule.

Although scarce, some evidence in medical journals suggests medical practitioners often relied on their sense of smell when no other methods of diagnosis existed. For example, in an article published by the *Lancet* on December 29, 1832, the case of a thirty-year-old laborer is recounted. Not surprisingly, after a hard day of labor, the man discovered an aromatic odor emanating from his forearm. More unusually, the smell increased the more his arm was rubbed and excited. Symptoms continued for two months, but then the patient underwent a strange attack of fever. Even more baffling, at the first sign of fever, the smell disappeared and did not return following recovery. Smell, it can be assumed, would have been taken more seriously by the doctor who treated the laborer, at least until more evidence could be provided, presumably by one of the journal's readers.

A decade later, on March 18, 1843, a similar episode again appeared in the *Lancet*'s pages. This time, the letter recounted the symptoms of a forty-one-year-old man who gave off a fetid odor while suffering from an unspecified digestive disease. Though this might not have been regarded as unusual, it was of considerable interest that the odor ceased shortly afterwards when the man was afflicted by an attack of typhus fever. By linking a smell with disease, the evidence seemed to suggest some hope of diagnosing by smell alone, a tendency that has since been described as unique to the Victorian period.[8] In this case, doctors simply added one more scent to a rapidly expanding list of diseases and their associated odors. For example, on another occasion, the journal's editors compared the odor of fever patients to that of mice.[9] Infantile cases, on the other hand, were described as being more acidic in their nature. In contrast, smallpox smelled of onions, though some argued its scent was more reminiscent of horse manure, while measles, again associated with children, tended to be more acidic.[10] In the first pages of his work, Corbin even refers to a characteristic smell associated with cancer.[11] One would assume that, like typhoid, and as opposed to typhus, cancer was characterized by a more putrid scent. Although fetid odors of any kind were generally associated with disease, slight variations were also noticed. Generally, some were deemed moldy, while others were described as acidic. For this reason, early work on arsenic poisoning is especially interesting. Recent work by Ian Burney, for example, suggests chemists during this period often tested for the poison using scent alone, as arsenic was said to be characterized by the smell of garlic, a more subtle odor than was otherwise used to describe illness.

The importance of smell in medicine, however, has been shown to have declined by the late nineteenth century as the medical community left smells behind and moved on to microbes. Equally, this may have been an attempt by doctors to consolidate their diagnostic powers, which, when it came to smell, were until this period more widely shared with lay members of the middle classes. New instruments, however, had been developed that allowed one to determine disease causation with greater certainty. Smell might still have been used to locate disease or the drunkard, but sight and a trained medical practitioner were now almost always necessary to confirm the existence of an illness.

Besides classifying primarily good and bad smells, most histories of smell also describe it as perhaps the most elitist of the senses. The factory, consequently, has very little role in the history of the olfactory, other than being a major source of pollution, but even smoke for a time was regarded as purifying and healthy. Nevertheless, the lower orders in general appear to have been oblivious to good and bad smells alike. As one Victorian perfumer put it, "noses they have, but they smell not."[12] They did, however, emit smells. During the Victorian period, most are to have spent too much of the day working to have had any time left over for practices of cleanliness. Generally, the working classes reeked of "poverty" and "coarseness."[13] In part, this malodor was due to the fact that manual laborers naturally perspired when they worked. Many others smelled of their work, though this could only be perceived by the middle classes, as laborers quickly became acclimatized to their workshops, their sense of smell often having become dull due to overexposure to offensive odors.[14] Few middle-class observers, however, overlooked the "stench of animal putrefaction" emitted by tanneries or the rotting emanations of the slaughterhouse. Not surprisingly, many workers could even be recognized from their workplace. Friedrich Engels drew attention to bleachers, whom most individuals would have recognized from their chlorine-scented breath.[15] In his popular novel *The Young Physician*, Francis Brett Young refers to the odor of stale oil exhaled by iron and brass workers.[16] Many other examples can be gleaned from records produced in these years. In general, the majority of workers were regarded as healthy and worked in odorless workshops. If there were any lingering smells, Charles Thackrah consoled the English public in 1832, that the smells of various workplaces, such as butcher shops and chandleries, though often vile and once regarded to be harmful to health, did not actually cause illness.[17] This, however, appeared to contrast with the worker's home environment.

Without a doubt, not a single history of public health does not refer to the stinking conditions in which the working classes lived during industrialization. Most draw liberally from the sanitary ramblings of such individuals as Hector Gavin and Friedrich Engels.[18] Gavin, who toured Bethnal Green in the footsteps of Southwood Smith a decade after the latter compiled his famous report for the poor law commissioners, found the regions to have declined further and was even more observant when it came to describing the parish's odors. Engels, like Gavin, "relied on his own eyes and ears," not to mention his nose, in order to gauge the condition of the working class in England from London to Manchester and describe how "intolerably bad conditions were for the great majority."[19] He described the foul, stagnant pools found in the streets of East London, recorded the "horrible smell" of the fish-dealers' stalls, as well as the "shocking stench" of workers' homes. Almost everywhere he traveled he discovered foul vapors that offended both sight and smell. Even Engels, however, fell into the trap of using smell and his other senses in order to rank members of English industrial society. For example, the unendurable stenches of the districts he visited were said to challenge the civilized in these areas, any remaining inhabitants having long reached the "lowest stage of humanity." According to Gavin, the "Disease Mist" that overhung Bethnal Green also "destroy[ed], and enfleeble[d], the population."[20] Corbin likewise draws attention to the notion that the stench of the poor was regarded as a mark of their decay.[21] Should they have been left alone, most would have perished given the state of their homes and diet. Middle-class intervention, on the other hand, promised reform. According to Engels, such efforts were necessary as the middle class could more easily detect adulteration "with their sensitive palates."[22] Presumably, most inhabitants of the worst districts only continued lodging where they did as they had long grown insensitive to their polluted environment. No longer simply the great unwashed, the working classes had become the great anosmic, their sense of smell having long abandoned them, somewhat curiously perhaps, given the other animal attributes they were said to possess.

Some laborers, however, like their middle-class contemporaries, relied on their sense of smell in order to work, even if they toiled in the most unhygienic of conditions. Take, for instance, Gervaise, the laundress protagonist whose decline is charted in Zola's *L'Assommoir*. Though a fictional character, Gervaise has been included here to acknowledge Zola's contribution to the study of smell; her use of smell also gains some credence given the

meticulous way the author researched his subjects before com-
mencing his novels. She, much like the hygienists in Corbin's
work, searched out the filth in the finery of her clientele, having
used smell to sort all the laundry her shop handled.[23] Rules for
the management of public washhouses also suggest the clothes
of dirty and clean customers were not to be laundered together,
but, unfortunately, these records do not indicate how this was
determined.[24] Interestingly, this is never mentioned in Patricia
Malcolmson's history of the English laundress. She does, however,
mention that many laundries smelled of urine, which was used
when sufficiently stale to get whites their whitest because it contained ammonia. As a result, she too seems to emphasize extremes
of smell, as has been the case in other historical studies. However,
her comment is then placed in a context that makes it extremely relevant to this study, for Malcolmson argues that many medical officers mistakenly believed the smell of laundry was the result of the
wearer's filthy state rather than the solution in which it was being
washed.[25] Though Malcolmson does not identify any specific cases
of such misunderstanding, a rereading of some well-known medical reports appears to substantiate her claims. Perhaps the most
interesting comes from Edwin Chadwick's report on the *Condition
of the Labouring Population of Great Britain* from 1842. The words
are John Liddle's, one of the medical officers of the Whitechapel
union, and once again refer to the deplorable condition of the working classes in this neighborhood and in particular lament the lack
of water for any purpose, especially laundering. Referring to washing specifically, Liddle gives more detailed evidence: "When I have
occasion to visit their rooms, they have only a very scanty supply
of water in their tubes. When they are washing, the smell of the
dirt mixed with soap is the most offensive of all the smells I have to
encounter. They merely pass dirty linen through very dirty water.
The smell of the linen itself, when so washed, is very offensive, and
must have an injurious effect on the health of the occupants."[26]

Corbin demonstrates that others, such as policemen, worked alongside medical officers, directly assisting these professionals as part of the movement to purify the urban environment of nineteenth-century France.[27] However, he does not, perhaps somewhat surprisingly, suggest they may have used their senses of smell on other occasions in order, for example, to fight crime. Consequently, though he refers to "smell" prints, which Barruel offered as an alternative to fingerprints, this discovery remains an unknown page in the history of identification.[28]

Evidence from a local archive, however, permits some elaboration on this interesting topic. Though the material recounts events that transpired in Paris in the 1830s, it is particularly suited to this discussion as it simultaneously combines the themes of English medical students and the stench of the dissecting room. Of most interest in the collection is a letter written by an English medical student, Thomas Southam Burman, to his mother in the Midlands. Given that his parents were paying for the young man's medical education, they must have been especially pleased to read a particularly enthusiastic report that referred to the great availability of body parts for dissection in France.[29] Not only could Burman dissect endlessly at the local anatomy school that he attended, but he had on several occasions taken organs and limbs to the lodging house where he resided to continue his studies into the early hours of the morning. While Burman does not disclose how he disposed of those body parts for which he no longer had a use, he does in one letter devote many lines to the antics of a close friend, who also took specimens home with him. On one occasion, the young medical colleague had obtained the arm of a woman, which he dissected for a number of days in his lodging house. When finished with this particular study, the young man searched the house for a means to dispose of the limb. Eventually, the pupil decided to deposit the arm through a hole in the wall at the end of the hallway outside his room. Given its great height, however, he was unable to see where the opening led before discarding his homework. Nevertheless, he managed to pass the arm through the damaged wall and in this way successfully launch it from the building. Unfortunately, the decaying limb dropped directly through a skylight of the neighboring house and ended its flight in a kitchen, where a servant was preparing soup. Not surprisingly, the distressed cook immediately communicated with the local police, who commenced to investigate what appeared to be an unusual case of murder. As there had been no witnesses, however, the police were forced to rely on alternative clues. Given the advanced state of decay the arm had reached, one brave officer decided to familiarize himself with its scent and proceeded through the neighboring lodging house, tracking the offender like a bloodhound, relying only on his sense of smell. This eventually paid off, for when he reached the upper floors, the scent was quickly identified and led him to the medical student's room. No other evidence was discovered, but the strength of the smell in the room was deemed sufficient to convince the police of the young man's guilt. In this case, the student was issued a fine and strong warning. The police, on the other hand, were satisfied with the outcome, having been convinced that a murder had not been committed. Finally, the tale also gives some credibility to the accusations made by the landlady, who, in the first pages of Corbin's study, regards the stench emanating from cesspools near her Parisian lodging house to have been the result of decaying body parts buried there by local medical students.[30]

Presumably, the police officers involved in either case were not trained to use their sense of smell, despite the development of Barruel's theory of smell prints. Many workers, however, were. For example, a number of guides produced in the Victorian period refer to the importance of smell in carrying out certain industrial tasks. More importantly, such advice continued to be of use long after the advent of the same diagnostic tools that had led to a decline in the importance of smell among medical practitioners and other professionals. For example, a twentieth-century hop text highlights a continued reliance on smell, especially when purchasing hops, despite the existence of microscopes and other more "scientific" tests. In his *Hop Judging for Brewers* (1910), C. Oscar Grindely suggests that "with care and little trouble a buyer by rubbing hops down and using his sense of smell together with his sense of sight can, in most cases, become a sufficiently good judge of the intrinsic value of hops to be a guide for his purchases."[31] Additional material pertaining to a related industry is of even greater interest as it suggests smell was required of those involved in production, and not simply by purchasers, who might also have been managers. Evidence from the English malt industry is of great importance to the history of smell, as it provides the sort of testimony that suggests that workers possessed very sensitive noses and responded to the subtlest of scents, even in those cases when their most valued attribute was strength. This, more than any other documentation, appears to challenge the notion that laborers lacked a refined sense of smell.

Most descriptions of the malting trade suggest workers were recruited for their strength alone. Above all, histories of the trade suggest the malthouse was a demanding environment.[32] The entire production process was labor intensive, a fact that was used to justify maltsters' very generous ale allowances. Soon after barley steeped in water and laid out on the malthouse floors, the germinating grain was turned frequently, often "violently tossed about," a practice that aided the evaporation of moisture over some ten days. Thereafter, the layers of grain were reworked with special forks every two hours during the last four days of malting.[33] After kiln drying, malt was packed into bags weighing at times more than sixteen stone (224 pounds). Based on previous histories of smell, one would assume that just this sort of laborer was implied by those who asserted that "strong arms precluded a delicate nose."[34] The quotation in this case refers to sailors, but similar descriptions reappear throughout historical texts. Nevertheless, although the entire malting process could not be measured as accurately as the average malting department's accounts, workers appear to have judged the quality of malt fairly accurately throughout production using only sight or even occasionally smell. For example, according to some maltsters and the editors of trade journals, the poorest malt smelled of rotten apples, while "good malting smell[ed] of cucumber."[35] While almost anyone might have been able to identify bad malt, the latter scent seems an unusually subtle scent that even many middle-class noses might have had some difficulty detecting. Presumably, given malting's links to the practices of a larger agricultural community, most workers in malthouses would have had fewer difficulties with such a description. It is much more likely that many of these workers' middle-class contemporaries would have been surprised at such a claim, as most clearly doubted the existence of such fine-tuned and delicate senses among workers who were generally known for their strength and stature.

A final example from another related industry, namely brewing, suggests smell was not only an important part of production but could at times be central to a laborer's particular post. In this way, smell might even be conceptualized as a neglected skill, surviving into a period often characterized by deskilling. Just as hops and malt are key ingredients of ale, so too was smell important to the success of provincial breweries. While most histories of the industry note the smell associated with brewing districts, very rarely is it anything more than a byproduct of the production process. Smell, however, was crucial to the distribution of ale, whether sold locally or shipped worldwide. After all, ale could only be shipped out to customers if the casks in which it was delivered were kept clean and in good condition so as to avoid secondary fermentations, wastage, or outright spoilage. At even a midsized provincial brewery, such as Flower and Sons in Stratford-upon-Avon, this involved approximately twenty coopers maintaining nearly sixty thousand casks.[36] Not only did coopers construct new casks, but they were responsible for the maintenance of all vessels in circulation. For example, after its contents had been consumed, a cask returned from customers was first handled by a cellarman and examined for cleanliness and any obvious damage. Though few casks were ever lost or damaged, all were cleaned since most came back to breweries "covered in filth and mud."[37] At some of the more modern nineteenth-century breweries, casks would have been transported to a scalding shed after their numbers had been recorded by a junior member of the cask department. Once in the shed, individual casks were placed over a nozzle, and their interiors were blasted with steam. At a number of provincial breweries, however, laborers continued to clean all casks by hand well after midcentury. This was still common, for example, at Steward and Patterson's Norwich brewery in 1885.[38] Despite the efficacy of both methods, many casks required more than a simple rinse before they were refilled. Occasionally, gravel or chains and other metallic objects were placed in barrels to remove hardened waste.[39] Violent action was needed "to work off the yeasty stuff left in the cask."[40] Those that stood empty longest before returning to breweries often reached more serious states of decay. Most nineteenth-century brewers struggled with infected, rotten casks, generally referred to in the trade as "stinkers."

The task of diagnosing a cask as rotten was delegated to the brewery smeller. Although technology had clearly been introduced to the cleaning of casks, diagnosis required less advanced hardware. Although contemporary descriptions of this laborer, reminiscent of Nicolai Gogol's most absurd writings, appear to minimize his role in the brewery, the importance of a good smeller is stressed in most discussions of brewery cooperages produced in these years. Most were senior and therefore high-paid members of staff. In general, smellers were to have developed their skills over time, and few were recruited from a cooperage's youngest members. Moreover, most men who worked in this capacity did so day after day, for it enabled them to overcome a recognized "critical period." For example, in an article on brewery cooperages, written quite appropriately by H. C. Sweatman, William Kinnear, a member of a London cooperage, described his first days as a smeller. Interestingly, Kinnear's testimony also suggests smellers were made and not born, a fact that only highlights smell's status as a skill. The article begins with the cooper's earliest recollections of the job, when "he could feel the muscles of his nose getting sore and his smelling power gradually diminishing."[41] As he kept on with it, however, his nose got stronger and much more sensitive. Naturally, when Kinnear took his holidays, his skills decreased somewhat but gradually returned again. As a result, many brewers, eager to prevent the infection of ale, believed it was in their best interests not to change their smellers.[42] Only when brewers turned away from wood and began to ship their product in steel or aluminum in the interwar period would the skills of the smeller become devalued and gradually disappear. The skill's survival, however, was ensured with a growth in the use of bottles, whether used for beer or other beverages. That it would be recognized as a skill was even less likely then, as most bottling plants were staffed entirely by women, generally regarded as unskilled labor throughout and beyond this period.

Despite not being alluded to in most histories of the sense, smell does appear to have had a productive purpose in Victorian England. Collecting just these few references relating to the laboring nose has itself been laborious and surely demonstrates the scarcity of such evidence. It is not, however, as rare as is suggested in the first pages of *Perfume*.[43] Clearly, smell does leave "traces in history." Not surprisingly, however, most surviving scents tend to be extremes or the highly unusual smells that people regarded as worthy of note. The existing historiography adequately demonstrates these were regularly identified as either spiritual delights or satanic stenches. While this in itself is understandable, historiographies of smell have also erected boundaries that have been very influential and have been unproblematically incorporated into other historical works.

That which differentiates the middle classes from the lower orders by way of scent, as well as their ability or inability to smell, is just one of these. Consequently, greater efforts must be made to uncover further evidence if we are to challenge such binary models of smell and their implicit assumptions and enrich our understanding of past scents.

NOTES

1. S. Halliday, *The Great Stink of London* (Stroud, 1999), xi.
2. Ibid., ix.
3. Ibid., x.
4. L. Granshaw, "Upon This Principle I Have Based a Practice': The Development and Reception of Antisepsis in Britain, 1867–90," in *Medical Innovations in Historical Perspective*, ed. J. Pickstone (Basingstoke, Hampshire, 1992), 17–18.
5. Birmingham Central Library (BCL), Queen's Hospital, Minutebook of Managing Committee, 1876–1880, HC/QU/1/1/3.
6. BCL, Post-mortem report book, Children's Hospital, 1862–1878, HC/BCH/ 3/6/1.
7. Ibid.
8. R. Palmer, "In Bad Odor: Smell and Its Significance in Medicine from Antiquity to the 17th Century," in *Medicine and the Five Senses*, ed. W. Bynum and R. Porter (Cambridge, 1993), 67.
9. *Lancet*, January 18, 1840, Among those diseases Corbin identified by their smells was jail fever, which was also characterized by its mice-like odor; see A. Corbin, *The Foul and the Fragrant: Odor and the French Social Imagination*, trans. M. Kochan (New York: Berg, 1986), 41.
10. Patrick Süskind, *Perfume: The Story of a Murderer* (Washington Square Press, 1985), 11.
11. Corbin, *Foul and Fragrant*, 4.
12. C. Classen, D. Howes, and A. Synnott, *Aroma: The Cultural History of Smell* (London: Routledge, 1994), 82.
13. Classen, Howes, and Synnott, *Aroma*, 161.
14. Corbin, *Foul and Fragrant*, 132.
15. F. Engels, *Condition of the Working Class in England* (1845), 208.
16. Francis Brett Young, *The Young Physician* (London, 1938), 359.
17. Charles Turner Thackrah, *The Effects of Arts, Trades, and Professions* (London, 1832), 11.
18. H. Gavin, *Sanitary Rumblings* (London, 1848).
19. Engels, *Condition of the Working Class*, 12–13.
20. Gavin, *Sanitary Ramblings*, 101.

21. Corbin, *Foul and Fragrant*, 164.
22. Engels, *Condition of the Working Class*, 106.
23. Emile Zola, *L'Assommoir* (Harmondsworth, 1970), 150.
24. See rules for Liverpool from 1844 in E. Royston Pike, *Human Documents of the Industrial Revolution in Britain* (London, 1966), 241.
25. P. Malcolmson, *English Laundresses: A Social History* (Chicago, 1986), 4–5.
26. See Liddle in Pike, *Human Documents*, 340–41.
27. Corbin, *Foul and Fragrant*, 129.
28. Corbin, *Foul and Fragrant*, 187.
29. Shakespeare Birthplace Trust Records Office (SBTRO), Correspondence of Thomas Southam Burman, 1835–1850, DR 469/61.
30. Corbin, *Foul and Fragrant*, 2.
31. C. O. Gindley, *Hop Judging for Brewers* (London, 1910), 10.
32. G. E. Evans, *Where Beards Wag All* (London, 1970), 243.
33. *Brewers' Journal*, October 15, 1904.
34. Corbin, *Foul and Fragrant*, 141.
35. *Brewers' Journal* 15 April 1881.
36. SBTRO, DR 227/82–5; and DR 227/118. In comparison, the Burton Brewing Company's inventory listed 75,893 casks in 1871, see BCL, Lee Crowden Collection, 1085.
37. H. C. Sweatman, "The Work of a Brewery Cooperage," in *JIB*, 175.
38. T. R. Gourvish, *Norfolk Beers from English Barley* (Norwich, 1987), 66.
39. Sweatman, "Work of a Brewery," 190; Diana Mary Knox, *The Development of the London Brewing Industry, 1830–1914* (PhD diss., University of Oxford, 1956), 153; Alfred Barnard, *The Noted Breweries, Volume 1* (Causton, 1889), 63 and 221.
40. Sweatman, "Work of a Brewery," 187.
41. Ibid.
42. Ibid.
43. Süskind, *Perfume*, 3.

CHAPTER 7

Reodorizing the Modern Age

Robert Jütte

The ovens, / the stench, / I couldn't repeat / the stench. You / have to breathe. / You can wipe out / what you don't want / to see. Close your / eyes. You don't want / to taste. You can / block out all the senses / except smell.

—Barbara Hyett, *In Evidence* (1986)

"Smells can still be agreeable or disagreeable," writes the French historian Annick Le Guérer, "but they have lost their powers of life and death."[1] And indeed, the miasmic "stench of plague," the sign of a very real menace in premodern times, is nowadays just a rather worn metaphor for any kind of bad smell ("it smells like the plague"). Thanks to a hundred years of popular campaigning against billowing factory chimneys, stinking rivers, and open sewers, smells have become an avoidable nuisance. At the beginning of the twentieth century, the German Association of Public Health conducted a survey of all German towns with more than fifteen thousand inhabitants that revealed that between a quarter and a fifth of the population was infected by the "smoke plague," as air pollution was then called.[2] Since then, the improvement of the quality of the atmosphere and the reduction of smell pollution have become major issues in science and technology and local and environmental politics.

Since industry was slow to install air filters to deal with oppressive smells and dangerous but odorless emissions and normally acted only in response to enormous pressure, the legislature was forced to intervene at an early stage. The Civil Code of 1900 expressly assured property owners that they were not obliged to put up with "excessive" nuisance, which included smells (§907). All the same, an owner could only seek legal redress if the smell interfered seriously with the use of his property or exceeded "normal local levels." After 1915, the courts no longer took as their yardstick the average use of the property but "what the residents of the area concerned regarded as normal."[3] This implied a new, "sensory" interpretation of "local norms" which remained in force until 1959, when the passage referring to "normal local levels" was amended. Since then, nuisances of any kind do not have to be tolerated "if they may be prevented by measures for which those who are responsible may reasonably be expected to pay."[4]

Translating all this into action was both crucial and difficult. The problem is highlighted by the so-called technical provisions of the 1895 trading regulations, which actually remained in force until 1964. The clean air provisions of these regulations deal with noise and smell pollution in very general terms and only specify limits in a few exceptional cases (such as sulfur emissions from glassworks). However, they did not preclude the prescription of limits in individual cases by competent licensing authorities. In the 1920s, for example, the municipal council of the city of Berlin considered the enactment of "municipal air-protection regulations" to stem a rising tide of dissatisfaction with the much-lauded "Berlin air." In the event, the chief constable of Berlin found himself forced to drop this impractical legal device "because it would be impossible to implement."[5]

But by the beginning of the twentieth century, it was not just smoking chimneys and car-exhaust fumes that were poisoning the air of urban conurbations and provoking ever more vociferous public protests. People had also had their noseful of the stenches issuing from rivers that had been turned into sewers and were in search of some form of systematic control. In 1901, the Prussian government issued a decree intended to produce cleaner water and effective protection against air pollution: "Clouded, discoloured, noxious and bad-tasting waters are aesthetically displeasing . . . and detrimental to hygiene."[6] A particularly poignant case was the struggle of the people of Wuppertal to clean up the stinking Wupper—a river that found literary fame in a play of the same name by Else Lasker-Schüler. A government bill presented in 1928 called for the observation of a minimum degree of cleanliness, though merely "to the extent of avoiding intrusive smells."[7] The authorities wished to do as much as was feasible to get rid of the smell of the Wupper, short of actually cleaning it up. The Wupper Association was founded in 1930 for the specific purpose of supervising the gradual implementation of these proposals. By 1944, the association was already operating four purification plants, though its successes in the campaign against the increasing pollution of the water and the smells that accompanied it were if anything rather modest during the period of National Socialist rule. The general confusion about who was responsible for what during the Third Reich was one factor in this; others were the "four-year plan" of 1936, which was primarily concerned with stepping up arms production, and the war economy established in 1939.

The monotonous "international" smell of car-exhaust fumes and industrial effluvia hung over industrial urban areas until well into the postwar period. Given that a large part of the population continued to be preoccupied with everyday cares, it was some time before environmental awareness was again strong enough in Germany to compel the attention of politicians. A similar phenomenon may be observed during the period between World War I and World War II. "Over the longer term," writes the environmental historian Dietmar

Klenke, "the growing prosperity of Western industrial societies and the increasing exploitation of their natural resources also generated a greater sensitivity to the negative aspects of this development."[8] In this context we might consider the election campaign fought by the SPD (German Social Democratic Party) in North Rhine–Westphalia in the 1970s, which promised the return of blue skies to the Ruhr. The date September 17, 1970, is often seen as a watershed in environmental politics, for it was then that the new liberal-socialist coalition introduced an immediate program for the environment aimed at the purification of air and water and the restriction of noise. By the time Willy Brandt resigned as federal chancellor, three important bills had cleared the parliamentary hurdles: the Leaded Petrol Act of 1971, the Waste Disposal Act of 1972, and the Federal Air Pollution Act of 1974.

It was unrealistic to expect rapid results. The 1970s and 1980s were a period of industrial resistance and administrative foot-dragging, and almost two decades elapsed before a German minister of the environment was able to demonstrate the improved quality of the waters of German rivers by bathing in the Rhine under the carefully staged gaze of the media. The clean air legislation was also slow to take effect.

A great deal has been achieved, however, and in industrial cities smog alerts and driving bans are now issued only in extreme weather conditions. It seems, therefore, that our sense of smell is no longer taking as much punishment as it did just a few decades ago. Indeed, people are now beginning to lament the "odourlessness of our cities." According to the Viennese social and cultural historian Peter Payer, "people are beginning to realize that thorough deodorization not only banished foul-smelling smog from the city but also got rid of pleasant scents, which can now be savored only in a few isolated 'smell reservations.'"[9] So city planners are now beginning to "reodorize" their cities by creating areas of greenery. The planning and development department of the city of Munich, for instance, is guided by a so-called scent map, on which such islands of fragrance are already marked out. The *Neue Zürcher Zeitung* of September 4–5, 1999, called for the creation of inner-city "islands of scent, where we can fill up and sharpen our senses."

Olfactory perception became a political issue in the twentieth century, and not only in the context of environmental protection. The German Jewish sociologist Georg Simmel rightly describes smell as a "dissociating sense," for it not only creates "much more repulsion than attraction" between individuals in everyday social life, but there is also something "radical and non-negotiable" about its emotional judgments.[10]

Turning up one's nose at someone is hardly a new phenomenon but is a behavioral gesture that may be encountered in almost all cultures throughout history. In the nineteenth and early twentieth centuries, for instance, the archenemies France and Germany "couldn't stand the smell" of each other—which did not prevent the middle classes of both countries from scorning the "stinking working class." In the United States the notion that the blacks stank and therefore had to be segregated persisted even after the abolition of slavery. Supporters of apartheid in South Africa followed a similar path of reasoning.

In Germany the idea that Jews were dirty and spread a repellent smell (*foetor judaicus*) was not invented by Hitler. "A bad smell is clearly an extension of the attribute of dirtiness," writes the American historian John Efron, "and the copious testimony of popular culture allows us to conclude that the foul-smelling Jew was largely the creation of the 'Christian olfactory imagination.'"[11] An anti-Semitic Franconian proverb runs: "Anständige Juden und Juden, die nicht stinken, / kannst du wohl suchen, aber nicht finden" (Decent Jews and Jews that don't stink / are harder to find than you think). Even children's rhymes played their part in carrying the negative stereo types deep into the twentieth century:

"Der Jude Isaak Meyer / Der stinkt wie faule Eier" (Isaak Meyer, the dirty Yid / Smells just like a pile of shit; lit.: "The Jew Isaak Meyer stinks like a rotten egg") could be heard from the mouths of children during the Third Reich. The traditional prejudice acquired a new and lethal resonance when Hitler used it as one of the building blocks of his racial anti-Semitism. In *Mein Kampf* the future dictator claimed that the smell of an orthodox Jew would often turn his stomach during his years in Vienna. One of the consequences of this "olfactory imagination" is now very well known: millions of Jews were murdered in gas chambers disguised as disinfection units.

Yet even though it was tackled with incredible bureaucratic energy and German precision, the "final solution" failed to deliver the National Socialists from "the smell of the Jew." One of the most striking manifestations of the Nazi regime's obsession with the sense of smell was its attempts to conceal from the outside world the smell of burning flesh issuing from the chimneys of the ovens of Auschwitz and other death camps. Most of these efforts were futile. One Auschwitz doctor said later that his wife had been given the usual "fiction" reserved for visitors: "in such a large place it was inevitable that many people died, so that a crematorium was needed, and the smoke was due to the fact that it was not working properly."[12] However, it was impossible to deceive the victims' sense of smell. As one Auschwitz survivor relates: "And then of course immediately you realized what the unbelievable smell was . . . that you have been smelling. . . . Somehow or other they [the inmates] were . . . already so inured."[13] Even the murderers themselves had needed time to adjust to it, as an anonymous Auschwitz doctor admitted in an interview with the medical historian Robert Jay Lifton: "When you have gone into a slaughterhouse, where animals are being slaughtered . . . the smell is also part of it . . . not just the fact that they [the cattle] fall over [dead] and so forth. A steak will probably not taste good to us afterwards. And when you do that [stay in the situation] every day for two weeks, then your steak again tastes as good as before."[14]

So for all their hankering after German perfection, not even the Nazis managed to find a way of disposing of corpses without creating a smell. Even in the murderous twentieth century, a monstrous and perfidious project of this kind could only be imagined as science fiction. Strangely enough, however, the idea actually appears as a theme in the work of a Jewish writer. In 1911, Salomo Friedländer (1871–1946), under the pseudonym Mynona, published a grotesque entitled *Von der Wollust über Brücken zu gehen* (On the Delights of Walking over Bridges). The plot is reminiscent of a modern science fiction novel. A German scientist named Dr. van der Krendelen discovers a chemical formula for ridding the earth of bad smells. But few manage to survive in the perfectly pure air. Most people die and have to be cremated. And then something quite miraculous occurs: "Furthermore, the corpses burned in the wonderful air of the early spring without giving off the faintest smell of decomposition."[15]

An openly anti-Semitic tract with the pseudoscientific title *Der Jude im Sprichwort der Zeitalter* (The Jews in the Proverbs of the Ages; Nuremberg, 1942) offers a "racial-biological" explanation of why a non-Jew can also suffer from bad breath: "He's been kissing a Jew." In the 1920s, the Odol company was still innocently advertising its famous mouthwash with the text, "Why doesn't he kiss me? Even the most beautiful woman is undesirable if she has bad breath."[16]

The story of the Germans' preoccupation with bad breath—that most intimate of physical subjects—would make a gripping study of mental attitudes. It is inextricably entwined with the history of a global company whose name is still on everyone's lips: Odol. Today around 20 million Germans use a mouthwash daily; 70 percent choose Odol, a brand with a hundred years of tradition and success.

Since the turn of the twentieth century, when Odol first became synonymous with mouthwash as such, bad breath has been a subject that could be talked about openly in Germany without giving rise to embarrassment. In England and the United States, on the other hand, people were still reluctant to talk about bad breath in the 1920s, so the advertising department of the Lambert Pharmaceutical Company had to find a scientific name for it. It quickly came up with the word "halitosis," which proved to be a great success. Following the launch of a mouthwash named Listerine, the firm's turnover rose from $100,000 in 1920 to over $4 million in 1927. However, the German manufacturer Karl August Ferdinand Linger had not needed to resort to this sort of euphemistic wordplay in order to make his fortune with Odol at quite an early date. As early as the winter of 1900–1901, the Dresden Chemical Laboratory founded by Linger was promoting itself as the world's largest producer of mouthwash. By 1924, the export share of product sales was already 60 percent. This success on the international market is reflected in the purposely more elaborate text of one of the company's newspaper advertisements in the 1920s: "Women of all races and nations pay tribute to Odol-Hygiene. We adore the blonde gentleness of the German woman, the cool elegance of the Scotswoman, the grace of the Frenchwoman, the bright freshness of Scandinavian femininity and the springy resilience of the women of the United States . . . But regardless of all differences of racial type, we adore a woman with a fresh mouth, beautiful, snow-white teeth and seductively pure breath."[17]

Just a few years later, advertising copy of this kind would no longer have been considered politically correct—always assuming that it had not already succumbed to self-censorship. The Odol advertisements of the Third Reich tended to emphasize the blonde Nordic type. The woman of these images is no longer a vamp or seductress but a housewife and mother who is pictured looking up at her husband with a radiant smile: "superb teeth and a fresh mouth, thanks to Odol." This covert sucking up to National Socialist ideology did not appear to disturb even those whom the regime had compelled to emigrate, for they remained loyal to the brand in their countries of exile, unwilling to renounce their beloved mouthwash. Among the items on view at an exhibition organized by the German Museum of Hygiene in 1993 was a post-card that gives a striking illustration of product loyalty. It reached Dresden from the United States shortly after the end of the war, and its writer wishes to know whether he can now count on receiving his precious Odol again.

The development of mouthwashes into mass-produced articles and the fashioning of brands into household names were not just the work of the advertisers. It is also necessary to take account of the general change of attitudes to oral health and hygiene fol-lowing the publication in 1883 of the pioneering research of the American dentist Willoughby Dayton Miller (1853–1907) into the microorganisms of the oral cavity that cause caries and bad breath. What had been hitherto an occasional cosmetic option now became a medically recommended prophylactic. As early as 1890, Carl Röse (1864–?), another pioneer in the field of oral hygiene, had examined Odol in his laboratory: "Setting aside the extravagant manner in which it is advertised, I find that with respect to harmlessness, germicidal efficiency and pleasant taste Odol is the best mouthwash I have come across."[18] To this day, there are few advertisements for toothpaste and mouthwash that do not include a scientific endorsement of the prophylactic effects of the product in question.

When you reach for a bottle of mouthwash such as Odol, you are not just following the disciplines of oral hygiene laid down by dentists. As the novelist Robert Walser (1878–1956) notes ironi-cally in one of his prose pieces, pure, fresh breath has been a pass-port to civilized modern living for quite some time: "Civilization is unthinkable without Odol. If you want to be regarded as a culti-vated human being and not just a barbarian, you'd better get hold of a bottle of Odol without delay."[19] Kurt Tucholsky (1890–1935) was also aware of the needs of the modern artist and intellectual: "Tinte, Rotwein und Odol / sind drei Flüssigkeiten wohl—/ Damit kann der Mensch schon leben" (With these three fluids, / Odol, ink and red wine, / I can get along just fine).[20] But the man or woman of the twenty-first century requires more than a mouthwash. Deodorants are now a scarcely less vital, if not indeed indispensable, article of hygiene. Fortunately, not everyone applies them with quite the zeal of the sixteen-year-old boy from Manchester, whose death in 1998 produced the following newspaper headline: "Clean Youth Poisons Himself with Deodorant" (*Stuttgarter Nachrichten*, November 16, 1998). Obsessed about body odor, this young teenager had sprayed himself from head to foot with deodorant at least twice a day, explaining to his worried father that he wanted to smell pleasant. He finally died from what the postmortem described as an overdose of propane and butane, the by no means harmless propellants used to spray the scent from the can onto the body. A representative of the British Association of Aerosol Manufacturers said at the time that she had never encountered a case like it.

Under normal circumstances, people are a little more sparing in their use of deodorants. According to an article in the *Frankfurter Allgemeine Zeitung* of November 23, 1998, only one in two Frenchmen uses a deodorant—and this in a country that is one of the leading consumers of perfume. A nonrepresentative survey conducted by the psychologist Ingelore Ebberfeld in 1998 revealed that people are particularly fond of smelling their partners just after they have emerged from the shower (61.6 percent). If this percentage seems rather high, we should bear in mind that in Germany and Britain no less than 70 percent of the population now baths or showers daily. The figure for France is said to be just 47 percent. Rising expenditures on body care products suggest that German citizens smelling better and attaching more importance to a clean appearance. Per capita spending in 1998 was DM 208, which was 3.9 percent more than in 1997. The two major items were skin and haircare products. In third place were toothpaste and dental products, followed by fragrances, on which women spent 3.5 percent more in 1998 than in the previous year.

Body odor is definitely "out" these days. Like almost everything else in our highly technologized and science-obsessed society, it has its own standard unit of measurement: 1 olf is the amount of air pollution produced by an adult in a sitting position with a hygiene rating of 0.7 baths per day.

In 1998, a new perfume appeared on the market almost every two days. Alcohol-based perfumes comprise one-quarter of the entire market. In France alone, the perfume industry now employs over thirty-six thousand people. Perfume now has a 40 percent share of the gift market, and the recipients have long since ceased to consist entirely of women. Competition is fierce in this expanding international market, despite growing demand. The market success of a perfume is determined not only by the way it is advertised but also by the prominence or otherwise of characteristics such as complexity, naturalness, and artificiality.

Perfume fashions changed during the course of the twentieth century, though not as much as dress fashions. Women still use the great perfume classic Chanel No. 5, the legendary "scent of a northern morning by a lake" first introduced in 1921 by the couturière Coco Chanel (1883–1971). Arpège by Lanvin (1927) and Joy by Patou (1935) are still popular brands. All the same, there have been certain noticeable changes in consumer attitudes. One of them was the change to musk, which first caught on in the United States. With their heavy emphasis of the physical element, perfumes with this base note broke all the classical rules of perfume production. Scent compositions with the word *musk* in their names were regarded as non-perfumes or at least as highly unconventional. At the end of the 1970s, leading fashion designers sought market success with heavy perfumes (Classic by Karl Lagerfeld, for example, or Opium by Yves Saint Laurent). Toward the end of the 1980s, these heavy

and bewitching scents made way for purer and clearer compositions. In the last decade of the twentieth century, light perfumes
finally prevailed. CK one by Calvin Klein became a market leader.

There have also been other developments during the last few
decades. According to the perfume expert J. Stephan Jellinek, "The
last few years have seen the development of a new attitude towards
perfume. Fragrances are now expected to be not only aesthetically
pleasing but also capable of altering our mood and state of mind."[21]
In Japan perfumed pillows have been marketed as aids to recupera-
tive slumber since the beginning of the 1990s. Meanwhile, the nose
has been discovered by the sales managers of German supermarkets. According to a report in *Die Zeit* (July 8, 1999), there are now
shopping centers in which so-called scent columns emit electroni-
cally controlled fragrances, which are said to put customers into a
buying mood. A study of more than a hundred shops, which was
completed by Paderborn Polytechnic, found that customers tended
to linger longer in supermarkets perfumed in this way. The willingness of customers to part with their money rose by 15 *percent*,
representing a 6 *percent* increase in turnover.

Although condemned as manipulation by consumer protection
organizations, the automatic fragrancing of spaces has already
entered offices and factory floors in Japan. Managers at the Toyota
car company claim that the scenting of the assembly areas with
the smell of lemon has reduced conveyor-belt errors by as much as
30 percent. When the miniature Smart Car (originally a German-
Swiss collaboration) was introduced to the public at the end of the
1990s, the ingenious advertising strategists came up with something special: the lemon yellow demonstration model had a pleasant lemony smell. It was a breach of the time-honored code of the
motor industry, which lays down that a new car must have a neu-
tral smell. This is why car manufacturers all over the world employ
highly paid olfactologists (professional "sniffers") to test each new
car for the unpleasant smell of plastic or rubber.

Although still a project of the future, the sensuous "scented TV," with a remote control unit containing aromatic capsules activated by a radio signal, already haunts the nightmares of the critics of our media society, who fear that the five senses are gradually being monopolized by the multimedia. However, the sense of smell has in fact already entered the world of cinema. As the Constance media specialist Anne Paech has noted, "In its pursuit of the ultimate illusion, cinema has already made several serious attempts to heighten certain visual effects for the spectator by introducing corresponding olfactory sensations."[22]

The first film to appeal to the olfactory nerves of the audience was screened at the New York World Fair in 1940. Its title, *My Dream*, alluded to a perfume that was very popular at the time. Using the "Odorated Talking Pictures" process developed by the Swiss Hans E. Laube, it first became possible to reproduce smells during the performance of a film using a fully automated system. A cinema of scent was a long-standing dream, and the reader may recall the synchronized olfactory experiences created by the famous "scent organ" in Aldous Huxley's dystopian novel *Brave New World* (1932).

There was another successful attempt to appeal to the filmgoer's sense of smell in 1960. The "Aroma-Rama" process developed by Charles Weiss involved piping smells into the auditorium through the air-conditioning system and was used in a film documentary about the Great Wall of China. However, owing to the "olfactory chaos," as Anne Paech described it, produced by the relatively primitive technology, it found no immediate imitators.

In the same year, another "smelly" made film history. This was Mike Todd Jr.'s thriller *Scent of Mystery*. The American producer had taken Hans E. Laube's process a stage further, renaming it "Glorious-Smell-o-Vision." However, this unique olfactory experience was available only to audiences at specially converted cinemas in Chicago, New York, and Los Angeles, where the seats were connected to a system of tubes. A signal on the film's soundtrack triggered the emission of the appropriate smell in the auditorium at a given point in the action. This was followed immediately by the release of a neutralizing scent, prior to the next sequence of smells. "The olfactory information," writes Anne Paech, "matched by and large the images on the screen, which were connected with things such as garlic, gunpowder, wine, peppermint, shoe polish, lemons, fish, bananas, pipe tobacco, perfume, and more than twenty other smells."[23] Despite all the expense, this state-of-the-art version of olfactory cinema was also only a modest commercial success.

The less elaborate process first used in 1981 by the American horror film producer John Waters, in a thriller entitled *Polyester*, is perhaps still the best known. To enable the members of the audience to savor the "evil smells" described in the film's plot (which included the hallucinations of a glue sniffer), Waters distributed scratch cards, which the audience was invited to smell when the numbers of the matching scenes appeared on the screen. The nauseating smells and brutal scenes of Waters's "shocker" apparently turned the stomachs of some of the more sensitive spectators.

What looks like the last attempt—at least for the time being—to create a sophisticated cinema of scent took place in Paris in 1989. On this occasion the "smelly" was a film about diving entitled *Le Grand Bleu* (The Great Blueness). The moment the blue sea appeared on the screen, the auditorium was pervaded by the tangy smell of sea salt, which was passed through the air-conditioning. So what does the future hold in store? The assault on the olfactory nerves is not the only one that devotees of the new visual medium have had to face since the 1950s. "Commercial cinema," notes the American film historian Patricia Mellenkamp, "bombards the senses of touch, taste and smell, as well as sight and hearing."[24] Yet this does not necessarily mean that we are moving toward new "sensuous" or even synesthetic cinematic experiences.

The rediscovery of the sense of smell in the twentieth century was accompanied by the revival of an ancient form of therapy, which acquired the special name of aromatherapy only in the 1930s. In the meantime, the word has come to mean more than just a simple therapy of scent. Its implications are now more general, and it is often taken to refer to "an integrated therapeutic method, which, with the assistance of essential oils, exercises an influence on both physical and mental processes."[25]

Essential oils are known to have been used for medicinal purposes in antiquity. Nowadays they barely get a mention in official pharmacopoeias, which simply note their aromatic effects and limited usefulness in certain treatments (e.g., for flatulence). But for the highly promising therapeutic experiments conducted at the beginning of the twentieth century by the chemist René-Maurice Gattefossé (1881–1950) in the small town of Grasse, one of the bastions of the perfume industry, the exploitation of essential oils would have been confined largely to the perfume industry. It was Gattefossé who coined the term *aromatherapy*, which we hear all around us today.

Still controversial, this alternative medicinal therapy enjoyed an early period of florescence in France before World War II. With the trend toward alternative medicine that spread to almost all the countries of the West in the 1970s, aromatherapy became known outside France. Marguerite Maury, who together with her husband championed and organized courses in the therapy, was for many years one of its leading exponents. Nowadays, the chemist or drugstore that does not stock a wide selection of essential oils is a rare phenomenon. Regardless of the method preferred (burning the oils in an essential oil burner or rubbing or massaging them into the skin), the aromatic substances released are supposed to have an immediate effect on the body, mind, and spirit. And, for "rapidly banishing unpleasant smells or negative vibrations [*sic*!] from the atmosphere of a room," one recently published handbook of esoteric therapies recommends the use of a room spray consisting of a mixture of essential oils (e.g., rose oil) and pure alcohol.

The signs are, therefore, that the process of deodorization, which the French cultural historian Alain Corbin has described as a product of the medical enlightenment and increasing hygienic awareness of the late eighteenth and early nineteenth centuries, is now giving way to a process of reodorization. This transformation is marked by the more or less definitive suppression of stenches of any kind by the latest modern technology. So regardless of where the nose pokes itself in, the only smells it encounters are fragrant. Viewing the long-term character of this development, Constance Classen, an American ethnologist and the author of a remarkable cultural sociology of smelling, poses the obvious question: "As odours, like roses, have long-standing associations with both spirituality and sensuality, one wonders if this post-modern interest in smell is evidence of a quest tor spiritual and/or sensual fulfilment."[26] The use of pheromones—mysterious, sexually enticing substances secreted by the body—in the production of perfume may perhaps be regarded as part of this quest.

NOTES

1.   Annick Le Guérer, *Scent*, trans. R. Miller (London, 1993), 205.
2.   Gerd Spelsberg, *Rauchplage: Hundert Jahre saurer Regen* (Aachen, 1984), 75.
3.   Quoted in ibid., 152.
4.   Quoted in ibid., 211.
5.   Quoted in Klaus-Georg Wey, *Umweltpolitik in Deutschland: Kurze Geschichte des Umweltschutzes in Deutschland seit 1900* (Opladen, 1982), 115.
6.   Quoted in ibid., 50.
7.   Quoted in ibid., 99.
8.   Dietmar Klenke, "Bundesdeutsche Verkehrspolitik und Umwelt: Von der Motorisierungseuphorie zur ökologischen Katerstimmung," in *Umweltgeschichte: Uniweltverträgliches Wirtschaften in historischer Perspektive*, ed. Werner Abelshauser (Göttingen, 1994), 184.
9.   Peter Payer, *Der Gestank von Wien* (Vienna, 1997), 13.
10. Georg Simmel, *Soziotogie* (Frankfurt am Main, 1992), 736.
11. John M. Efron, "Der reine und der schmutzige Jude," in *"Der schejne Jid": Das Bild des "jüdischen Körpers" in Mythos und Ritual*, ed. Sander L. Gilman, Robert Jütte, and Gabriele Kohlbauer-Fritz (Vienna, 1998), 76.

12. Quoted in Robert Jay Lifton, *The Nazi Doctors: Medical Killing and the Psychology of Genocide* (New York, 1986), 319.

13. Ibid., 164.

14. Ibid., 197.

15. Mynona [Salomo Friedländer], *Rosa die schöne Schutzmannsfrau und andere Grotesken*, ed. Ellen Otten (Zurich, 1965), 20.

16. Martin Roth, Manfred Scheske, and Hans-Christian Täubrich, eds., *In aller Munde: Einhundert Jahre Odol* (Ostfildern-Ruit, 1993), 110.

17. Ibid., 155.

18. Ibid., 99.

19. Robert Walser, *Prosa-Stücke* (Berlin, 1978), 360.

20. Kurt Tucholsky, *Gesammelte Werke*, ed. Mary Gerold-Tucholsky and Fritz J. Raddatz (Reinbek, 1975), vol. 9, 206.

21. Stephan J. Jellinek, "Der Planet der Parfums im Sternbild der Düfte," in *Das Riechen: von Nasen, Düften und Gestank*, ed. Kunst- und Ausstellungshalle der Bundesrepublik Deutschland (Göttingen, 1995), 128.

22. Anne Paech, "Das Aroma des Kinos: Filme mit der Nase gesehen: vom Geruchsfilm und Düften und Lüften im Kino," www.uni-konstanz.de/FuF/Philo/LitWiss/MedienWiss/Texte/duft.htm.

23. Ibid., 2.

24. Quoted in ibid., 5.

25. Werner Kühni-Ramisch, *Sanftes Heilen mit edlen Düften: Ein praktisches Handbuch der Aromatherapie* (Heidelberg, 1993), 9.

26. Constance Classen, *Worlds of Sense: Exploring the Senses in History and across Cultures* (London, 1993), 35.

CHAPTER 8

Making "Others" Smell

Mark M. Smith

They look like marmalade jars, stuffed with pieces of fabric. To specially trained dogs, the jars and their containers were "the odour of dissent." Or so East Germany's secret police, the Stasi, hoped.[1]

Of the many records released following German reunification, perhaps none is as curious—or sinister—as these jars. The Ministry of State Security (the Stasi) collected so-called smell probes from hundreds of suspected political dissidents. How, precisely, the Stasi collected the scent of such suspects varied. Some suspects were made to hold special tissues under their armpits during interrogation, the tissue subsequently jarred and recorded; other suspects had their scent harvested without their knowledge, with Stasi agents lifting suspects' smell from work chairs and clothing. Dogs were essential to the project. As one Stasi officer told his staff in 1978, "The protection of the socialist order demands the use of all available means, especially the decisive use of the canine nose." And so the Stasi built an extensive "scent archives" in the belief that individual scents could be preserved and that trained canine noses could detect them.[2]

Whether or not the Stasi enjoyed success with the method is not really my concern here. Certainly, we know that canine ability to detect an individual scent is extraordinarily potent; we also know that dogs' noses are able to smell scents—including the smell of disease—entirely beyond the ability of the human nose.[3] But my point here has less to do with the efficacy or accuracy of the Stasi olfactory technique than it does with the fact that the experiment happened at all. The Stasi experiment grants us access to a fundamental but revealing point concerning the historical meaning—and use—of the sense of smell: it has proven an immensely fugitive sense, one deployed throughout the centuries in a wide variety of contexts, expressly for othering, for designating class, gender, and status in a variety of societies, Western and non-Western, and, in the modern period especially, for surveillance.[4] For the Stasi, smell was used to identify those who would otherwise remain anonymous and unidentifiable in their modern society, and they placed enormous faith in the capacity of scent to reveal truth and generate knowledge. The long- and short-term origins of such an assumption may well have had a great deal to do with the deep historical roots that associated smell with truth.

Drawing on the olfactory stereotyping of European Jews and black Americans, this chapter traces those roots and argues, at the broadest level, that olfactory othering was a product of particular cultural imperatives born of particular historical contexts. I also make the case that there was a shift in the way smell, beginning in the late nineteenth century, was used to not simply demarcate groups but, in addition, to supposedly detect "race" and ethnicity. If there was a modern quality to the sense of smell, it is to be found less in its putative dilution and supposed subordination to sight and more in a growing belief—one utterly unproven, mind you—that the sense of smell could be used to reveal the truth about a person's race and ethnicity.

Plainly, there is no genetic basis to smell—we have studies enough to show, for example, that "black" people do not smell differently from "white" ones—hardly a surprising finding given that the very notion of race is itself a historically specific cultural construction and not biologically classifiable.[5] Yet the idea that race and ethnicity could be detected by scent has, in a wide range of historical contexts, held enormous power in the popular imagination. For a good deal of history, the deployment of olfactory stereotypes, especially with regard to European Jews and African Americans, was used by elites and those in power to justify degradation and othering and, in the modern period especially, as a way to detect, locate, and fix blackness and Jewishness.

It is something of a commonplace observation among historians of the senses to make the point that the sense of smell is one of the most transgressive senses. Sans nose-lids, scents invade and trigger, frequently indexing memory and emotion. While this is certainly the case, smell also operates in a cultural context, functioning frequently to demarcate difference and serve as an arbiter of power.[6] Here, I wish to suggest how the culturally framed (and historically situated) sense of smell has been deployed in radically different contexts to achieve similar ends. My approach is loosely comparative: I explore the enduring deployment of the *foetor judaicus* stereotype from the medieval period to the modern era and the racialization of olfaction, particularly with regard to African Americans in US history. I stress that the way the stereotype was used against both groups raises meaningful questions concerning the appropriateness of the great divide theory, which claims that the invention of print and the larger forces animating Enlightenment thinking functioned to dilute the nonvisual senses and elevate the eye over the nose, mouth, skin, and even the ear. Attention to the transcendent quality of olfactory stereotypes should caution us against making emphatic claims about the supposed eclipse of the proximate senses following the print revolution and the Enlightenment, especially since print, in the modern period, managed to capture and arguably disseminate sensory stereotypes to audiences who in an earlier age would rarely have encountered those stereotypes.[7]

In other words, if Marshall McLuhan, Walter Ong, and other distinguished theorists[8] were right to claim that modernity denigrated the proximate senses, rendering the sense of sight the principal arbiter of truth, knowledge, and reason, then the Stasi smell experiments and a host of other olfactory beliefs should not have happened. But they did, and I want to suggest how and why that was the case.

Let me be clear about my aims here. I am not offering a causal argument, at least not directly. Although there might well be empirical evidence connecting medieval olfactory stereotypes directed against Jews and those deployed during the Third Reich, for example, I am less interested in excavating that evidence—which is beyond the scope of this article—and more interested in simply establishing the sheer historical range and forms of olfactory othering. I am also interested in trying to detect shifts in the way that olfactory stereotypes were applied over time. At one level, the application of the stereotype to Jews and African Americans was fairly constant—the argument that they possessed a distinctive and increasingly innate odor can be found in the early modern as well as the modern period. But the function of the stereotype did change, and those authorities deploying it in the modern period, especially in the late nineteenth and early twentieth centuries, of necessity had to press the stereotype into service for reasons quite different from its use in earlier periods. In other words, the olfactory stereotyping of Jews and African Americans certainly transcended the putative great divide between the premodern and modern eras, but it is nonetheless the case that modernity, while keeping alive earlier sensory iterations, dragooned the olfactory stereotype into service of a slightly different, though certainly related kind.

Foetor Judaicus

Among the raft of anti-Semitic stereotypes used to justify Jewish exclusion and persecution, the idea that Jews possessed a distinctive odor was among the most tenacious. Although the specific foundation underwriting the stereotype changed over time, the essential idea that Jews were fetid remained remarkably consistent from the medieval to the modern period.

The origins of the stereotype of *foetor judaicus*, as Trachtenberg showed in his seminal *The Devil and the Jews*,[9] have a great deal to do with medieval identification of Jews with Satan and his evil stink. Although this association may have been made even earlier—courtesy of the Roman indexing of Jews with the god Saturn and "a Saturnine or melancholic odor"—the stereotype seems to have gained concrete, reproducible credibility in the medieval mind when Guido Bonatti elaborated it to describe the stench as "goat-like," an odor that "would only vanish upon baptism."[10]

The idea that the putative stench was religiously generated and not inherent (in other words, that it would evaporate upon baptism) was subject to debate, though, and seems even during the medieval formulation of the stereotype to have been eclipsed by a broader and tenacious association with Jews, filth, and impregnated (and thus indelible) odor. How, precisely, the association between Jews and inherent odor became solidified is unclear, though it was probably courtesy of applied overlapping stereotypes, beginning with the religious justification, then continuing in the high Middle Ages with an increasing association between Jews and stereotypes of filth and diabolism (which was also attached to lepers and heretics),[11] and capping in the late medieval period by a shift in political economy.[12] Regardless of the specific reasons, it remains clear that by the time of the Enlightenment, Jews were believed to have an innate smell. As Cohen remarks: "The Jew was often associated with stench (the *foetor judaicus*) and impurity. While during the middle ages this stench was supposed to disappear automatically at the baptismal font, by the seventeenth century it clung also to converted Jews, a quasi-genetic rather than religious characteristic."[13]

Felsenstein's important study of anti-Semitic stereotypes in England offers some insightful interpretations about how olfactory Jewish stereotypes persisted even as they changed form—how they remained doggedly alive and reconstituted by changing context.[14] As late as the seventeenth century, the *foetor judaicus* retained currency and was informed very much by theological beliefs imported from the Middle Ages. By the eighteenth and nineteenth centuries, the stereotype that Jews possessed a distinctive and repulsive odor was still alive and kicking but for markedly different reasons. The same or similar descriptions prevailed: Jews smelled, with a "stink" sufficiently powerful to mark off certain neighbors in London as smelling Jewish. Yet the writers who offered such laden descriptions did so with "little or no awareness of the mythical *foetor judaicus*."[15] Now the stereotype was more carefully indexed to social and economic factors: the establishment of crowded Jewish neighborhoods and their status as impoverished urban slum dwellers. Such a reconfiguration of the stereotype makes sense, especially in the context of an increasingly secular England where even those well versed in theology became more inclined to look to secular explanations for modern conditions. Even the "liberal intelligentsia" of the nineteenth century did their bit to perpetuate the stereotypes of *foetor judaicus*. *Kidd's London Directory* maintained in the 1830s that the scent was beyond erasure: "their skin [is] so impregnated with filth as to defy the power of suller's soap."[16]

Yes, the stereotype was irrational, jarring to the gestalt of the Enlightenment, with its reliance on "empiricism and common sense," its visualist emphasis clashing (at least seemingly) with the frequency with which the nonvisualist stereotype was peddled.[17] But understood another way, it isn't surprising that olfactory stereotypes should have outlasted the Enlightenment. After all, and as I and others have argued in another context, the senses helped inform some of the most fundamental categories of modernity, including industrialization, class formation, race-making, and colonialism.[18] Olfaction especially informed these larger developments, functioning to demarcate "others" both within a particular society and without. Indeed, even as olfactory stereotypes lived on, some thinkers realized the simple, if reconfigured, basis for its tenacity. As one English writer put it simply in 1830: "All the persecuted stink. One of the first receipts for having a man persecuted, is to impugn the credit of his corporal presence."[19]

For this reason, in ways both quiet and loud, the *foetor judaicus* stereotype both lurked and lunged, populating popular discourse and becoming, in some minds, a truism. Kept alive through various religious and, increasingly, secular stereotypes, the idea that Jews stank became a genetic argument: theirs was a scent they could not eradicate. Nowhere did this association gain greater traction or with such appalling consequences than under the Third Reich. Adolf Hitler believed firmly in an innate Jewish scent and repulsive odor. Hitler apparently believed in the medieval origins of the stereotype,[20] and his own obsession with personal cleanliness seems at some level to have been indebted to this belief. But he also embraced the idea because he needed to. He loathed the application of aftershave or perfume in part because "he was afraid that either the smell of body odor or the use of perfume to cover it up might make people think he was a Jew."[21] The Third Reich had to be able to detect Jewishness if its logic was to remain intact Jews could never be part of the German nation, Hitler maintained. "The Jews [have] a different smell," he argued, consigning them to perpetual outsiders, strangers."[22] Neither were these beliefs reserved for private musings. In a speech in Munich in November 1939, he elaborated: "Racial instincts protected the people; the *odor* of that race deterred Gentiles from marrying Jews."[23] Critically, modern olfactory masking demanded olfactory vigilance: "At present in these days of perfume, where any dandy can assume the same *odor* as anyone else, the feeling for these finer distinctions between peoples is being lost. The Jews count on that" (Waite, 1993, 131; emphasis added).

On the whole, it seems that *foetor judaicus* evolved in overlapping fashion, the stereotype remaining constant over several centuries, with the justification underwriting the idea shifting and cobbling onto prior iterations. In the medieval period, a broadly theological justification was joined by cognate elaborations concerning filth and later money, and all three associations proved quite tenacious, lasting at least until the eighteenth century. To some extent, the religious underwriting seems to have been diluted in the nineteenth century and replaced with a vague, inchoate idea, one very likely informed by pseudoscientific, early eugenic thinking about a putatively "innate" Jewish smell which certainly informed Nazi stereotypes in the twentieth century. In each instance, the generation and application of the Jewish olfactory stereotype functioned to justify exclusion, persecution, and, in the case of the Third Reich, genocide. But the Nazi idea that scent functioned as locator of Jews was important and rather different from earlier stereotypes. As we will see, it was arguably a product of a modern moment.

The Smell of Race

Stereotypes concerning smell, then, were used to anchor beliefs about Jewish otherness from the medieval through to the modem period. Jews were not alone in this regard. In the context of US history, African Americans were similarly othered by olfactory stereotyping, also over a long period of time. Although one scholar has argued that after World War II in the United States, "the slur of racial smell had been (unconsciously) transferred from Jews to blacks,"[24] the notion that black people possessed a peculiar and, increasingly, innate odor predated the mid-twentieth century.

Although the idea that black people stank seems to have had little basis in religious discourse, the application and reiteration of the stereotype operated on the knife-edge of environmental and genetic thinking. As early as the eighteenth century, when whites were becoming increasingly exposed to West African slaves, efforts to explain why black slaves in the United States and elsewhere supposedly possessed a distinctive odor flitted between environmental explanations (they came from hot climates, they did not wash, their food was different) and quasi-genetic ones (their skin simply emitted a rank, fetid odor, the olfactory signature of blackness). Even the most enlightened thinkers of the period helped endorse and disseminate the widely held stereotype. Dr. Benjamin Rush, a well-respected humanitarian, antislavery supporter, and Philadelphia physician, tried to explain black sensory difference in environmental terms but ended up coming extremely close to an argument that made blackness and its associated smell unalterable. For Rush, diet, custom, and especially disease—most notably leprosy—were the underlying causes of African blackness, rendering their skin "black, thick, greasy" and causing it to "exhale perpetually a peculiar and disagreeable smell, which I can compare to nothing but the smell of a mortified limb."[25] But Rush then argued that since black people were especially prone to leprosy and its associated smell and since reversing the disease was impossible, the smell was likely to remain, somehow locked in the skin.[26] Rush, though, was one of the more subtle thinkers about race; others, including statesman Thomas Jefferson, historian Edward Long, physician Charles White, and philosopher Lord Karnes—all respected eighteenth-century thinkers—claimed to varying degrees that, as Karnes put it in the 1770s, "The black colour of Negroes . . . and rank smell, distinguish them from every other race of men."[27]

By the time US slavery had become a distinctly southern phenomena, giving rise to an aggressive proslavery ideology in the 1840s and 1850s, the idea that black scent was impregnated in skin had wide currency. At work here was a sustained attempt at othering and, ergo, the continued justification of enslavement. Religious justifications for the smell of blackness were relatively few[28]; even less common by the mid-nineteenth century were environmental ones. Instead, a roughly conceived and poorly articulated but nevertheless deeply persuasive (to southern whites) belief that black people possessed an innate odor had infected popular discourse. This notion was tightly knitted with a host of other sensory stereotypes about how they sounded and about how their skin—insensitive, tough, leathery—was well suited to manual labor. These sensory stereotypes worked to make blackness synonymous with enslavement.

There was something else at play here, a factor that reached its zenith not under slavery (though the idea was born then) but, interestingly enough, after the Civil War, during freedom. This was the notion that black people, regardless of how light-skinned they were, could always be detected through their scent. This thinking became a matter of some urgency, especially after the Civil War, when the very basis of southern segregation rested on the assumption that bodies should be arranged in public space according to race.

Here, the application of the reconfigured *foetor judaicus* belief under the Third Reich and the olfactory stereotype concerning race under modern US segregation shared something important—and something distinctly "modern." For Hitler, recall, smell supposedly allowed him to identify Jews. The same argument was applied in the late nineteenth- and early twentieth-century US South against black people. Just as Hitler argued that the presence of a Jew could be detected through the nose, so southern segregationists maintained that race, even when visually muddied (as was the case increasingly after the Civil War with rising numbers of light-skinned "black" people) could always be spotted and verified by smell.

In fact, the very basis of southern segregation, the infamous 1896 Supreme Court case *Plessy v. Ferguson*, was built on the premise that the nose and not the eye could detect racial identity. The case involved a visually ambiguous man, Homer Plessy, who though visually "white" was, under Louisiana state law, technically "black." In 1890, Louisiana instituted segregation on some of its railroads. Black passengers had to sit in one railroad car, white ones in another. Elite blacks—many of whom were visually white or very light-skinned—were quick to challenge the legislation and, with the support of some white lawyers, elected to challenge the very basis of the statute by having Plessy sit in a "whites only" car. According to Louisiana law, Plessy was technically "black" because of his proportion of African ancestry, but the train conductor's eyes couldn't detect it, and Plessy himself had to tell him that he was in fact legally "black." In court, Plessy's attorney maintained that the statute itself was unenforceable because racial identity could not always be seen. The logic was impeccable: if you couldn't see race, how on earth were people charged with enforcing segregation going to reliably confine black people to exclusively "black" public spaces?

Louisiana's prosecuting attorney, John H. Ferguson, replied by drawing on centuries of racial, sensory stereotypes. It did not matter that the conductor couldn't see Plessy's race; instead, Ferguson insisted, he could smell Plessy's racial identity. The argument, as later psychologists showed, was hardly empirical—there never was, nor has there ever been, an olfactory signature to race.[29] But that didn't matter. That whites had the authority to designate race as a culturally stable category by appealing to smell was, in the context of 1896, enough to make Homer Plessy black. The specific context of power relations dictated that southern whites could invoke the stereotype, one cultivated under slavery, to effect a stabilization of race.[30]

The *Plessy* case and the deployment of the Jewish olfactory stereotype under the Third Reich had much in common. Although modernity supposedly empowered vision, there is a strong case to be made that certain habits and technologies of the modern era undermined the reliability of sight. When it came to the modern compunction to classify and categorize people, old stereotypes regarding the proximate sense were resurrected and recruited in an effort to reestablish truth. As a number of scholars have shown, key elements of modernity often masked differences among people and functioned to render invisible what had once been obvious.[31] Smells were driven underground into sewage systems; the mass movement of people, courtesy of modern transportation systems, made it harder to place strangers, to fix them socially and racially; and a whole range of modern technologies, such as the photograph and radio, made it difficult to say with any certainty whether someone was, for example, Jewish, black, or white. Into this era of visual uncertainty stepped the old sensory stereotypes, especially the stereotype of smell. To claim that a certain person "smelled" was not simply a way to denigrate them (although it almost certainly was that); it was also a way to locate and fix them, to categorize them. From there, they could be othered and degraded.[32] The Stasi understood this only too well; hence their belief in their scent experiment. That it was impossible to actually identify race or ethnicity according to smell mattered little to those deploying the argument because the aim of the argument was, at base, to reempower long-held beliefs in the context of a modern world that threatened to undermine those same beliefs. The reiteration of the argument was sufficient to preserve the power of the stereotype and reassure elites that important aspects of their changing world remained stable and predictable.

Tenacity, Transcendency

To what extent the othered—either Jews or African Americans in the context of this essay—have accommodated to or resisted the consistent application of the olfactory stereotype is difficult to gauge. Although there are some examples in post–World War II Jewish literature depicting the Nazis stinking of excrement, Jewish intellectuals seem to have resisted the temptation to ricochet the olfactory stereotype back onto their oppressors.[33] Rather, wry humor and hard-headed common sense were used to combat the stereotype. For example, Bella Fromm, the self-proclaimed Jewish social reporter in Berlin during the years leading up to World War II, had trouble believing the gullibility of the German people and their anti-Semitism. Fromm voiced her disbelief during an official reception. Hitler was present. "Your Führer must have a cold," she told the chief of Hitler's Reich Chancellery, Heinrich Lammers. Lammers asked why. Fromm answered: "He's supposed to smell a Jew ten miles away, isn't he? Apparently his smell isn't working tonight."[34] Likewise, African Americans in the segregated South emphatically rejected the argument that their scent was innate. Rather, they argued that if they did smell it was courtesy of wretched living conditions, the form of labor they were required to perform (largely manual and outside), and the fact that they simply did not have access to amenities.[35]

Such arguments, of course, held the intellectual edge and mocked the illogic of the olfactory stereotype. But intellectual muscle proved ineffective against the power of a stereotype that had assumed axiomatic status in the minds of many, courtesy of centuries of perpetual elaboration and reiteration: witness the odd experiment of the Stasi. It was this very transcendent quality of the olfactory imagination, combined with the cultural power underwriting the claim that Jews and blacks smelled for various reasons, that rendered it such a difficult stereotype to combat. Claimed by political and social elites as a truism, applied to achieve their particular, context-specific ends, and able to satisfy specific cultural and political imperatives in both the premodern and modern eras, the olfactory stereotype proved tenacious, transcendent, and incredibly durable. That fact is important less because it mocks the intellectual validity of great divide theory and more because of the ways in which it was used and the wretched causes for which it was recruited.

NOTES

1. U. Kornmeier, "Smells of Treason," *Exberliner: The English-Language Paper for Berlin* 5 (2003): 16.

2. Ibid.

3. D. G. McNeil Jr., "Dogs Excel on Smell Test to Find Cancer," *New York Times*, January 17, 2006.

4. A. Corbin, *The Foul and the Fragrant: Odor and the French Social Imagination* (Cambridge, MA: Harvard University Press, 1986); M. M. Smith, *Sensing the Past: Seeing, Hearing, Smelling, Tasting, and Touching in History* (Berkeley, CA: University of California Press, 2008), 65–70.

5.   Morlan, "An Experiment on the Identification of Body Odor," *Journal of Genetic Psychology* 77, no. 2 (1950): 263–64; B. J. Fields, "Slavery, Race and Ideology in the United States of America," *New Left Review* 181 (May–June): 95–118.

6.   C. Classen, D. Howes, and A. Synnott, *Aroma: The Cultural History of Smell* (New York: Routledge, 1994); M. M. Smith, *How Race Is Made: Slavery, Segregation, and the Senses* (Chapel Hill, NC: University of North Carolina Press, 2006), 59–64.

7.   Smith, *Sensing the Past.*

8.   M. McLuhan, *The Gutenberg Galaxy: The Making of Typographic Man* (Toronto: University of Toronto Press, 1962); W. J. Ong, *Orality and Literacy: The Technologizing of the Word* (New York: Methuen, 1988).

9.   J. Trachtenberg, *The Devil and the Jews: The Medieval Conception of the Jew and its Relation to Modern Anti-Semitism* (New York: Meridian, 1961), 47–49.

10. E. Zafran, "Saturn and the Jews," *Journal of the Warburg and Courtauld Institutes* 42 (1979): 18.

11. R. I. Moore, *The Formation of a Persecuting Society: Authority and Deviance in Western Europe, 950–1250* (Malden, UK: Wiley-Blackwell, 2007).

12. L. K. Little, *Religious Poverty and the Profit Economy in Medieval Europe* (Ithaca, NY: Cornell University Press, 1978).

13. E. Cohen, *The Crossroads of Justice: Law and Culture in Late Medieval France* (Leiden, The Netherlands: E. J. Brill, 1993), 86.

14. F. Felsenstein, *Anti-Semitic Stereotypes: A Paradigm of Otherness in English Popular Culture, 1660–1830* (Baltimore, MD: Johns Hopkins University Press, 1995).

15. Ibid., 258.

16. Quoted in ibid.

17. Ibid., 49.

18. Smith, *Sensing the Past.*

19. Quoted in Felsenstein, *Anti-Semitic Stereotypes*, 259.

20. K. Fischer, *The History of an Obsession: German Judeophobia and the Holocaust* (New York: Continuum, 1998), 454n62.

21. R. G. L. Waite, *The Psychopathic God: Adolf Hitler* (New York: Da Capo Press, 1993), 131.

22. I. Kershaw, *Hitler; 1889–1936: Hubris* (New York: W. W. Norton and Company, 1999), 66.

23. Waite, *Psychopathic God*, 131; emphasis added.

24. Felsenstein, *Anti-Semitic Stereotypes*, 318.

25. Quoted in Smith, *How Race Is Made*, 18.

26. Ibid.

27. Quoted in ibid., 14.

28. Ibid., 42.

29. Morlan, "An Experiment"; E. T. Prothro, "Ethnocentrism and Anti-Negro Attitudes in the Deep South," *Journal of Abnormal and Social Psychology* 47, no. 1 (1952): 108.

30. Smith, *How Race Is Made*, 70–72.

31. K. Flint, *The Victorians and the Visual Imagination* (Cambridge, UK: Cambridge University Press, 2000).

32. Smith, *How Race Is Made*, 67–71.

33. S. L. Gilman, "Jewish Writers and German Letters: Anti-Semitism and the Hidden Language of the Jews," *Jewish Quarterly Review* 77, no. 2/3 (1986–1987): 137.

34. B. Fromm, *Blood and Banquets: A Berlin Social Diary* (New York: Citadel Press, 2002), 98.

35. Smith, *How Race Is Made*, 96–114.

Epilogue

Futures of Scents Past

David Howes

The exhibition *Belle Haleine: The Scent of Art* at the Museum Tinguely represents an important turning point in the history of aesthetics. It inspired many laudatory reviews and sparked considerable interest in the media.[1] I was reminded, as I prepared this paper for the interdisciplinary symposium held in conjunction with the show, of another such historic exhibition three years ago, when the New York Museum of Arts and Design put on *The Art of Scent, 1889–2012*, curated by Chandler Burr. The latter exhibition's stated objective was to "situate olfactory art within the larger historical context of the visual arts." Burr accordingly assembled twelve perfumes, from *Jicky* by Aimé Guerlain to *Angel* by Olivier Cresp and *Osmanthe Yunnan* by Jean-Claude Ellena, in a bid to put perfumery on a par with painting.

A colleague of mine who attended the Chandler Burr show was not, however, impressed, either by the selection or the presentation. "How sweet," she drawled when talking to me about it, echoing that line in *The Foul and the Fragrant* where Alain Corbin speaks of the bourgeois seizure of control of the sense of smell and the construction of "a schema of perception based on the pre-eminence of sweetness" as being one of the defining developments of modernity.[2] *The Art of Scent* exhibition was indeed very bourgeois, very "nice." It did not include any scents that pushed the envelope, none of the compositions of, for example, the renowned Norwegian smell artist

Sissel Tolaas.[3] By contrast, Tolaas's installation *The Smell of Fear—The Fear of Smell* (2006–2015) figures as one of the centerpieces of *The Scent of Art.* For this piece, Tolaas collected the sweat of twenty paranoiac men during periods of crisis and incorporated its smell into the walls of the ten-by-ten-meter room where the installation is housed, with each subject's smell identified by a number. To experience the individual smells the visitor must scratch the walls, but there is also a composite odor that has a distinct edge.

The exclusion of Tolaas's work from *The Art of Scent* exhibition raises interesting questions concerning its status as art. Can a work such as *The Smell of Fear* be considered aesthetic? At first blush, one might be inclined to answer "no," because *The Smell of Fear* is not very beautiful and, if anything, inspires only nausea. However, I would suggest that while Tolaas's installation may not be very nice, it *is* aesthetic, profoundly aesthetic, like all the other works by avant garde artists that surround it at the Museum Tinguely exhibition. These range from Marcel Duchamp's *Air de Paris* (1919) and Piero Manzoni's *Merda d'artista* (1961) to more contemporary works like Clara Ursitt's *Eau Claire* (1992–1993), composed of vaginal secretions; Ernesto Neto's *While Nothing Happens* (2008), redolent of turmeric, saffron, and other spices; and Carsten Höller's pheromone-spewing scent machine, *Hypothèse de grue* (2013). All of these works could be considered olfactory art *avant la lettre*, since the category did not exist prior to the Museum Tinguely curatorial team's staging it.[4]

Now, the avant garde has of course been preoccupied with (and famous for) shocking the senses of the bourgeoisie from the start.[5] Were it not for their efforts the art world would have remained stuck in a rut. We should be thankful to them for their dogged determination to extend the bounds of the aesthetic. What is not so commonly recognized, however, is that in doing so they have also been reclaiming something of the original meaning of the term *aesthetic*. In other words, there is a retro aspect to their forwardness.

The term *aesthetic* was coined by the eighteenth-century German philosopher Alexander von Baumgarten. He actually took it from the Greek *aestheta*, which refers to things perceived by the senses as distinct from *noeta*, or "that which can be known intellectually, through logic," like the truths of mathematics.[6] "Baumgarten was determined to raise *aestheta* to a science with its own rules and truths, which might be comparable to the rules and truths of logic, although not as clear."[7] To this end, Baumgarten held that the aesthetic is rooted in the body and senses—that is, in perception rather than reason, and that beauty is in the senses of the beholder, rather than an inherent quality of the art object. To put this another way, the aesthetic has to do with the perfection of perception first and only secondarily with the perception of perfection or "beauty." Properly understood, then, the aesthetic is a way of sensing that involves grasping "the unity in multiplicity of sensible qualities."[8] Significantly, there is no specification as to the modality of aesthetic perception in Baumgarten's *Aesthetika* (although most of his discussion centers on the distribution of light and shadow and so evinces a visualist bias).[9]

Unfortunately, Baumgarten's sensuously minded definition was not long for this world. It quickly got tidied up (purified of "confusion") and objectified by Immanuel Kant. For Kant as for his legions of followers, the aesthetic is supposed to involve the "disinterested contemplation" of some object and issue in the passing of a judgment that is in principle free and universalizable. This redefinition not only paved the way for the bourgeoisification of "taste" (in the metaphorical sense), as Pierre Bourdieu has shown in his social critique of the judgment of taste, it also opened the way for the disqualification of smell.[10] "To what organic sense do we owe the least and which seems to be the most dispensable?" Kant asked, and answered, "The sense of smell. It does not pay us to cultivate it or to refine it in order to gain enjoyment; this sense can pick up more objects of aversion than of pleasure (especially in crowded places) and, besides, the pleasure coming from the sense of smell cannot be other than fleeting and transitory."[11] Kant's disqualification was the first blow against smell, not just as an aesthetic sense but also as a cognitive sense. This prejudice has persisted. For example in *Visual Thinking*, the art psychologist Rudolf Arnheim writes, "one can indulge in smells and tastes, but one can hardly think in them."[12] This is in contrast to the senses of sight and hearing, the aesthetic and cognitive or "intellectual" vocation of which has always been treated as given in the Western tradition. The curious thing is that smell was also seen as an intellectual sense in premodernity. For example, *nose-wise* (now obsolete) could mean either "clever" or "keen-scented," and the words *sagacious* and *sage* derive from Latin words meaning "to have a good sense of smell."[13] Moreover, on account of its identification with the breath (Latin *spiritus*), smell was widely understood to be the most spiritual of the senses.[14] Thus, Kant was out of line.

The second strike against smell was leveled by Sigmund Freud. In a lengthy footnote to *Civilization and Its Discontents*, Freud made much of the "diminution of olfactory stimuli" that resulted from man's assumption of an upright posture. No longer would humans go about on all fours, like dogs, sniffing everything in their path (particularly the genital regions of other humans). This "fact" of human evolution has been taken up and repeated endlessly. But the supposed diminution of olfaction had more to with Freud's personal history than human history.

It has been conclusively established that Freud had a nasal complex.[15] This was due to a traumatic incident involving his close friend Wilhelm Fliess, author of *The Relationship between the Nose and Female Genital Organs* (1897). It is not commonly recognized how deeply the young Freud's thoughts on human sexuality were influenced by his friend's bizarre theory of "nasal reflex neurosis," nor how dependent Freud was on Fliess to minister (with cocaine and various surgical interventions) to his numerous nasal complaints. The break-up of their relationship came after Fliess persuaded Freud to let him operate on the nose of one of the latter's female patients in order to cure her of certain sexual complaints, and the operation went terribly wrong due to Fliess's incompetence. The one positive thing to come of this fiasco was "The Dream of Irma's Injection," which Freud had in the early hours of July 24, 1895, and in which, upon reflection, he could see how he unconsciously wished to exculpate himself of blame. (The details of the dream need not concern us.) This self-analysis gave rise to the "wish-fulfillment theory of dreams" which is a cornerstone of psychoanalysis. But the crisis also appears to have led Freud to write the nose out of psychoanalysis and human sexuality generally because it was such a sore spot for him, and he wanted to put his association with Fliess (which centered on the nose) behind him. Freud's subsequent repression or denial of nasality can be seen in his theory of the erotogenic zones of the body, where he lists the mouth, the anus, and the genitals but makes no mention of noses. Similarly, Freud devoted a section to "Touching and Looking" in his *Three Essays on the Theory of Sexuality* (1954) but says nothing of smelling.

The curious thing is that Freud's anosmic theory of human sexuality was accepted without much question by the general public, in the same way the public acquiesced to his theory of the Oedipus complex. In the result, smell was marginalized, and the full erotic potential of the nose has never been thought through or tested. All we have is intimations here and there of a vast universe of olfactory desire. For example, a white Russian émigré interviewed by Margaret Mead in *The Study of Culture at a Distance* (1953) observed that many Russian poets have composed odes to the palms of their mistress's hands on account of their scent. How delightful! Who would have thought the scent of a palm could be an aphrodisiac? There is also that odd remark about not washing that the Emperor Napoleon wrote in a letter to Josephine (which would not seem so odd in retrospect were it not for Freud's denigration of olfaction). Probing further, we know from the anthropological literature that nothing prevents the nose from being an erotogenic zone: consider the widespread custom of the nose kiss, which has basically to do with scenting the other in addition to the tactile pleasure of rubbing.

The third strike against smell was delivered by the man who, paradoxically, is commonly considered its greatest champion, Marcel Proust. Consider what is known as the "Proust effect" in honor of the author of *À la Recherche du Temps Perdu*. It would be more accurate to call it the "Proust syndrome" for all its limiting effects on our smell life, but it has become too entrenched in the discourse of psychologists and neuroscientists, not to mention the general public, for that.[16] The incident involving the madeleine cake dipped in tea is too well known, even by those who have never read Proust, to require quoting here. Suffice it to say that the taste of the madeleine precipitated a moment of "total recall" in the author, suffused with the sentiments of childhood, and gave rise to the doctrine of smell being the sense of memory and emotions.[17] It is the charter myth of that doctrine.

While the madeleine incident might seem like a celebration of smell, it was actually a demotion that compounded the Kantian devaluation of olfaction on cognitive and aesthetic grounds. No good for thinking, at least smell is good for emoting and remembering, the doctrine insinuates. And so smell has come to be known as the "affective" sense, with the result that the gap between it and the intellectual and aesthetic senses of sight and hearing grows even wider.

This is not to suggest that smell is not good for stimulating recall or triggering emotions (it is in the West), only that that is not all that smell is good for. By way of example, consider Francis Galton's invention of a smell arithmetic. It employed scents in place of written numerals but was just as effective at facilitating calculations, he found.[18] The idea that mathematical operations could be conducted olfactorily did not catch on, though. Why? Because of the countervailing influence of the Proust effect (read: syndrome) on the representation and representational possibilities of smell.

To arrive at a proper understanding of the aesthetic and cognitive potential of smell, we must look outside the Western tradition, to those traditions where it does not carry all the baggage, all the disqualifications that Kant and Freud and Proust have saddled it with. Let us turn to consider how the sense of smell and the art of smell (perfume) have been elaborated in Indian culture. We shall be relying on James McHugh's masterful analysis in *Sandalwood and Carrion*, which focuses on premodern India.

To recap, we have seen how in the West after Proust the dominant understanding of smell is as a temporal sense, the sense of recollection. Smell acts inwardly, it bridges time, and it resonates through the corridors of memory. In India, by contrast, smell is a spatial sense. It acts outwardly and is a force either for attraction or repulsion, on the analogy of the way a bee is drawn to a flower by its scent or the smell of carrion is found repellent. As a spatial sense, smell is not primarily concerned with recollection. McHugh is very clear on this. He observes that "in Sanskrit literature, smells are no more prominent than other sensory stimuli when it comes to memory (e.g., in contexts of remembering and longing for absent lovers). . . . It is not the case that when smells are present memories are automatically triggered."[19] This information will come as a shock to many a psychologist and neuroscientist, but so be it. If they were more sensitive to cultural diversity, they wouldn't make such grand pronouncements regarding "the nature of smell" in the first place.

While not particularly implicated in processes of recollection, being a spatial sense, smell is good for navigation. By way of illustration, McHugh points to a scene in a well-known play, *Ratnāvalī*, where a king sniffs his way around the royal pleasure garden on his way to a secret tryst in the dead of night: "This is surely the border of *campakas*; this is that beautiful *sinduvāra*, and this is the dense hedge of *bakula* trees; this is the row of *pātalas*. The path in this place, though concealed by double darkness, becomes clear by means of the signs of the trees recognized by constantly sniffing the varied perfume."[20] Here, smell has replaced sight (disabled by darkness) as the sense that orients a person in space and leads them to their destination. This scenario introduces us to a very different way of thinking about the cognitive potential of smell. It is positively geographical.[21]

Indian perfumery practices also disrupt deep-seated assumptions. In the West perfume is normally consumed in the form of a textureless, mildly tinted liquid. It is basically a unimodal art. In India perfume normally takes the form of a paste and has a plethora of sensible qualities. Consider the following description of *candana* (sandalwood): "Light, unctuous, not dry, smearing oil like ghee, of pleasant smell, suitable for the skin, mild, not fading, tolerant of warmth, absorbs great heat, and pleasant to touch—these are the qualities of sandalwood."[22] Preparations involving sandalwood are thus valued not only for their smell but also for their light white or yellow color (sight), cooling potency (temperature), pleasing feel (touch), and longevity (other aromatics fade), in addition to being exotic and expensive. This explains their vaunted status alongside gemstones in royal treasuries and their use to cut fever, incite pleasure, and for visual body decoration. Perfumery in India is thus a multimodal art. To prepare or appreciate the effects of sandalwood involves grasping "the unity in multiplicity of sensible qualities," as Baumgarten would put it.

Another example of this notion of smell as the sense of navigation—that is, a spatial sense that acts outwardly rather than a temporal sense that unfolds inwardly—is given in the Japanese incense ceremony known as *kōdō*.[23] Briefly, the ceremony involves the participants being introduced to an assortment of scented woods by the master of ceremonies. These are circulated, one at a time, in a censer during the first round, with each wood being designated by an evocative name, that is keyed to the theme of the ceremony. The master of ceremonies then mixes up the order of the woods, and they are circulated in the censer a second time. The participants guess which wood they are smelling and write their responses down on paper. Their responses are then tabulated and judged by the master of ceremonies.

In one version of *kōdō*, known as "The Three Scenic Spots," the woods are assigned the names of three famous sites: Matsushima (an archipelago), Amanohashidate (a white spit of land covered in pine trees) and Itsukusjima (a majestic Shinto gateway). The idea is that the participants are to imagine themselves on a boat ride to these spots. It is the scent of the wood that transports them to each destination, providing they guess correctly. The interest of this ceremony lies in the way it uses the medium of smell to visualize spaces, rather than relying on photographs or verbal descriptions. It is a way of developing the olfactory imagination, both the capacity to discriminate smells and the capacity to form associations through scents. There is nothing resembling this form of mind-travel in Western culture, except perhaps for cinema, but then cinema only traffics in visual and acoustic images; it has no smelltrack. Little wonder that smell has become the least educated of the senses in the modern West.

By contrast, people take an interest in the education of olfaction in Japan. There is a way of smelling in the context of *kōdō*. This involves inclining one's head, lifting the censer to one's nose with one hand while cupping the smoke with the other, sniffing three times, then turning one's head to the side so as not to disturb the ash in the censer when one breathes out. There is a special quality to the attention shaped by this way of smelling too. The Japanese refer to it as "listening to the incense" (*ko wo kiku*). This is to underscore the difference between it and normal, everyday smelling, in the same way that listening differs from (mere) hearing, but this usage also imparts a multisensory dimension to the participants' attention.

The one final thing that it is important to note about the Japanese incense ceremony is that its name, *kōdō*, means "way of fragrance"— that is, it is a practice, a way (*dao*), or performance art, if you will, rather than an art *form*, such as painting or perfumery.[24] *Kōdō* is a practice informed by the ideal of the perfection of perception, which may also involve the perception of perfection. Baumgarten would approve. Kant would just turn up his nose. For Kant to approve, he would first have to recant his dismissal of olfaction.

We have seen how smell is the sense of space in India and Japan, but it can also function as the sense of time, as in the case of the incense clocks of imperial China. But before discussing the Chinese example, we need to briefly reflect on the history of the sense of time and timekeeping in Western culture. We moderns are used to looking at a clock or watch to find out what time it is, and even to an image of a clock face being used as a symbol for time itself. It was not always this way, though. In premodern Europe timekeeping was largely sonic: the day was ordered by church bells ringing out the hour. The importance of such sonic methods of timekeeping is evidenced by the fact that the English word *clock* originally meant "bell." With the invention of the mechanical clock, this began to change, since it became possible to visualize time in addition to hearing it when the clock struck.

Mechanical clocks were one of the items which the first European missionaries to China brought with them for the edification and entertainment of their hosts. In China in the sixteenth century, there were a variety of ways of telling time.[25] Astronomical and water clocks were both used, while gongs and drums were employed to mark off periods of time within cities. The most widespread method of telling time, however, involved the use of incense. A popular expression in China was "in the time it takes to burn an incense stick."

Burning incense was a common religious ritual in China and its association with the passage of time may well have led to the development of the incense clock. These incense clocks, which could be simple or very elaborate, measured time in two basic ways. One way was that a passage of time would be indicated by an incense stick of a certain length burning out. Another way was that the fragrance emitted by the incense would change after a certain amount of time. Such incense clocks were widespread in China in early modernity and used in both homes and temples. This smell-infused understanding of time, as can be appreciated, provided a highly engaging experience: time was "in the air," one "breathed" it in and did not simply "read" it on a clock face. The experience of time as mediated by the incense clock was thus qualitative instead of purely quantitative and immersive rather than objective. The cultural significance of this olfactory way of imagining time was also informed by the way the Chinese regarded the fragrance of incense as an aid to thoughtfulness, a stimulus to conversation, and a mental and physical purifier. Obviously, Western mechanical clocks, while very efficient at keeping time, could fulfill none of these other roles of the incense clock.

When mechanical clocks were first introduced to the Chinese by the Jesuits, they aroused great interest, if not for the reasons we moderns might expect. The interest was due to their novelty, but that novelty had primarily to do with the clocks' ability to ring out the hours rather than their visual features. One sixteenth-century Chinese official, for example, eagerly asked the Jesuit missionaries to send him "a big self-sounding clock." This Chinese interest in the mechanical production of sound through clockwork meant that European trade to China from the seventeenth to the early nineteenth centuries was dominated by what the British called "sing-songs": clocks and other devices—such as snuff boxes with mechanical birds that sang when the lid was opened—that appealed through their novel auditory effects. Mechanical clocks were not, therefore, regarded as the practical, everyday devices Europeans took them to be but rather as novelties and luxury objects.

Early modern European travelers to China, for their part, often remarked on the importance of fragrance in Chinese culture. But while the Chinese might think of fragrance as a way of clearing and elevating thoughts, to the Europeans it seemed a sign of irrational sensuality. One missionary wrote, for example, of "hot wafts of scent from flowers or incense working on minds open to bewitchment."[26] The Europeans prided themselves on their rationality and spirituality in contrast to the supposed overweening sensuality of the Chinese (also signaled by the Chinese craving for opium, with its sickly sweet smell, which the British actually forced on the Chinese, but that is another story). This prejudice prevented the Europeans from ever coming to appreciate the potential of incense as a trade good alongside the other goods they sought (tea, silk, porcelain), which was a pity considering the high quality of the incense produced in China. This lack of European desire for incense indicates a decline in the importance of the sense of smell in modern Europe.[27] Chinese incense was an interesting novelty, but it did not have the attraction of other Chinese trade goods.

This essay has tracked the devaluation and dismissal of smell as a spiritual, intellectual, or aesthetic sense in modern European history. It has also disclosed aspects of the elaboration of smell in diverse Asian cultures—India, China, and Japan—and thereby (hopefully) enlarged our sense of what smell is good for. Meanwhile, *Belle Haleine: The Scent of Art* has opened a breach in the web of prejudices that has come to surround smell in the modern period, and thereby contributed substantially to the expansion of aesthetic experience and the recovery of the original meaning of the category of the aesthetic, as envisioned by Baumgarten, before Kant got hold of it. Significantly, it has done so by exposing visitors to a full range of smells, not just the nice smells of *The Art of Scent* exhibition. This is what makes this exhibition a truly historic occasion.

NOTES

This essay is a product of an ongoing program of research sponsored by the Social Sciences and Humanities Research Council of Canada and the Fonds de Recherche du Québec—Société et Culture. An earlier version of this essay was presented at the interdisciplinary symposium held in conjunction with the exhibition *Belle Haleine: The Scent of Art* at the Museum Tinguely, Basel, in April 2015 and published in the catalog of the same title. I wish to thank the organizers of the *Belle Haleine* exhibition and symposium for inviting me to participate in this historic occasion and Sissel Tolaas for all the inspiration I have derived from following her work. I am grateful to the director of the Museum Tinguely, Roland Wetzel, for permission to reuse this material here.

1. E.g., Ashraf Osman and Claus Noppeney, "Review of Belle Haleine," Basenotes, basenotes.net/features/3049 (accessed May 15, 2015).

2. A. Corbin, *The Foul and the Fragrant: Odor and the French Social Imagination*, trans. M. Kochan (New York: Berg, 1986), 141.

3. With the possible exception of Daniela Andrier's *Untitled*, which uses galbanum and which must be considered borderline.

4. There are those who may question whether the Museum Tinguely exhibition is a first. Whatever, as Osman and Noppeney state in "Review of Belle Halleine," it is "not only the biggest of its kind so far, but indisputably the best as well." There are also those who may attribute the invention of the notion of "olfactory art" to Edmond Rourdnitska, author of *L'Esthétique en Question: Introduction à une Esthétique de l'Odorat* (1977), but he borrowed his analytic framework from Kant, which must be regarded as suspect.

5. Constance Classen, "Art and the Senses: From the Romantics to the Futurists," in *A Cultural History of the Senses in the Age of Empire, 1800–1920*, ed. Constance Classen (London: Bloomsbury, 2014); Hannah Higgins, "Art and the Senses: The Avant Garde Challenge to the Visual Arts," in *A Cultural History of the Senses in the Modern Age, 1920–2000*, ed. D. Howes (London: Bloomsbury, 2014).

6. Jennifer Allen, "The Beautiful Science," *Frieze Magazine* 113 (March 2008), frieze.com/issue/article/the_beautiful_science/ (accessed May 20, 2015).

7. Allen, "The Beautiful Science." Why "not as clear"? Because the truths of, for example, mathematics are self-evident (logical) whereas the evidence of the senses is always suspect, "confused and indistinct" by comparison, according to a long-standing prejudice, which was expressed most forcefully by Descartes.

8. M. J. Gregor, "Baumgarten's Aesthetika," *Review of Metaphysics* 37 (1983): 367–85.

9. I freely admit that my reading of Baumgarten's *Aesthetika* is overdetermined. This is only partly because I do not read German and so must rely on secondary sources (Baumgarten has yet to be translated into English). It is mainly because I have sought to fill in what Baumgarten might have said, from the cross-cultural, multimodal perspective I have staked out elsewhere (Howes, "Hearing Scents, Tasting Sights: Toward a

Cross-Cultural Multimodal Theory of Aesthetics," in *Art and the Senses*, ed. Francesca Bacci and David Mellon (Oxford: Oxford University Press, 2011).

10. Pierre Bourdieu, *Distinction: A Social Critique of the Judgment of Taste* (Cambridge, MA: Harvard University Press, 1984).

11. Immanuel Kant, *Anthropology from a Pragmatic Point of View* (Carbondale: Southern Illinois University Press, 1978), 46.

12. Rudolf Arnheim, *Visual Thinking* (Berkeley: University of California Press, 1969), 19.

13. Constance Classen, *Worlds of Sense: Exploring the Senses in History and across Cultures* (London: Routledge, 1993), ch. 3.

14. Constance Classen, *The Color of Angels: Cosmology, Gender and the Aesthetic Imagination* (London: Routledge, 1998), ch. 2.

15. Annick Le Géurer, *Scent: The Mysterious and Essential Powers of Smell* (New York: Turtle Bay Books, 1998); David M. Howes, "Freud's Nose: The Repression of Nasality and the Origin of Psychoanalytic Theory," in *Nose Book: Representations of the Nose in Literature and the Arts*, ed. Victoria de Rijke, Lene Ostermark-Johansen, and Helen Thomas (London: Middlesex University Press, 2000); and David M. Howes, *Sensual Relations: Engaging the Senses in Culture and Social Theory* (Ann Arbor: University of Michigan Press, 2003), ch. 7.

16. Jonah Lehrer, *Proust Was a Neuroscientist* (New York: Mariner Books, 2008); Chretien van Campen, *The Proust Effect: The Senses as Doorways to Lost Memories* (Oxford: Oxford University Press, 2014).

17. It will be noticed that the Proust effect was produced by a taste, not a smell. This distinction is commonly disregarded in most discussions of the topic, since smell and taste are both "chemical senses," hence interchangeable. From a cross-cultural perspective, however, this distinction should not be trivialized. For example, in many sacrificial traditions, the smell of smoke (i.e., the essence) of an offering is consumed by the gods, while the human participants are free to eat the leftovers.

18. Francis Galton, "Arithmetic by Smell," *Psychological Review* 1 (1894): 61–62.

19. James McHugh, *Sandalwood and Carrion: Smell in Indian Religion and Culture* (Oxford: Oxford University Press, 2012), 14.

20. Ibid., 28.

21. Among the Ongee of the Little Andaman Islands, space and time and personhood are all mediated by smell. Their cosmology is a veritable osmology (see C. Classen, D. Howes, and A. Synnott, *Aroma: The Cultural History of Smell* [London: Routledge, 1994]).

22. Quoted in McHugh, *Sandalwood and Carrion*, 187.

23. Howes, "Hearing Scents, Tasting Sights."

24. See further David Howes and Constance Classen, *Ways of Sensing: Understanding the Senses in Society* (London: Routledge, 2014).

25. Silvio Bedini, *The Trail of Time: Time Measurement with Incense in East Asia* (Cambridge: Cambridge University Press, 1994).
26. Ibid., 48.
27. Classen, *Worlds of Sense*, ch. 1.

ACKNOWLEDGMENTS

Elements of this reader, especially parts of the editor's introduction, benefited from several conservations, public and private. I'm especially grateful for helpful audience feedback from the Austrian American Studies Association meeting in 2015 held at the University of Graz, Austria; for commentary offered at the Vanderbilt University History Seminar in 2017; and for the recommendations of students and faculty following my presentation at Concordia University, Montreal, Quebec, Canada, also in 2017. Andrew Kettler and David Howes helped me think carefully about the content of this reader, and they, like the two readers for West Virginia University Press, offered extremely thoughtful recommendations. Thanks too to Derek Krissoff, director of the WVU Press, for being wholly supportive and encouraging during the entire process. Jonathan Reinarz deserves more than a nod for his help in securing permission to republish his fine essay. My sincere thanks to the University of South Carolina for helping fund the reprint costs associated with the book. I'm particularly grateful to Abby Callahan of the University of South Carolina History Department for her invaluable help processing the permissions.

Further Reading

Many important and useful articles, chapters, and books not listed below can be found in the notes that accompany the editor's introduction and the chapters themselves. What follows is a brief but I hope helpful guide to key texts reading.

Barnes, David. "Confronting Sensory Crisis in the Great Stinks of London and Paris." In *Filth: Dirt, Disgust, and Modern Life*, ed. William Cohen and Ryan Johnson, 103–29. Minneapolis: University of Minnesota Press, 2005.

———. *The Great Stink of Paris and the Nineteenth-Century Struggle against Filth and Germs*. Baltimore: Johns Hopkins University Press, 2006.

Betts, Eleanor. "Towards a Multisensory Experience of Movement in the City of Rome." In *Rome, Ostia and Pompeii: Movement and Space*, ed. Ray Laurence and David Newsome, 118–32. Oxford: Oxford University Press, 2011.

Bradley, Mark, ed. *Smell and the Ancient Senses*. London and New York: Routledge, 2015.

Brown, Michael. "From Foetid Air to Filth: The Cultural Transformation of British Epidemiological Thought, ca. 1780–1848." *Bulletin for the History of Medicine* 82, no. 3 (Fall 2008): 515–44.

Caseau, Beatrice. "Euōdia: The Use and Meaning of Fragrances in the Ancient World and their Christianization (100–900 AD)." PhD diss., Princeton University, 1994.

Chiang, Connie Y. "The Nose Knows: The Sense of Smell in American History." *Journal of American History* 95, no. 2 (September 2008): 405–16.

Classen, Constance, ed. *A Cultural History of the Senses. Volume 5: A Cultural History of the Senses in the Age of Empire (1800–1920)*. New York: Bloomsbury, 2014.

———. "The Aromas of Antiquity." In *Aroma: The Cultural History of Smell*, ed. Constance Classen, David Howes, and Anthony Synnott, 13–50. London: Routledge, 1994.

———. "The Breath of God; Sacred Histories of Scent." In *The Smell Culture Reader*, ed. Jim Drobnick, 375–90. Oxford: Berg. 2006.

———. "The Deodorized City: Battling Urban Stench in the Nineteenth Century." In *Sense of the City: An Alternate Approach to Urbanism*, ed.

Mirko Zardini, 292–99. Montreal: Canadian Centre for Architecture and Lars Muller Publishers, 2005.

———. "The Odor of the Other: Olfactory Symbolism and Cultural Categories." *Ethos* 20, no. 2 (June 1992): 133–66.

Classen, Constance, and Anne C. Vila, eds. *A Cultural History of the Senses. Volume 4: A Cultural History of the Senses in the Age of Enlightenment (1650–1800)*. New York: Bloomsbury, 2014.

Classen, Constance, and David Howes, eds. *A Cultural History of the Senses. Volume 6: A Cultural History of the Senses in the Modern Age (1920–2000)*. New York: Bloomsbury, 2014.

Classen, Constance, David Howes, and Anthony Synnott. *Aroma: The Cultural History of Smell*. London and New York: Routledge, 1994.

Classen, Constance, and Herman Roodenburg, eds. *A Cultural History of the Senses. Volume 3: A Cultural History of the Senses in the Renaissance (1450–1650)*. New York: Bloomsbury, 2014.

Classen, Constance, and Jerry Toner, eds. *A Cultural History of the Senses. Volume 1: A Cultural History of the Senses in Antiquity (500 BCE–500 CE)*. New York: Bloomsbury, 2014.

Classen, Constance, and Richard G. Newhauser, eds. *A Cultural History of the Senses. Volume 2: A Cultural History of the Senses in the Middle Ages (500–1450)*. New York: Bloomsbury, 2014.

Clay, Richard. "Smells, Bells, and Touch: Iconoclasm in Paris during the French Revolution." *Journal for Eighteenth-Century Studies* 35, no. 4 (December 2012): 521–33.

Cockayne, Emily. *Hubbub: Filth, Noise, and Stench in England, 1600–1770*. New Haven: Yale University Press, 2007.

Cohen, William A. "Introduction: Locating Filth." In *Filth: Dirt, Disgust, and Modern Life*, ed. William A. Cohen and Ryan Johnson, vii–xxxvii. Minneapolis: University of Minnesota Press, 2005.

Drobnick, Jim, ed. *The Smell Culture Reader*. Oxford: Berg, 2006.

———. "Towards an Olfactory Art History: the Mingled, Fatal, and Rejuvenating Perfumes of Paul Gauguin." *The Senses and Society* 7, no. 2 (July 2012): 196–208.

Dugan, Holly. *The Ephemeral History of Perfume: Scent and Sense in Early Modern England*. Baltimore: Johns Hopkins University Press, 2011.

Evans, Suzanne. "The Scent of a Martyr." *Numen* 49, no. 2 (2002): 193–211.

Fantham, Elaine. "Purification in Ancient Rome." In *Rome, Pollution and Propriety: Dirt, Disease, and Hygiene in the Eternal City from Antiquity to Modernity*, ed. Mark Bradley and Kenneth R. Stow, 59–66. Cambridge: Cambridge University Press, 2012.

Fox, Cora. "Isabella Whitney's Nosegay and the Smell of Women's Writing." *Senses and Society* 5, no. 1 (March 2010): 131–43.

Foyster, Elizabeth. "Sensory Experiences: Smells, Sounds, and Touch." In *A History of Everyday Life in Scotland, 1600–1800*, ed. Elizabeth Foyster and Christopher Whatley, 217–33. Edinburgh: Edinburgh University Press, 2009.

Gavrilyuk, Paul L. and Sarah Coakley, eds. *The Spiritual Senses: Perceiving God in Western Christianity*. Cambridge: Cambridge University Press, 2012.

Grasse, Marie-Christine, ed. *Perfume: A Global History*. Paris: Somogy, 2007.

Green, Deborah A. *The Aroma of Righteousness: Scent and Seduction in Rabbinic Life and Literature*. University Park: Pennsylvania State University Press, 2011.

Hallett, Nicky. *The Senses in Religious Communities, 1600–1800: Early Modern "Convents of Pleasure."* Farnham, England: Ashgate, 2013.

Jenner, Mark. "Follow Your Nose?: Smell, Smelling, and Their Histories." *American Historical Review* 116, no. 2 (2011): 335–51.

———. "Tasting Lichfield, Touching China: Sir John Floyers' Senses." *Historical Journal* 53, no. 3 (2010): 647–70.

Lilja, Saara. *The Treatment of Odours in the Poetry of Antiquity*. Helsinki: Societas Scientiarum Fennica, 1972.

Martin, Bronwen, and Felizitas Ringman, eds. *Sense and Scent: An Exploration of Olfactory Meaning*. Dublin: Philomel, 2003.

Mattingly, D. J. "Paintings, Presses, and Perfume Production at Pompeii." *Oxford Journal of Archaeology* 9, no. 1 (March 1990): 71–90.

McHugh, James. *Sandalwood and Carrion: Smell in Indian Religion and Culture*. Oxford: Oxford University Press, 2012.

McVaugh, Michael R. "Smell and the Medieval Surgeon." *Micrologus* 10 (2002): 113–32.

Milner, Matthew. *The Senses and the English Reformation*. Farnham, England: Ashgate, 2011.

Nugent, Joseph. "The Human Snout: Pigs, Priests, and Peasants in the Parlor." *Senses and Society* 4, no. 3 (November 2009): 283–302.

Parr, Joy. "Smells Like?: Sources of Uncertainty in the History of the Great Lakes Environment." *Environmental History* 11 (2006): 269–99.

Pentcheva, Bissera V. *The Sensual Icon: Space, Ritual, and the Senses in Byzantium*. University Park: Pennsylvania State University Press, 2010.

Press, Daniel, and Steven Minta. "The Smell of Nature: Olfaction, Knowledge and the Environment." *Ethics, Place and Environment* 3, no. 2 (2000): 173–86.

Rindisbacher, Hans J. *The Smell of Books: A Cultural-Historical Study of Olfactory Perception in Literature*. Ann Arbor: University of Michigan Press, 1992.

Rudy, Gordon. *Mystical Language of Sensation in the Later Middle Ages*. New York: Routledge, 2002.

Saucier, Catherine. "The Sweet Sound of Sanctity: Sensing St. Lambert." *Senses and Society* 5, no. 1 (March 2010): 10–27.

Smith, Jeffrey Chipps. *Sensuous Worship: Jesuits and the Art of the Early Catholic Reformation in Germany*. Princeton: Princeton University Press, 2002.

Smith, Mark M. *How Race Is Made: Slavery, Segregation, and the Senses*. Chapel Hill: University of North Carolina Press, 2006.

———. "Making Scents Make Sense: White Noses, Black Smells, and Desegregation." In *American Behavioral History: An Introduction*, ed. Peter Stearns, 181–98. New York: New York University Press, 2005.

———. *Sensing the Past: Seeing, Hearing, Smelling, Tasting, and Touching in History*. Berkeley: University of California Press, 2007.

———. *The Smell of Battle, The Taste of Siege: A Sensory History of the Civil War*. New York: Oxford University Press, 2014.

———. "Transcending, Othering, Detecting: Smell, Premodernity, Modernity." *Postmedieval* 3, no. 4 (Winter 2012): 380–90.

Stamelman, Richard. *Perfume: Joy, Obsession, Scandal, Sin—A Cultural History of Fragrance from 1750 to the Present*. New York: Rizzoli, 2006.

Stanev, Hristomir A. "The City out of Breath: Jacobean City Comedy and the Odors of Restraint." *Postmedieval* 3, no. 4 (Winter 2012): 423–35.

Stevens, Benjamin. "The Scent of Language and Social Synaesthesia at Rome." *Classical World* 101, no. 2 (2008): 159–71.

Thurlkill, Mary F. "Odors of Sanctity: Distinctions of the Holy in Early Christianity and Islam." *Comparative Islamic Studies* 3, no. 2 (2007), 133–44.

Tullett, William. "The Macaroni's 'Ambrosial Essences': Perfume, Identity and Public Space in Eighteenth-Century England." *Journal for Eighteen-Century Studies* 38, no. 2 (2015), 163–80.

SOURCES AND PERMISSIONS

Introduction—Why Smell the Past?: Corbin, Alain. "Introduction." In *The Foul and the Fragrant: Odor and the French Social Imagination* (Harvard University Press). Copyright © 1986 Alain Corbin. Reprinted with permission of Berg Publishers, an imprint of Bloomsbury Publishing Plc.

Chapter 1: Harvey, Susan Ashbrook. "The Olfactory Context: Smelling the Early Christian World." In *Scenting Salvation: Ancient Christianity and the Olfactory Imagination* (University of California Press). Copyright © 2006 The Regents of the University of California. Reprinted with permission of The Regents of the University of California; permission conveyed through Copyright Clearance Center, Inc.

Chapter 2: Morley, Neville. "Urban Smells and Roman Noses." In *Smell and the Ancient Senses*, ed. Mark Bradley (Routledge). Copyright © 2015 Routledge. Reprinted with permission of Taylor and Francis Books UK.

Chapter 3: Woolgar, C. M. "Smell." In *The Senses in Late Medieval England* (Yale University Press). Copyright © 2006 C. M. Woolgar. Reprinted with permission.

Chapter 4: Dugan, Holly. "Discovering Sassafras: Sassafras, Noses, New World Environments." In *The Ephemeral History of Perfume: Scent and Sense in Early Modern England* (Johns Hopkins University Press). Copyright © 2011 Johns Hopkins University Press. Reprinted with permission of Johns Hopkins University Press.

Chapter 5: Evans, Jennifer. "Female Barrenness, Bodily Access and Aromatic Treatments in Seventeenth-Century England." *Historical Research* 87, no. 237 (August 2014): 423–43. CC BY-NC-ND 3.0.

Chapter 6: Reinarz, Jonathan. Chapter 7 in *Sense and Scent: An Exploration of Olfactory Meaning*, ed. Bronwen Martin and Felizitas Ringham (Philomel). Copyright © 2003. Reprinted with permission.

Chapter 7: Jütte, Robert. "Scenting—or From Deodorization to Reodorization." In *A History of the Senses: From Antiquity to Cyberspace* (Polity Press). Copyright © 2005 Robert Jütte. Reprinted with permission.

Index